W9-DDO-378

AUNTING

AUNTING
CULTURAL PRACTICES THAT SUSTAIN FAMILY AND COMMUNITY LIFE

*Laura L. Ellingson
& Patricia J. Sotirin*

BAYLOR UNIVERSITY PRESS

Cover Design by Nicole Weaver, Zeal Design
Cover Image: "Family Talk" by Bob Dornberg. Used by
permission of the artist.
Book Design by Diane Smith

Library of Congress Cataloging-in-Publication Data

Ellingson, Laura L.
  Aunting : cultural practices that sustain family and community life /
Laura L. Ellingson and Patricia J. Sotirin.
      p. cm.
  Includes bibliographical references and index.
  ISBN 978-1-60258-152-4 (hardcover : alk. paper)
  1. Aunts. 2. Families. I. Sotirin, Patricia J. II. Title.
  HQ759.94.E45 2010
  306.87--dc22
                                2010000764

Printed in the United States of America on acid-free paper with a
minimum of 30% pcw recycled content.

For Florence, Kay, June, Janice, & Joan, who aunted me,
and for those whom I am blessed to aunt—
Zachory, Jamie, Miette, Sam, Marissa, Matthew, & Nina
L.E.

For my parents, Paul and Muriel
P.S.

CONTENTS

PREFACE

Whenever we tell people that we research aunts, their eyes light up and they inevitably launch into stories about their favorite, most eccentric, or most nurturing aunts. Aunts often play key roles in our lives, but seldom does anyone think to ask about them. Since this project began seven years ago, we have been overwhelmed with people's desire to share their memories of aunts and, for many, to describe the importance being an aunt has for their own lives.

The topic resonates with popular culture as well; several popular tributes to aunts now appear in bookstores, and aunts are frequent characters in novels, children's literature, films, and television. Yet while aunts are everywhere, they tend to draw little notice as aunts per se. Likewise, when we turned to kinship research in communication, sociology, anthropology, and family studies, we found much about motherhood and the extended family, but little explicit focus on the role of the aunt.

Thus, we decided to launch our own exploration of the experience of aunts and aunting practices in the contemporary United States. We intend this study to provide a more nuanced and critical view of aunts than those offered in contemporary nonfiction trade books that celebrate our aunties, contributing to the work of scholars and practitioners in family communication and family studies, sociology and anthropology of kinship, and women's studies. Notably, family relations scholar Robert Milardo recently published research on aunts and uncles that complements many of the findings in our study. Like us, he enriches current understandings of family life by contending that aunting and uncling are transactional and responsive relational modes that contribute significantly to individual and family well-being.[1] We endeavored to make our account accessible to a wide audience of those interested in evolving family structures, the forging and maintenance of community ties, and relational communication more broadly by placing the majority of our research citations and theoretical discussions in an extensive notes section where they will not interrupt readers more interested in a good read than in the contextualization of our findings within larger academic discourses.

The result of our research has been a sense of wonder at the vital nature of aunts that cuts across regional, ethnic/racial, economic, and cultural divides. Moreover, we are tremendously excited about the possibilities for extending the communication practices found in aunt relationships in order to support families and communities of many types.

We could not have accomplished this research, nor written this book, without the support of our academic community. Parts of this project were presented in the Family Communication and Feminist and Women's Studies Divisions of the National Communication Association; we appreciate the constructive feedback we received from our colleagues. We also wish to thank the members of the Organization for the Study of Communication, Language, and Gender, who supported this work since its inception and shared their energy, scholarship, and friendship with us for more than a decade. In particular, we thank Lynn Turner, Jane Jorgenson, and Robin Remke, who combined scholarly expertise with friendship, thus improving our work immeasurably. Our thanks to our tall and handsome editor, Carey Newman at Baylor University Press, whose analogies motivated us to write a more engaging book.

Both of us wish to thank those who encouraged our scholarship and supported us personally through this project.

Patty wishes to thank members of the Gender Writing Group in the Department of Humanities at Michigan Tech for unwavering encouragement and insightful comments; they are my intellectual sisters: Vicky Bergvall, Heidi Bostic, Beth Flynn, and Diane Shoos. Thanks as well to colleagues and friends in the Humanities Department, especially Ann Brady and Glenda Gill (now at the University of Alabama, Huntsville). I appreciate friends working in communication and gender studies whose scholarship and affection have been sustaining: Linda Seward, Cynthia Stohl, Linda Putnam, Deborah Ballard-Reisch, Patrice Buzzanell, Alice Deakins, Anita Taylor, and Suzanne Walfoort. Fond thanks to Jennifer Slack, whose strength and laughter sustain me through whatever projects I undertake, scholarly and otherwise.

I am grateful for the two Faculty Scholarship Grants awarded by the Office of the Vice President of Research at Michigan Technological University that made possible my trips to California to collaborate on this manuscript. I am grateful as well to Ercerla Miller and Marisa Valdez, my undergraduate assistants during 2003, who collected interviews and narratives and reviewed children's books about aunts. Their assistance was funded by the Michigan College/University Partnership Program (MICUP) sponsored by the Department of Career Development's King-Chavis-Park Initiative.

I thank my own aunts—Pat, Tess, Stacia, and my great-aunt Gert—as well as my nieces and nephews—Mikhail, Nikolai, Andrea, Paige, and John—for firsthand experiences with aunting. My brother Rob remains a marvel, and brothers-in law Scott and Baylor are fine uncles, although the best is still my Uncle Sam. My mother Muriel would have loved this book and her memory is part of it. My father, Paul, has been my first and greatest supporter throughout my life, and I am grateful to him and Lorraine for their ongoing enthusiasm. My sisters are dear to me and are themselves wonderful aunts: Barbie, Chris, Paula, and sister-in-law Jill. Thanks for camping trips, family reunions, sisters' weekends, and a guaranteed welcome no matter when or why. I am grateful for Aunt Barbie's help with silly gifts, college expenses, and internships, but especially for our Saturday morning phone calls. Finally, everything I do is inspired by my love for my children and enabled by their patience and support: Elena, Tara, Tavis, and Zakris.

Laura wishes to extend a heartfelt thanks to my colleagues in the Communication Department and the Women's and Gender Studies Program at Santa Clara University. My gratitude goes also to the SCU Women's Faculty Group and Women's Reading Group members who keep me going when I am worn out, and to many colleagues/friends who inspire me to create. I gratefully acknowledge the Thomas Terry Research Grant awarded to me by the SCU Provost's Office and the Paul Locatelli, S.J. Junior Faculty Grant awarded by the Office of the Associate Vice-Provost for Faculty Development, which covered research expenses related to this project. I further acknowledge the assistance of undergraduate research assistants Roselyn Debhavalya, Kristina Salcido, and Kathleen Peabody, who contributed greatly to my productivity by handling countless details, and my Department Goddesses Chris, Helen, and Jessica for reminding me so nicely every time I forgot something.

To my friends, whom I treasure: Matt and Mary, Lisa, and the amazing early morning Crew, especially Kim, Pauline, Sarah, Robin, Gail, and Connie. To my family, for their love and support: Jim and Brigitte, Mark and Diane, my parents Jane and Larry, Genni and Steve, Eric and Elizabeth, Dennis and Becca, and Barbara. Thanks to my colleagues/friends in the Communication field, especially Patrice Buzzanell, Carolyn Ellis, Lainey Jenks, Lynn Harter, Kathy Propp, Deb Walker, Elizabeth Curry, Melanie Mills, Shirley Drew, and Nicole Defenbaugh. To my academic nieces Maggie and Marie, who give me more than I could ever give them—blessings upon you.

My aunts, nieces, and nephews inspired this book. I grew up with wonderful aunts who taught me so much. Aunt June taught me about survival, and Aunt Florence about being tough while sounding sweet. Aunt Kay taught me to spit watermelon seeds and gave me the useful phrase, "Twist my arm and beat me with the bloody stump!" Aunt Janice modeled independence as a leader in the League of Women Voters and as an executive director, balanced with loving motherhood and short-cut cooking; reconnecting with her as an adult has been a joy. Beloved Auntie Joan has been my dear friend, confidante, and cheerleader for as long as I can remember; her unshakeable belief in me is an incredible blessing, and growing up to be her friend is a gift.

My nieces and nephews are amazing, and I am deeply grateful to them for allowing me to aunt them. Zac was the first to call me auntie; his sister Jamie came along a year later, and the two of them taught me how to be an aunt. Miette burst onto the family scene with energy and enthusiasm several years later and made me see the world differently. Sam and Nina are my New England nephew and niece; seeing or hearing from them is truly coming home. Marissa and Matthew gave me the wonderful experience of local aunting; being part of the furniture of their lives is one of life's great blessings.

Finally, I could not write about aunting or anything else without the love and support of my partner Glenn. He uncles as I aunt, makes me laugh and think, and loves me even when I have a writing deadline that coincides with the end of an academic term, which is saying quite a lot.

WHY AUNTS?

In writing about aunts, we necessarily explored personal experiences, family networks, social conditions, and cultural relations. A person cannot be an aunt without a recognized connection to others. So a book about aunts is a book about the dense, complex, and necessary relationships that support personal and family life. The answer to "Why aunts?" is that our experiences of family life are not just about the nuclear family but about extended family and community. We think that the aunt is a critical node in our kinship networks and one that, if we are concerned about the well-being of families in this country, deserves closer and more appreciative examination.

After all, families are in trouble. We hear it all the time—the family is declining, neighbors do not know each other anymore, no one has time to volunteer in their communities, mobile families move away from their extended family networks as they pursue careers (or paid employment) in an increasingly desperate economy.[1] Stresses on the family are almost too numerous to mention: the decline of real income, the lack of affordable child care and health care, the "sandwich generation" of adults parenting their kids while caring for aging parents. As a nation, we face a crisis of nearly one in every five children living in poverty.[2] At the same time, family forms have proliferated, challenging our local and national policymakers to support divorced and blended families, chosen families, lesbian/gay families, single-parent families, foster families, and adoptive families.

In the face of these very real social problems facing families of all types today, American families remain resilient. We contend that while understanding problems is critical, vigorously examining how families survive and even thrive in challenging times is just as critical to our collective well-being. As we took a closer look at what, how, and why aunts contribute to family life, we became convinced that the aunt relationship should not be overlooked when we study the problems and resilience of families today. Our project explores how the aunt relationship works to support family functioning and individual family members; how playing an aunt role in the neighborhood can create enduring ties; how mobile families may construct chosen families (often referred to as "fictive kin") wherever they land; and why people volunteer in official and unofficial "kin-like" capacities to serve others. In talking with people, we often found them referring to their aunt as the person doing the work, making the phone calls, babysitting the kids, and mentoring the next generation. Whether that aunt connection is through biology (a mother's sister), marriage (a father's brother's wife), or choice (a family friend, a neighbor), aunts and their nieces and nephews relate to each other in a variety of ways that matter—tangibly, emotionally, and significantly—in their daily lives. If it takes a village to raise a child,[3] many of the villagers are, or can be thought of as, aunts. And the benefits are multidirectional; while the nieces and nephews obviously benefit from aunts' caregiving, the village "aunties" benefit from their involvement with nieces and nephews, and these relationships strengthen the entire village. We do not exaggerate when we claim that aunts can and are shaping our collective social and cultural lives as they support a wide variety of family forms. In a very real sense, aunts—in the many ways they respond to interpersonal, familial, and communal issues and opportunities—are a relational bulwark against the threats of disintegration and disillusion that undermine our collective experience of contemporary family and social life.

In championing the aunt relationship, we want to complicate the idea of "the family." Despite the tremendous proliferation in family forms, the popular image associated with "the family" is still over-whelmingly that of the heterosexual nuclear family with a husband, wife, and children.[4] Many family communication researchers, particu-larly feminists, are committed to honoring a plurality of family forms and relationships, both for ideological reasons and for pragmatic ones, since families that deviate from the idealized nuclear norm now actu-ally out-number the supposedly normative families.[5] Communication researchers have begun to argue that the rich communication practices of alternative and extended families are different but not deficient in relation to the practices of normative and nuclear families.[6]

One important aspect of many families is extended kinship resources, yet that topic has been under-studied by family researchers who remain more focused on the heterosexual, intact nuclear family.[7] Anthropological studies of the significance of kin exist, but contempo-rary studies demonstrate a decline in families' involvement with, and scholarly interest in, kinship ties.[8] At the same time, we found in the course of writing this book that people were eager to talk about their experiences with and as aunts, suggesting that scholarly disinterest in kinship is out of step with current family practices. The place of aunts in extended family relations deserves more careful study. Evidence of the centrality of aunts in family relations abounds in family stories, everyday conversation, and popular tributes to aunts.[9]

Along with complicating the idea of families and kinship, our focus on aunts encourages a more expansive appreciation for the mul-tiple roles and contributions of women in family life. Family com-munication researchers typically study women as daughters, sisters, mothers, or grandmothers. Yet many, if not most, women in these roles also are aunts. Aunts are, after all, usually a sibling from a par-ent's immediate family of origin or otherwise closely connected. With few exceptions, studies of kinship relationships gloss the aunt role in favor of framing motherhood as the essential role of women.[10] Our study begins to counteract the overemphasis in family communica-tion studies on the nuclear family, mothers, and parenthood, and the neglect of kin relations and the aunt relationship in particular, by exploring what makes the aunt relationship meaningful to people in their own words.

REIMAGINING THE AUNT

Given our perspective on families, kinship, and women's roles, we encourage readers to think a bit differently about families in order to appreciate our argument for the pervasiveness and importance of the aunt relationship in contemporary United States families. We hold that the aunt is woven into the fabric of U.S. society, yet remains a largely taken for granted family figure. Our goal is to make explicit the lived realities of aunts, nieces, and nephews. In drawing out these realities, we identified three important threads, or themes, that we wove throughout this book.

First, we encourage readers to think of the aunt not as a person or even a role, but as a practice, as something people *do*. That is, we think of aunt as a *verb*; to aunt, to engage in *aunting*. Rather than rely on traditional models of family structure, we follow recent research that emphasizes family as a dynamic experience rather than as a static accomplishment and that focuses on "doing family."[11] Hence, we have organized this book around communicative practices that people enact in particular moments, rather than focusing on static and predetermined family roles. It is easy to fall back into treating the aunt as a prescribed role—an aunt should be or do this and that—because cultural norms dictate family roles. However, the norms governing aunts are often ambiguous, and we prefer to study the actual communication practices through which any particular aunt, niece, or nephew enacts that relationship. That is, aunts' communicative actions constitute direct and/or indirect messages about an aunt's personality; her relationships to particular nieces or nephews; her place within a family network; her embodiment of (or resistance to) cultural norms, values, and rituals; and so on. These messages collectively construct images of what it means to be an aunt in a given culture. Such images, or cultural narratives, both reflect and influence individuals' enactment of aunting with each biolegal (that is, biologically related or formalized via marriage) or honorary niece or nephew.

Accordingly, we asked our research participants to tell us their personal stories of aunting and being aunted. In these stories, participants described their relationships by telling us what aunts and nieces/nephews *do* and *do not do* together. Whether "just" talking with each other, or performing actions that in turn demonstrate the nature and value of their relationship, aunts and nieces/nephews construct their relationships to each other through communication. By asking about having and being aunts, we allowed our participants to describe in their own words the meaningfulness of aunting and what aunts do that contributed to their own well-being and to their experience of family life.

Second, aunting is a *choice* that is available to *everyone*—women, of course, but also men, children, and people in all walks and seasons of life. Biology and legal ties (i.e., marriage, divorce, adoption) are not destiny. A primary goal of this book is to reframe aunting as a way of nurturing, leading, encouraging, mentoring, teaching, and listening beyond traditional family structures to include friends, neighbors, and other close relationships. Aunting in this sense entails a repertoire of communicative practices. In addition, reframing aunting as a relational practice puts the focus on choices in kin relationships. Researchers use a variety of terms to refer to voluntary kin-like relationships, such as fictive kin, quasi-kin, chosen family, pseudo-family, ritual kin, intentional family, and constructed kin ties.[12] We prefer to call such relationships *chosen* kin because that phrase embodies the agency of individuals who create and sustain kinship. Finally, choice is critical to what and how people enact aunting. For example, aunting may be enacted as a lifelong, intense relationship or a series of brief encounters or a single but significant interaction. Chosen families evolve over time, just as biolegal ones do. Sometimes a relationship becomes more salient at one period and then fades, perhaps to resume at a later time. While circumstances may condition the choices available to us, we can nonetheless make choices within those constraints. Even choosing to think of nurturing others (and being nurtured) as aunting can open relational options, for example, in mentoring or teaching relationships.[13] We can choose not to have close relationships with others, or to allow relationships to fluctuate in intensity. Thus, we focus on the choices people make about how to enact their relationships as and with aunts.

Third, aunts embody *flexibility*. By this we mean that aunting is not "fixed" by any particular cultural meanings or norms; an aunt's

enacted identity as an aunt depends on the particularities of that relationship. Additionally, aunting is a responsive personal and familial
resource that can be adapted to a variety of material, social, and historical needs and circumstances. We see aunting as a model for a range
of family, community, professional, and organizational relationships
because this practice can be adapted to relational opportunities and
needs. Unlike our cultural ideas about what makes a "good mother,"
a wider range of possibilities is open to aunts to enact a feminine role
within families. The aunt relationship is uniquely unburdened by normative expectations and role prescriptions. Even very "bad" behavior
may be deemed indicative of a "good" aunt. Some "good" aunts see
their nieces/nephews only once a year, let them run wild and stay up
late, feed them junk food, bestow fun and impractical gifts, and model
a form of excessive and permissive nurturance. Clearly, a pattern of
caretaking such as this by a mother would not garner general societal
approval. We take this as evidence that the aunt enjoys much more
cultural flexibility than the mother, a role that is governed by strict,
albeit often paradoxical, cultural (and legal) sanctions. What counts
as "bad" aunting depends on the particular perspective. Our point is
that what is "good" or "bad" aunting is a flexible, contingent determination, shaped by personal, familial, social, cultural, and historical
considerations and responsive to those contexts as well.

Aunting is not only flexible and responsive to personal and cultural preferences and perspectives but to the material and social circumstances and needs of family members as well. For example, aunts
have long served as sources of material aid to families in need of
support—the babysitting aunt, the "rich" benefactress aunt, the aunt
who sponsors the immigration of the rest of the family.[14] Further, even
aunts who violate norms of feminine conduct and decorum may serve
as models of paths not to take, as embodiment of a family and cultural heritage, or as people who help maintain extended family ties.
In short, aunting is shaped by circumstances as much as we enact it in
ways that respond to those circumstances.

Further, aunting offers a flexible model for many other interpersonal relationships. For example, stepmother/stepdaughter relationships
often become fraught with tensions and role conflicts. Reframing this

relationship as an "aunting" relationship frees both parties from the expectations and tensions of mothering and daughtering while retaining a sense of connection and mutual accountability. We celebrate the multiplicity of ways aunts and nieces/nephews relate to each other and urge a broad adoption of aunting as a model for doing relationships in a responsive and flexible manner.

NARRATIVE PERSPECTIVE

We take a narrative approach to exploring aunting. In listening to our participants' stories of aunting, we sought to understand what made these stories "habitable," that is, how these stories made sense of the experiences of aunts and aunting and the ways of living in and through aunting relationships that they suggested.[15] Stories pose real and imagined possibilities, affecting expectations, beliefs, and relationships. Family stories "locate" us both spatially and temporally. For example, one of the most fascinating and unforeseen of our findings was participants' apparent need to situate themselves and their aunts in the constellation of their family. With no prompting whatsoever, participants introduced each aunt, niece, or nephew by explaining—often in lengthy detail—which parent's side of the family they were on, where in the birth order they fell, who they were married to, whose son or daughter they were. Clearly, mapping ourselves into the family presents an important aspect of stories about aunting. We have a need to know who we are, and aunts are an important part of the mapping process. In addition, stories of aunts often bound different generations of a family together; aunts and their siblings are typically members of one generation, while their children, nieces, and nephews are members of a different generation. Stories bind these generations to each other and affirm, celebrate, or contest their family ties. Indeed, through family stories, people can feel connections with—get guidance, inspiration, and strength from—ancestors they had known barely, if at all.[16]

Family storytelling reflects both creative and ritualistic communication. That is, it both produces our understandings of everyday family experience and reproduces "The Family" as a cultural product and ideal. Considerable cultural and social knowledge about family relationships and how to enact them exists. These implicit models affect behavioral expectations, choices, and interpretations in the conduct of daily family life.[17] Both as individual stories that unfold as we live them and as larger, cultural narratives, families are shared, internalized, and enacted in storied form.

The dominant cultural narrative of families remains the heterosexual nuclear family, with a breadwinning father, a nurturing mother, and two children. This stubborn image persists despite the fact that this is not the dominant family form any longer, if indeed it ever was. Copious evidence substantiates that the story of the family popularized by *Leave it to Beaver* and *Father Knows Best* is a sham—a whitewashed, suburban myth of "the way we never were."[18] A cultural nostalgia for this impossible mode of living remains a pervasive trope of conservative family values rhetoric. Although we disagree with many of their political and policy initiatives, we nonetheless feel a deep sympathy with the longing that underlies conservative groups' fantasy of a time in which families (or at least most families) were (imagined to be) healthy, happy, and self-sufficient.

Whether or not all families *should* conform to a particular narrative ideal is irrelevant. Pandora's box has been opened, and the reality is this: the heterosexual, intact, nuclear family is not the normative family, nor is it a workable model for the majority of people living in the United States today.[19] Hence, any social and policy initiatives predicated on the belief that we must do all we can to squeeze all families into a single nuclear family box are doomed to failure. We keep repeating the story of the nuclear family as our only hope for a healthy and productive society that embodies "family values." Yet this idealistic obsession serves to obscure far more pragmatic alternatives for addressing family problems. Flexibility is how families have always survived, and it is how they continue to survive now. We propose that the aunt embodies a uniquely valuable way to tell an alternative, sustainable story of family life in contemporary Western cultures, one that many more of us can live in than can fit within the romantic fantasy of the heterosexual nuclear family.

By telling a more expansive story of aunts, we hope to reframe the story of family life. We want to honor multiple ways of being a family and building connected communities, rather than reducing the complexities and rich possibilities of contemporary life to one model. Family research is itself a story about families; what we offer in this book is a story of aunting as a way of doing family and community.[20]

OUR STORIES

To understand our perspective on aunting, readers should know something about us as authors. This has been a truly collaborative project to which we have contributed equally and which reflects the benefits of our complementary scholarly profiles and personal experiences. We are both professors of communication, and our focus on the ways that communication creates, sustains, repairs, and transforms culture—as it plays out on global, national, local, and interpersonal levels—determined the point of view that underlies this book. We start from the premise that meaning is created through interaction,[21] including the meaning of family, and of the aunt/niece/nephew bond in particular. Most work on kinship reflects a sociological, anthropological, or human services perspective. We enrich current perspectives with our exploration of aunts' and nieces'/nephews' verbal and nonverbal communication. We have explored elsewhere topics such as the representation of aunts in popular culture, the aunt as a way of rethinking mentoring within higher education, niece/nephew perspectives on aunts, and the aunt/niece/nephew bond as an under-studied extended family relationship.[22] Our previous work contributed to the ideas expressed here, as does a wealth of existing research, particularly from feminist scholars of the family who have sought to enlarge the boundaries of what counts as worthy of research and recognition to include a variety of prevalent family forms and domestic practices beyond the heterosexual nuclear unit.[23]

Our personal experiences also shaped our approach to aunting. We are both European American women who are, or have been, in committed heterosexual partnerships. Patty has four children, while Laura has chosen not to be a mother. We are both nieces and aunts; our experiences of being aunted, and of aunting our nieces and nephews, share some similarities and yet diverge in many ways. Being an aunt is a crucial nurturing role in Laura's life, while it takes a distant second place to mothering and sistering in Patty's life. Laura's aunt Joan is one of her closest friends, and she has enjoyed warm relationships with other aunts; Patty remembers her aunts fondly from childhood experiences and family reunions, especially as sources of family stories and legacies of her heritage.

OUR STUDY

This book draws on a large set of data that we collected between March 2003 and February 2008. We conducted in-depth interviews with aunts, nieces, and nephews representing a rich cross section of ethnicities, age cohorts, regions of the United States, religions, sexual orientations, socioeconomic classes, and citizenship/immigrant statuses. We also collected written accounts of communication with aunts from students at three different universities in three geographic regions of the United States and gathered every discussion we could find of aunts in scholarly books and journals, as well as in the popular press to contextualize our findings. We then conducted a systematic qualitative analysis of our data, analyzing emergent themes and patterns to construct a cohesive account of the diversity of aunting experiences in the contemporary United States.

In our research, we privileged personal narratives, asking our participants to "tell us about your aunt" in whatever ways were meaningful to them. We deliberately cast a wide net rather than developing a standardized set of questions, in order to avoid constraining participants' beliefs about, and experiences of, aunting with preconceived notions about family based upon scholarly definitions or particular cultural traditions. Our open-ended approach was rewarded with an abundance of stories that reflected the experience of particular individuals, networks of extended family, and diverse cultural legacies. For those interested in further methodological details of our study, please see the book's appendix.

We offer one other comment here on the intellectual contributions of this work: we chose to place most of the scholarly research, reference citations, and discussions of the relationship between our findings and family communication theory and research in a robust notes section at the end of the book. In this way, we sought to highlight readability while still providing a sound, scholarly context for our findings and implications. Another way we enhanced readability was to include a cast of recurring characters over the course of the book.

OUR MAIN CHARACTERS

To illustrate our findings about aunts, nieces, and nephews, we included examples from dozens of participants. However, the stories of a number of key participants recur throughout the book, demonstrating the richness of aunt/niece/nephew relationships and the complexities of extended family networks within different co-cultures. Their sustained stories provide an ongoing narrative thread that weaves together with the excerpts we draw from others' narratives. We introduce these central characters and some of the aspects of aunting that they illustrate as a preface to the chapters to come.

Christine lived with her aunt Wilaluk throughout high school and college. Wilaluk immigrated to the West Coast of the United States from Thailand more than twenty years ago through the sponsorship of one of her aunts. As a child, Christine had lived with her mother and father, both Thai citizens, in the United States. Upon her parents' divorce, Christine returned to Thailand with her mother. As Christine neared the age to begin high school, Wilaluk invited her niece to return to the U.S. to live with her family and attend school. At the time of our interviews with both aunt and niece, Christine was 21 years old and a junior in college, and her aunt Wilaluk, a married mother of two, was working as a software licensing coordinator at another local university. Wilaluk functioned as a "second mother" to her niece, caring for her alongside her own daughters.

Teresa was a vigorous woman in her early sixties who belonged to a large Mexican American extended family. She worked as a housekeeper and a babysitter and spent a lot of time with her grandchildren, as well as her nieces, nephews, and their children. She spoke of honoring blended families by welcoming new nieces and nephews when her brother married a woman with children, and of the caring way in which one of her sisters took in her drug-addicted niece and helped her straighten out her life. For Teresa, extended family was both her primary source of social support and the primary recipient of caregiving from her.

Elise was part of a large French Canadian community in northern New England. Growing up, her family maintained close ties with both her mother's and her father's kin, and Elise had many memories of enjoying her aunts at large family gatherings and holiday celebrations. Elise worked for a large discount retailer, was married with two children, and enjoyed spending time with her nieces and nephews, including a chosen niece.

Camile, an African American professor, grew up with a chosen aunt who was a close friend of her parents and a loving presence in her and her sister's lives. Camille also described the many ways in which her father, designated the extended family's caretaker, provided care for his elderly great-aunts.

Betty grew up in the southwestern United States, the daughter of European American parents. She became an aunt at a very young age, as her sister and brother were fifteen and eleven years older than she, respectively. Her brother had six children for whom she regularly babysat, and she maintained a close, big-sister-type relationship with her sister's daughter. Betty was married and worked as a medical transcriptionist.

Rose was the daughter of Portuguese immigrants. She had two daughters and worked as a bookkeeper. Rose had close relationships to her aunts, one of whom was her godmother. Aunts as godmothers within the Catholic Church played an important part in their extended family traditions. Rose and her husband chose from among their biolegal aunts as godmothers for their own daughters, and Rose was a godmother to one of her nieces, her brother's daughter.

We chose two nephews to highlight as well. Interviewed as a 21-year-old college senior, Tim grew up in Hawaii as part of a large extended family network that included many neighbors and family friends. His aunties were an integral part of his daily life —both his biolegal aunts and the community women he called his "calabash aunties" as a term of affection and respect.

Likewise, 20-year-old college student Joshua grew up in a close-knit Mennonite community in the Midwest where aunts were expected to provide care for their nieces and nephews whenever the need arose. One of his aunts helped him to cope with his evolving identity and to maintain family ties as he struggled to establish his own life path out-side that insular community.

In the chapters that follow, readers will meet these and many other characters in our story of aunting. We hope their insights will inspire a broader appreciation for the potential of aunting as a communicative relational practice to sustain family and community life.

1

CARING FOR KIN

My aunt, she's like a mother. Oh goodness! "Make sure you have
enough to eat. Eat your breakfast. How's your grades? You don't
have a boyfriend, do you?" . . . That's the house everybody goes to
when, you know, they need a place to stay for awhile, they go over
there. She take care of 'em. So she's real good.

This description of a nurturing aunt from Celia, a 19-year-old African American niece, richly illustrates the importance of aunts to many
nieces and nephews, as well as the value many aunts place on nurturing their kin. In addition to making caring inquiries and offering a
refuge to family members in need, her aunt Janet serves Celia as
a trusted confidante and advisor. This aunt further functions within the
niece's kin network as a caring force that keeps family close, drawing
together extended kin in frequent, casual family gatherings, particularly in the summer.

This chapter argues for the significance of aunts in contemporary
kin networks. We found that aunts play vital roles in their nieces' and
nephews' lives, crossing boundaries to overlap with the nurturance provided by nuclear families. The mundane nature and taken-for-granted-
ness of aunts as part of extended kinship networks should be taken not
as devaluing them but rather as a testament to their enduring presence

in many families, despite dire predictions of the decline in social capital within kin networks by some scholars.[1] Aunts continue to supplement and fill gaps in nurturance inevitably left by nuclear families, which cannot possibly meet all members' needs without support.[2]

Social support is often discussed in terms of illness, death, birth, or other significant, stressful life events. However, giving and receiving support does not occur only in times of crisis and upheaval, but also manifests within ongoing personal relationships.[3] In other words, support is embedded in daily, mundane communication among kin. In simple ways, aunts fill gaps left by parents trapped in the "time bind" of work/family demands, for example, by driving kids to and from school and activities.[4] Along with such small but significant support, aunts are called on at times to redress more demanding circumstances that constitute significant gaps in family and kin resources. Such needs include regular or even daily childcare; providing a temporary home for troubled adolescents; and providing significant support or acting as "other mother," by offering a "home away from home" for nieces and nephews attending college. Finally, our data show that aunts may bridge broken relationships when nuclear family structures falter or collapse. Clearly, aunts remain a responsive resource for many families, performing what scholars call "kinwork" or "kinkeeping." Of course, no one aunt fulfills all roles, nor do all families include an aunt who functions in the ways described in this chapter. Nonetheless, instances of aunts' caring work permeated our data.

Juggled alongside paid employment, housework, and child care, "kinwork" involves "the collective labor expected of family centered networks across households and within them," including child and dependent care, wage and nonwage labor[5] and relationship-maintaining communication and tasks such as "visits, letters, telephone calls, presents, and cards to kin; the organization of holiday gatherings; the creation and maintenance of quasi-kin relations."[6] We will discuss the work of communication and relationship maintenance in the next chapter; here we concentrate on detailing the many ways in which aunts provide material, or tangible, care and instrumental support to nieces, nephews, their parents, and other extended family members.

Far from reflecting "only" physical labor, the performance of tasks as mundane as picking children up from school or cooking a meal communicates a great deal about the value of relationships between aunts and their kin. They also provide spaces in which interpersonal communication between aunts and their nieces/nephews occurs.

Communication scholars describe communication as always having two levels of meaning within every verbal and/or nonverbal message: the content level and the relationship level.[7] That is, when someone communicates the content of a message—for example, I will pick up my niece from her swimming lesson today—she or he transmits more than a fact or intention. It is impossible to share information without also communicating something about the relationship between the people involved. If an aunt offers to pick up her sister's child (the aunt's niece) after school, she communicates the significance of the relationship with her sibling (and possibly the sibling's spouse or partner) and with the child. Of course, she also may communicate a whole range of meanings. Caring for the needs of kin shows them and the larger community that meeting such needs is worthy of time and effort and embodies respect for a family and/or community tradition of caregiving (or possibly an exception to a trend against providing such caregiving). It may communicate a closeness between the aunt and her sister or brother (parent of a niece/nephew); a special bond between the aunt and her niece or nephew; a more general emphasis on the importance of actively caring for all members of an extended kin network; the aunt's identity as a nurturer, organizer, or problem solver; and so on. Of course, aunts may also communicate resentment, guilt, or other, less appreciated emotions when they provide material care. Nonetheless, the doing of the task speaks of the priorities in the aunt's life.

In the remainder of this chapter, we explore some of the many ways in which aunts' kinwork is practiced today, such as carpooling, child care, nurturing nieces or nephews attending college away from home, and providing support during family crises. We then turn to a discussion of nieces and nephews who choose to provide care to their elderly aunts.

CHAUFFEURING

A mundane but necessary way in which aunts provide nurturing to nieces and nephews and support to their parents is through carpooling. Driving kids around constitutes a key form of kinwork now, particularly in suburban areas that developed post-World War II in the automobile era. Public transportation is often lacking, and children need to be shuttled from home to school and among sports and other activities. Overscheduling organized activities is a problem in many families. "Kids today have very little time for a life of their own" because they participate in so many activities, and parents often end up driving children around for hours each day, a time-consuming and often stressful task.[8] Carpooling provides one way to make busy schedules possible, particularly in families with two employed parents or in single-parent families. Tim, a young man who grew up in Hawaii, explained:

> Auntie Vicky, who's my dad's brother's wife, they lived two doors down from us growing up, and I have a cousin that's twenty-six days older than me, so we grew up together and went to the same school. And so we'd end up carpooling together and Auntie Vicky would give me a ride to school and coming back from school, so she's [the aunt] I've spent the most time with.

Vicky's role in her nephew's life, while valued, was also framed as part of the normal pattern of his days. His parents presumably appreciated the labor aspect of the aunt's kinwork, but the nephew expressed a more relational view of his aunt as spending time with him, rather than as performing a task. Of course, work and relationships are not mutually exclusive, but complementary aspects of kinwork. We point to the aunt's chauffeuring as work as a way of signifying its social value.

Wilaluk, a first-generation Thai immigrant, explained that she spent a lot of time picking up her children from school and other activities, and that she included her niece in the car pool:

> We all go together. In the morning, you know, . . . [my niece] goes to a different school . . . so I had to drive her to school and then I would drop off [my daughter], so I was kind of running in and out, and we had piano lessons, [and] you know—me the driver!

She also had two nephews, sons of her sister who lived on the same street, and for years they took swimming lessons together. She would pick up both nephews after lessons, along with her two daughters. Similarly, Margaret, a recent college graduate and the daughter of Portuguese immigrants, explained that various aunts, uncles, and cousins had been responsible for picking her up after school, sports, and activities. Recently, she volunteered to drive her godchild (her youngest aunt's child) to swimming lessons while his mother worked, because she wanted to continue the tradition of helping with her nieces and nephews. "It's important, you know," she said. "I want them to have what I had growing up."

Aunts filling small gaps in family care by assisting with carpooling may seem at first glance to be relatively inconsequential. However, our data do not support such a conclusion. On the contrary, when we asked participants broad, open-ended questions about communicating with their aunts and nieces/nephews, they frequently mentioned these sorts of small actions as meaningful to them and their families. Participants clearly framed aunts' actions as indications that their aunts cared for them. Likewise, in discussing their efforts to care for nieces and nephews, aunts mentioned specific acts they performed as evidence of their caring. Such small gestures appeared to matter because they provide tangible evidence of a more abstract feeling. They remind people that they are loved, and that their needs matter to someone who cares enough to try to fulfill them.

SECOND MOTHERING

Participants described their nurturing aunts with terms such as "second mother," "other mother," and "like another mother to me," and described themselves as being like an aunt's child: "I'm her other daughter." One nephew stated that he often stayed at his aunts' homes, where his aunts "were parents to me." Another college-aged nephew wrote of one aunt, "I believe she looks at me as another son of her own," and of another aunt, "We spent so much time together that she developed a 'mother's sense' (the sense that a mom just knows) and helped me through those tough times." A niece explained that her aunt "seemed more of a motherly type toward me than the other aunts;

she took more of a motherly role." For our participants, aunts often figured as supplementary mothers. Lacking a language for aunting, people in the dominant United States culture often reach for the language of motherhood.[9] The language of parenting reflects a deep connection in which the aunt nurtures the child. Likewise, aunts that we interviewed expressed maternal feelings toward one or more of their nieces and nephews, referring to them as essentially another of their children. Wilaluk said of the niece who lives with her, "she's like my other daughter but you know; instead I have two, now I have three girls" and "I'm probably like her second mother; I think I understand her." Aunts who functioned as second mothers provided regular childcare for their nieces and nephews, took over as a mother during a crisis or time of upheaval, or provided a "home away from home" for young adults attending college far from home.

Providing childcare is a common way of embodying the second mother role. Aunts in our study often felt a duty to assist with domestic labor, particularly childcare. Such labor is necessary to the functioning of families but is devalued by a capitalist system that ignores the unpaid domestic labor that makes capitalist production possible.[10] Our participants, particularly those who grew up in working-class families, reported that as children, they were often cared for by their aunts who were obligated to provide free or low-cost childcare within the extended family, usually with expectations of reciprocity. Joshua, a young Mennonite nephew, explained that his Mennonite aunts were expected to help raise and care for him and other children in the community:

> [Aunts] are expected to be there for a family when they are needed. So before babysitters were ever thought of, that's what their role was. To step in and be the moms. . . . And I don't think [my mother] ever felt like she was in a position where she had to go find a sitter. She could always just call [my aunts] and say, "Hey, I need you." And just like that they'd be there.

He reported that his mother reciprocated in kind: "there's a feeling of, you know, 'we have to do this for each other because we're family.'" Mothers frequently barter other services and/or rely on the generosity of their sisters, sisters-in-law, and chosen kin to care for their children.[11]

For middle-class and affluent families, shared childcare may have less to do with meeting the basic needs for survival than with increasing quality of life, for example, by enabling a mother to work outside the home confident that her children are well cared for by a loving family member. Many aunts provided childcare for young nieces or nephews that perhaps was not economically necessary but nonetheless was highly valued within the extended family network. A 20-year-old niece described her aunt's role:

> [My aunt] is someone who cared for me when I was little when my mother would work, and I needed a sitter. She is a very nice, caring person, who treated me as if I was one of her own children at times. She always was looking out for me, and she treated me like I was very special.

Another niece recalled that her aunt regularly provided childcare: "[My aunt is] in a lot of ways, my mother. She took very good care of me when I was a little girl and my mom was at work." A nephew stated, "My mother was busy taking care of her career as a pediatrician, so [my aunt] frequently looked after us." Gretchen, a 50-year-old Polish/Irish American woman from the Midwest, said of her aunt:

> She was always in the kitchen cooking and cleaning. And we were always playing. She would always [watch me]—she was the babysitter. She would take care of everybody's kids. To this day, she still takes care of all her grandkids. And great-grandkids—everybody's mom.

Betty, a medical transcriptionist, spoke of having become an aunt at a relatively young age; she was fourteen when her first niece was born. Her brother and his wife eventually had six children.

> I babysat all the time. I was the live-in babysitter practically. . . . I would go and stay with them a lot. One year I went to Disney World with them and then I stayed with them when we got back . . . for a couple more weeks with them at their house and . . . we'd go [to] movies, shopping and just general type things, but it was a lot of fun. They were good kids.

For this young aunt, helping with childcare was set in the context of familial experiences and enjoyable activities. With six young children, Betty's brother and sister-in-law needed the assistance that Betty provided by caring for the children and doing basic household chores, and they made an effort to ensure that she also had fun and felt appreciated.

Childcare and assistance are common among chosen kin (particularly chosen aunts) as well. Researchers have documented a significant decline in neighborhood social capital in traditional urban neighborhoods, and a distinct lack of neighborhood networks for social support in suburban neighborhoods.[12] Yet exceptions to this rule exist, and researchers have sought to understand how supportive environments arise. "Caring neighborhoods" are characterized as those in which neighbors help to care for each other's children in formal and informal manners, including sharing childcare, carpooling, and other kinwork.[13] Reciprocity formed the foundation for providing support, knowing that it would be offered when it was needed. We found ample evidence of chosen aunts providing meaningful assistance to participants. Chosen aunts gave and received help, enacting caring relationships, particularly in assisting each other in childcare. One niece, Ella, who grew up in Hawaii, explained that in Hawaii women in the community, such as neighbors and parents' friends, are addressed as "aunty." She describes one aunt who has been her neighbor "since the day I was brought home from the hospital" and who continues to be an important source of support. Camille, an African American professor, spoke fondly of a neighbor who was an integral part of her childhood as a chosen aunt:

> She owned a duplex, [and] when my parents got married . . . they moved into her duplex. . . . We always called her Aunt Nancy and her husband Uncle Roland . . . she was really like my mother's mother, like she helped her. So we lived there for about, I guess, seven years and then they moved to the house where I grew up . . . but we used to go over to their house all the time, all the time, like holidays. We'd stay over there if my parents wanted to be alone, we'd go over after church, we'd go to the swap meet on Saturdays, we'd go to

McDonalds. Yeah all of those things and she was an amazing chef.
She was like the best. . . .

In Camille's case, her chosen aunt performed important kinwork. She
and her husband provided childcare and other domestic assistance,
cooked, took the kids for fun outings. Now that she has been dead for
quite awhile, the family still misses her—"We miss her so much . . .
we still talk about her food now and she's been deceased for maybe
ten years . . . [our loss when she died] was a really big deal"—signifying the chosen aunt's importance in Camille's life.

SUSTAINING SINGLE MOTHERS

We turn now to a particular family configuration that benefits from
aunts' support: single parents.[14] Illustrating a different level of obligation and support, Jill, a 21-year-old European American niece, related
that her mother had been sent to a home for unwed mothers and was
expected to give up her baby. A week before giving birth, her mother
left and went to her sister's home to stay with her. Jill said of her
mother's sisters:

> My mom's sisters are my closest aunts. They had a hand in raising
> me. They were my second mothers and my best friends. . . . For the
> first six months of my life, my aunt, and a pseudo-aunt took care of
> me along with my mother.

In this case, the aunts preserved the bond between the mother and
child by making it possible for them to remain together and for both
Jill and her mother to receive the care and support they needed. Second mothers generally do not replace people's mothers, but they provide valued nurturing to supplement and complement what mothers
are able to give.

Janice and Chris, a middle-aged lesbian couple who have been in
a committed partnership for seventeen years, chose not to have children, even though they enjoy them. Chris was part of a fairly small
cohort in a graduate program and was friendly but not particularly
close with Eileen, the mother of the girls she and her partner now
aunt. When Eileen decided to become a single mother, others closer

to her organized help, to give her some relief. Janice and Chris call themselves the "Tuesday night aunties," a term which hails from their ritual of going over one evening a week to give their friend, a single mother of twins, a break when the babies were little. They still spend a lot of time together, which has made them feel close to their chosen nieces. Janice and Chris both have good relationships with their biolegal nieces and nephews but do not live close to them. In part because of the geographic proximity of their friend and her children, they simply are able to spend a lot more time with their chosen nieces than with their biolegal nieces and nephews.

> Chris: [Eileen] basically [has] always been single, but had decided that she wanted to have a baby, and you know, being a modern woman, she went to the sperm bank ha . . . and got pregnant, and then once she found out that she was gonna have twins, a bunch of people started making plans to help out for the first few months. . . . There were close friends who like each came and stayed with her for a few weeks and then once the kids were two or three months . . . the friends who tended to be academics also, you know, were done being able to spend their vacation time here and a number of us who are local each took a different night. . . . Our thought was so she could, like, take a shower or leave the house or whatever, but what ended up happening is that—well, I think partly because she was so happy to have adults around—we hung out, and we would bring over dinner or order dinner in . . . and hang out with the babies, and it just sort of stuck.

> Janice: . . . So we're their sort of "official," regular aunties now. And it switched to Sundays finally, because . . . it became much easier for us to go on weekends. And so we now go usually between 3:00 p.m. and 4:00 p.m. every Sunday . . . and she actually makes dinner for us now, which is the shift, and we play with the kids.

Interestingly, their friendship with the mother actually grew out of their aunting, rather than the other way around, as is more common. Janice and Chris agreed to participate to support her, and the relationship really blossomed from there.

A long tradition of chosen family exists within LGBTQ (lesbian, gay, bisexual, transgender, and queer) communities, among people who identify as any of a variety of nonheterosexual orientations or gender identities. Indeed, the term "chosen family" became popularized within the dominant U.S. popular culture largely through the advocacy of LGBTQ rights advocates and their allies.[15] Many LGBTQ people construct their own families in part because of the still common rejection of their nonheteronormative identities and ways of life by their biolegal kin. In addition, like most people, they create chosen family out of a desire to build a supportive network for enjoyment and to help them cope with life hassles, crises, and, for an increasing number, parenting.[16] These family networks "typically include partners, former partners, and friends and may also include biolegal family members."[17] Members of LGBTQ communities also form chosen kin networks that include straight people.[18] In some cases, the practice of constructing chosen aunt relationships for children of lesbian and gay parents has been formalized through programs that assist in the initiation and development of caring relationships, much like the Big Brothers Big Sisters organization.[19]

Caring during College

For many participants, attending college was their first significant move away from home. Aunts filled in the gaps of the absent nuclear family by providing fun, encouragement, and nurturing to the young people as they transitioned to adulthood and encountered the challenges and opportunities of college life.[20] While not childcare, such nurturing might be termed young adult care, or *transitional nurturing*, and certainly it represents one way of manifesting the second mother practices of aunting. One nephew reported that he turned to his aunt for comfort while away from home:

> I am closest to her because she was there for me when I first went away to college. I was homesick and she would pick me up and I would stay weekends at her house. . . . *Every* time I go to her house she makes a gourmet meal, something I really enjoy. . . . Whenever I go over to her house, that room is "my room," and I love it, I feel like I have a home away from home.

Tim, the nephew we mentioned earlier from Hawaii, explained how one aunt supported him while he attended college. She was an aunt he had not spent much time with previously because she lived so far away from his immediate family in Hawaii.

> One aunt in particular among my mom's sisters took me under her wing . . . when I went to college in Washington, because that was a real hard transition for me to make. . . . She was like a surrogate mom in a lot of respects you know. I mean I'd come over and do laundry at their house. She'd call to check up on me. She'd bring me food. She would, you know, she'd take care of me when I was sick, bring me medicine. . . . I spent Thanksgiving there and Easter there, and sometimes when I had free time I'd spend the weekend at their house, you know, and go to soccer games and that kind of stuff— just having a family when I didn't have a family . . . [and] really making me feel at home.

Ellen, a West Coast office manager in her mid-thirties, fondly remembers an aunt and uncle who "adopted" her when she attended college near them:

> I like hadn't heard from [my aunt Florence] in years, and then I got a graduation present from high school from her, and she wrote me this long letter . . . 'cause she knew I was coming down that way, so she wanted me to know that if I, you know, needed anything or wanted anything, that her door would always be open . . . [the first time I visited] I was very nervous . . . and not sure how it was going to go. . . . But they adopted me and from that point on I spent a lot of time, and then when I had my own car I went over there a lot and I just spent a lot of time with them . . . sometimes doing nothing much at all. She taught me to cross-stitch—we'd do our stitching and bitching and just talk. . . . We liked crafty things, you know, we liked going shopping [and] to craft fairs and things like that.

While none of these nieces and nephews were suffering from lack of money or other resources, they nonetheless felt a sense of familial deprivation that was alleviated greatly by aunts' efforts to embrace them. Geographic proximity is often sufficient to activate latent kinship relationships. For many, those relationships then became inactive again once the college student graduated or left the nearby university. However, our participants framed this flux as normal, and some, including Ellen, maintained active connections after relocating through regular phone calls and e-mail.

Sometimes the support given to nieces and nephews seems quite minor. Wilaluk, the Thai immigrant aunt, said of one of her nephews in her husband's family: "once every two weeks he will stop by or he will call . . . this past year he came more often, because every time he comes, he wants to do laundry. And then he will stay one or two nights and then go back [to college]." Her nephew's regular visits to do laundry signified to his aunt his desire to touch base with family members and to get a little nurturing. She accepted this behavior as normal and welcomed his visits, even though she did not feel particularly close to him. The aunt felt a definite sense of "family obligation" that she seemed happy to fulfill by supporting her nephew. By opening her home to her nephew, she assured him of his ongoing family membership and offered him the mundane comforts of family life. In contrast to special occasions and holiday celebrations, being welcomed into an aunt's home can provide a sense of personal security, self-worth, and nurturance for a niece or nephew away from home.

An aunt's proximity may also alleviate parental anxieties about a son or daughter in college. Betty explained that her sister allowed her daughter to attend a college in a city far from home because Betty and her husband would be located close by:

[My husband] and I are [my niece's] guardians. If anything were to happen to [my sister and her husband], they've listed us as her guardians, which is really nice because we've always been really close. Our relationship has really stayed close, and we get together all the time and do things, and the reason they had her come out here is because we were so close. Because if we weren't, they would have been really worried since she's only twenty and living on her own in an apartment. They really want us to be here. She probably wouldn't have come if it wasn't for us, so that's nice.

In this way, the aunt performs nurturing kinwork toward her niece while also alleviating her sister's anxiety about her daughter's safety and well-being. While the niece is now an adult who depends on Betty and her husband only for emotional support and minor practical assistance, the legacy of her aunt and uncle's formal designation as her guardians in the event of her parents' death when she was growing up persists in their close relationship.

FACING A CRISIS

Despite incredible resilience on the part of many nuclear families, parents' inability to care for their children due to death, incarceration, drug addiction, or other problems sadly is not uncommon. Sometimes small family rifts necessitate a cooling off period between parents and children, while other situations demand longer commitments to nurture children. While grandparents form the largest group of kincare providers, aunts' assuming temporary or permanent custody of their nieces or nephews is a growing trend.[21]

Crises may strengthen aunt/niece/nephew relationships as an aunt assumes a surrogate parental role. For some nieces and nephews, aunts provided a temporary home in times of trouble during their teen years. A Latina college student described her aunt's kindness in taking her in for awhile:

> I lived with [my aunt] and her two children (my cousins) for a short period in high school when I wasn't getting along with my parents. . . . This was an important time in our relationship because we both agree that a whole lot of bonding went on during that period.

This aunt allowed breathing room for her niece and the niece's parents until their differences could be resolved. For those months, she served as a surrogate mother to her niece. In another instance, a divorce spurred a separation between mother and daughter when the mother sought to return to her native country and the daughter wished to attend high school in the United States, where she had been living prior to the divorce. Christine has lived with her aunt Wilaluk throughout high school and college: "She acts on behalf of my mother who lives overseas; she is my guardian. . . . Basically, I treat her like another mother."

As is evident in Wilaluk's earlier excerpts, both aunt and niece view this relationship as similar to a mother/daughter relationship.

Teresa, a Mexican American housekeeper, told a story of one of her granddaughters, who became a drug addict and lost custody of her children. Many members of the family reached out to this young woman but had been unsuccessful in helping her to recover from her addiction. Over time, she lived with several of her aunts, but each of them kicked her out eventually because of her continued drug use. Finally, the troubled young woman's great-aunt, Teresa's younger sister, took her in.

> My little sister said, "well I can't give up on her." She goes, "I got to help her," but she gave her the "this is the last time, three times, that's it!" Well actually with a lot of talking with her, a lot of letting her know her kids will be better off with her, otherwise they're gonna be put in a shelter, and she thought better of it. She, you know, [realized] this is not a game anymore. She was really heavy into drugs for years. So my granddaughter, she just turned twenty-two, so [her aunt] talked to her, she said, "this is what I'm going to do for you. I'm gonna help you, you're gonna go back to school, I'm babysitting your kids, and after that you're gonna get a job." And so she gave her the opportunity . . . and she just became a nurse! And that's wonderful because nobody else gave her that opportunity, but [her aunt] did, [and] she's got a good job right now.

These stories of aunts helping during family crises reflect larger social trends. Studies of kinship foster care show that aunts are second only to grandmothers in numbers of kin who function voluntarily (although increasingly regulated and, in some states, compensated) as foster caregivers for children removed from their parents' custody.[22] Research on African American aunts documents the joys and sacrifices of aunts who raise their nieces and nephews.[23]

Another crisis-related kincare option for aunts is to act as co-parents. Tamara, a college student, described her aunt Ella as her primary caregiver. Tamara's teenage, unwed mother lived at home with her parents and sister, and Ella took over much of the parenting responsibilities for Tamara.

In many ways [Ella] has been more of a motherly figure in my life than my biological mother. . . . My aunt has always been more responsible and trustworthy than my mother. . . . It was my aunt who took me to church every weekend; it was my aunt who spent time with me to learn my ABCs and numbers; it was my aunt who bought me my first bike and taught me how to ride it; it was my aunt who I turned to when I needed anything, from advice to money; it was my aunt who instilled the values I now have in me . . . . It was my aunt who disciplined me throughout my teenage rebel years and who got me back in line. All in all, my aunt has always played the role of my own mother. . . . I look to her for both financial and emotional help. . . . [During a family crisis] I isolated myself from my mother because she didn't know what I was going through. That time period was the toughest time of my life, and it was my aunt who I turned to. . . . From the day I was born, she's always been there for me and always will be. (European American niece)

This niece's mother was present but unable or unwilling to provide parental guidance and support to her child, and her sister stepped in as an aunt to raise Tamara. Tamara eloquently articulates her aunt's contribution not only to material assistance, but to helping her to become who she is today.

Other aunts provided a form of foster care and significant assistance with cultural adaptation to their nieces and nephews. Wilaluk, who now cares for her niece, Christina, as we noted above, came to the United States in a similar manner herself, more than twenty-five years ago. She had an aunt living in Berkeley, California, who offered to help her. Her aunt had married an American citizen and welcomed her niece to the United States. Wilaluk explained how much her aunt did for her:

They don't have any children so I'm closer to her. When I came to California, she was like my guardian, took care of me. If she wasn't here, [my parents] would not have sent me to the States. . . . She's the one that looked for a school for me . . . and she helped me apply to the school.

After she was accepted to and enrolled in a nearby university, she lived in a dorm but continued to spend weekends with her aunt.

Margaret, who lived with her Portuguese American family while attending college, explained that her family of first- and second-generation immigrants was very close-knit, and that her contact with aunts occurred within the context of her immediate family's close association with the larger extended family. Immigration from the Azores Islands in Portugal had begun with the immigration of Margaret's father's sister, who sponsored her father to come to the U.S. They continued to sponsor various relatives as they raised their families, and in time, a large extended family network developed in close proximity to one another.

> So then when they all came [to the U.S.], they lived in the same block or they lived in the same house before they sort of migrated out, but we also lived in the same area practically, and so that sort of started the closeness. And then growing up we would get together, you know, if somebody was rebuilding their garage or someone was remodeling a kitchen, everyone would come together and help. The men would do the labor. The women would cook, care for the kids, so we were always together. There would be picnics, birthdays, communions, you know confirmations, baptisms, funerals, weddings, all the time . . . and it was just always, always together.

Margaret's aunts functioned as part of the vibrant extended kin network that formed the foundation for her childhood.

Research documents the importance of kinship networks for new immigrants needing financial and social support. People often activate latent relationships with extended kin in times of migration. Kin may provide family members with emotional support, financial assistance, companionship, and information on finding jobs and housing.[24] For example, aunts were featured prominently in one study of the accounts of Mexican migrant women about their experiences as they relocated, found work, and established households in the U.S.[25] Aunts may also be the immigrants taken in and supported by other family members, to whom they in turn provide domestic assistance.[26] Whether sponsoring or being sponsored, aunts continue to play a critical role in the saga of immigrant families in the U.S. and in kin networks essential to the immigrant experience.

TRADING PLACES: RECEIVING ELDERCARE

Kincare takes on material, social, and symbolic significance as family members age. Care responsibilities for the "sandwich generation"—adults who parent children and have primary responsibility for aging parents or other relatives—entail major financial, workplace, and personal adjustments.[27] Aunts, nieces, and nephews indicate that at least some adult nieces and nephews feel an obligation to and/or take pleasure in materially and emotionally giving to their aunts.[28] One story that dramatically demonstrates this sense of kincare as a reciprocal intergenerational obligation comes from Carol, a woman who had returned to earn her undergraduate degree as a nontraditional student. The story is of a distant relative that Carol knew as her aunt; this woman was the wife of Carol's grandmother's brother's brother-in-law. As a young woman, Carol moved to the city where this chosen aunt lived to look for work and stayed with her for a few months. Her aunt was strict with Carol, taking care of all her needs and managing her money for her.

> She made me give her every paycheck I received and would only give me enough money for the transportation to get to work. She would give me some allowance on the weekend to go out. She made all of my meals, packed my lunches, did my laundry, and mended my blouses and skirts (I had no choice in this matter). I had heard that Jewish mothers can be overbearing but hearing it and living it are two different things. But as a result of her diligent discipline, I quickly had the money to rent a decent apartment.

Carol lived in the city for the next several years and recalled fond memories of bringing her friends to her aunt's home for German meals, of attending German festivals and restaurants in the city, and of spending holidays with her aunt. Eventually, the aunt and her husband and daughter had health problems and the husband died. The theme of paying back (see an expanded discussion in chapter 6) featured prominently in Carol's story: "This is when I began to repay her for all of her kindness towards my family and I." Interestingly, her aunt framed her assistance to Carol as a matter of repaying Carol's grandparents for their kindness to her when she was younger by giving their granddaughter a helping hand. Carol helped with the daughter's illness and assisted her aunt with home repairs and daily living chores. After several years, the daughter died. Carol quit her part-time job for the summer to help her aunt put the daughter's affairs in order.

> I can tell that she feels guilty at the amount of time and money it has cost myself, [my partner], and my father, because she keeps crocheting afghans for all of us. This makes her feel better about everything I think, even though we tell her that we don't mind helping her.

The sense of paying back continues to be a major motivation in Carol's relationship with this elderly aunt.

> Over the years, this "want-to" slipped into "ought-to" as she started to age and started wanting me around a lot and if I couldn't come (I did have to work during the day!) she would try guilt trips. I found myself making an effort to go and see her. Later, after her husband died and then her daughter died unexpectedly, I found myself in have-to mode and that's where I am today. She depends on me regularly for fixing things in her house, cleaning, or keeping her company. Now she is showing signs of dementia as well as other severe health problems. She falls regularly and shouldn't be in her house alone. Still she resists any change whether it be moving in with us, a retirement home, or in-home care.

Carol's sense of family obligation and the responsibilities of intergenerational care seemed well-defined: "Besides my aunt, we have other elderly in our family in similar circumstances so we are fully experiencing the have-to part of relational commitment but in a way, even though it is demanding, we don't mind. It's just the way it is." Sometime after telling this story, Carol finished her educational program and moved closer to her aunt to help with her care.

Not everyone takes on such a tremendous responsibility for the care of aging aunts, but kincare for elderly family members is becoming a more visible element in American family life. While there is little research that addresses care of aunts directly, there has been some research into kinship support. Some of this research has shown cultural differences: in African American families, elderly aunts and uncles considered nieces and nephews to be close family members and reported receiving assistance from them, while elderly Caucasians reported no expectations of assistance from their siblings' children.[29] Clearly, more research is needed on reciprocal intergenerational obligations and changes in aunt/niece/nephew relationships over time.

Among our African American participants, the expectation that kincare would occur across generations within the extended family network was thematic. Camille noted that her father had taken on care responsibilities for his aunts: "He definitely feels like he's their caretaker, and it's weird because some of them have kids but they trust my dad." Camille's parents were seniors too, but her father felt obliged to help his older aunts; as she explained it, "He has this big aunt obligation." She described helping her father with these responsibilities:

> When I am home though I will run around and do stuff, and my dad is so relieved. I'm like "I'll take her to the cardiologist this morning" 'cause then my dad has to go to his own cardiologist. And they go ahead and make appointments to see the doctor without telling my dad ahead of time like, "Oh is this a good time for you?" "Well, I have to be there tomorrow at 10." He's like, "Well, I have to be at my thing tomorrow at 10." So and it's difficult for them to call and remake appointments 'cause they're old and they can't hear, and it's just like a mess, so I do help when I go home.

While Camille described helping her father out with the care of his elderly aunts, she did not envision taking on this kincare responsibility primarily herself. Rather, she was quick to say that her sister "gladly will" take on the kincare her father had been doing, even moving from one side of the country to another to care for her aunts if it became necessary: "My sister is much more family oriented, like she talks about it like, 'Yeah when this happens, I'm going to come down.'"

Audrey, a 60-year-old African American professor from Alabama who had lived and worked for many years in the Midwest, recalled her relationship with an aunt who expected her to provide financial assistance. For this niece, the expectation developed from a class-based misperception—the aunt believed that her niece earned more money and was more financially secure than she actually was.

> Aunt Fiona married Uncle Dell when she was fourteen years old. He was older than she, and I now know that he was born in 1895. She died in 1983, and we had become estranged by then, although at one time, I loved her more than I did most people. I believe that she was not a very elderly woman at her death. Our estrangement was due, not to my neglect or an argument, but a strange class difference. She believed I was earning lots of money and was failing to send her money which she sorely needed, at a time I was earning $8,000 a year, with my own mother in the midst of a catastrophic illness. Language and explanations often do little to change deeply entrenched perceptions. . . .

In looking back at this ill-fated relationship, Audrey felt both affection and regret for the estrangement: "I have accepted the blessings of our kinship and still regret that her expectations were those that, at the time, I could not meet." Not only did her aunt perceive class-based differences, but Audrey herself admitted that she had been aware of her aunt's limited literacy skills, which made her feel distanced from her aunt. She recalled that her aunt had written her letters, "which I am now ashamed to say, I threw away because they were so poorly written. I did answer all of them, and I initiated letters and cards and visits. We simply grew apart, in education and understanding." The obligations for kincare within the extended family network remain an important theme in Audrey's narrative despite the sad fate of her relationship with her aunt.

Another example of a niece expecting to give care to her aunt and uncle was Isabel, a 24-year-old Mexican American niece. She noted that she expected to take on kincare responsibilities for her aunt/godmother. According to Isabel, her relationship with her aunt had always been close, "so I was kind of chosen by her and her husband that when they get older they're gonna need somebody, and they asked me to do it a few years ago on my visits for the summer." Aunts acted as godmothers to many nieces and nephews in our study, which appeared to further the sense of mutual obligation and expectations for enduring relationships and responsibilities. We further reflect on the practice of choosing aunts as godmothers in chapter 6.

These stories of kincare among nieces and nephews demonstrate that across ethnic groups, expectations that aunts and nieces/nephews will care for each other across generations of kin vary but also clearly are present. Recent research suggests that increased life expectancy, changing family roles and work relations, lower fertility rates, geographic mobility, and emerging patterns of immigration have created more complex multigenerational family structures in the U.S.[30] Developing support systems is critical, both within kinship networks as well as across civil institutions and at policy levels. The obligations and expectations of aunting relationships seem particularly useful in addressing the need for social support and social capital in the contemporary period.

Feminine Kinworking

Despite reports of the decline of social capital, we found ample evidence that aunts and nieces/nephews perform regular, even daily, support for extended family members in ways that ranged from small to hugely significant. In asking nieces/nephews and aunts about their relationships, we were both unsurprised that aunts play formative and substantive roles in the lives of their nieces/nephews and, at the same time, overwhelmed by the wealth of stories, descriptions, and details that participants readily volunteered.

Yet it also became clear to us in our analysis that aunting remains a deeply gendered practice. Kinkeepers are most likely to be mothers, aunts, or grandmothers.[31] Given current research on extended family dynamics, this aspect of our findings did not surprise us. Many scholars associate the evolution of women as primary kinkeepers with the Industrial Revolution and the cult of domesticity that entrenched the notion of women as linked with the domestic sphere and men with the public.[32] Despite dramatic changes in families, work places, churches and other religious organizations, and communities, material caregiving work remains largely women's work; women are the primary "kinkeepers" in extended families.[33] The work of kinship is part of the feminine sphere of "psychological responsibility" that is embraced primarily by women.[34]

> Affluent women can "buy out" of housework, child care—and even some kin-work responsibilities. But they, like all women, are ultimately responsible, and subject to both guilt and blame, as the administrators of home, children, and kin network. Even the wealthiest women must negotiate the timing and venue of holidays and other family rituals with their kinswomen. It may be that kin work is the core women's work category in which all women cooperate.[35]

This is not to say that all women participate in kinwork, or that no men are involved, but men tend to go along with the plans made by their wives, mothers, grandmothers, sisters, and aunts rather than instigate or organize kinwork tasks independently, and they tend to leave the bulk of the work to the women who embrace it. Men with feminine styles of communicating and egalitarian beliefs about marriage were the most likely to share more equally in providing kincare than more traditionally masculine men.[36] Nonetheless, researchers found that wives spent almost three times as many hours per month as their husbands helping kin with domestic and practical tasks and were significantly more likely to provide material assistance to kin.[37]

In understanding the gendered nature of aunting and kinkeeping more broadly, we neither blame men nor frame women as victims, but join with other feminist scholars in reclaiming—or advocating the value of—women's common focus on kin networks as potential sources of personal satisfaction, empowerment, and, at times, vital material and emotional resources.[38] Performing kinwork can be burdensome, routine, satisfying, joyful, or all of the above. In such work (and/or through the absence of same), aunts "do family," constructing through communicative acts and interactions the meanings of aunt, niece, nephew, kin, and care.[39] Repeated performances of kinwork shape both aunts' own sense of their identity qua aunts and perceptions of them as aunts by their nieces, nephews, and other kin who witness or take part in the doing of kinship. While other roles assume kinwork responsibilities, we see the aunt as the one with the greatest liberatory potential. The aunt is feminine, yet she is not the mother; she does caring work, yet she enjoys a great deal more choice, freedom, and flexibility than nuclear family members. Expectations exist, but they are formed and continually revised within the ongoing enactment of aunt/niece/nephew relationships.

LOOKING AHEAD

Aunting kinwork for the most part is conceptualized as a hands-on practice; it may be performed from a distance, but most of what our participants talked about were immediate and concrete practices. The next chapter focuses on what we call "kin connections." In it, we explore ways in which aunts participate in, maintain, and even create or transform connections among family members that bridge geographical, generational, biolegal, or experiential gaps. This moves from the communicative value of everyday practices to those activities, rituals, and relational forms that are taken to communicate family.

Constructing Kin

Scholars note that "contemporary extended family does not simply persist. Someone expends a great deal of time and energy to maintain it."[1] Aunts often function as that "someone." Gretchen, a 50-year-old Polish/Irish American woman, described her role as primarily one of preserving family connections:

> My role as aunt? Try to encourage them of the importance of family, when we get together—to encourage an atmosphere of family, right. To encourage them to continue to get together as a family and to rely and count on your cousins and aunts and family connections—that they are the most important, that they should come first.

In addition to preserving and strengthening family bonds, aunts often initiate or participate in the formation of chosen kinship ties that extend family networks, blurring distinctions among family, friends, neighbors, and significant others. Kinkeeping communication maintains family relationships in ways that coordinate, supplement, and even substitute for the more material forms of care discussed in the previous chapter.

In this chapter, we explore how aunting creatively constructs and maintains kinship connections and networks by organizing and participating in family rituals, keeping in touch across long distances, functioning as information sources and influences within the family network, and establishing and maintaining chosen family ties. These creative relational configurations attest to the importance of nonnuclear family connections and extend the benefits of kinship beyond biolegal relations.

GATHERING TOGETHER

Rituals are often an important aspect of aunts' interactions with their nieces and nephews. Families create their own rituals, sometimes within the celebration of larger cultural events, such as religious ceremonies (e.g., bar mitzvah) or holidays (e.g., Thanksgiving Day). While rituals vary widely in form and content, they have certain elements in common: they involve "an act or actions intentionally conducted by a group of people employing one or more symbols in a repetitive, formal, precise, highly stylized fashion."[2] Symbols can be language based (that is, written or spoken words, such as the Torah), or involve another medium such as dance or music (e.g., Mendelssohn's wedding march), or they can involve interacting with an object imbued with symbolic value (e.g., heirloom serving dishes). Facilitating rituals is one of the primary outcomes of kinkeeping communication among biolegal and chosen family.[3] Rituals play a central role in forging and maintaining connections among aunts and nieces and nephews.

> Rituals affirm the reality of abstract meaning for daily living, and they define the continuity of experience between past, present, and future . . . family rituals are part of the ongoing process by which a private sphere of intimate ties is continuously constructed and reconstructed.[4]

Sharing family rituals was an important element of the relationships of some nieces/nephews with their aunts. A Latina college student noted: "Tía [Spanish for "aunt"] is the aunt that I know the best. Our family spent numerous holidays with her family." For other participants, family gatherings were among the only occasions in which they interacted with their aunts. One European American woman stated: "The only time I ever really see [my aunts] is during the winter holidays."

Aunts often play a vital role by simply attending events that mark turning points or accomplishments of their nieces and nephews. A 21-year-old niece observed that her aunts have been there for all the important rituals of her life:

> I just feel like they've known me since I was born. They've seen me go through every stepping stone and they've been to the baptisms and the graduation, all the birthday parties . . . it's like I'm used to seeing them everyday; we're always close like when we come in contact with each other.

For this niece, the participation of her aunts in periodic rituals is so meaningful that she describes her relationships with them as being as close as relationships that involve daily contact (even though she does not see her aunts that often). By affirming her stages of growth and accomplishments, her aunts made her feel that they appreciate and care about her. Another young niece, Ruth, grew up in a Catholic family with seven children and close extended family ties, particularly among her mother's relatives. Regular visits to her grandparents' home for holidays and summer vacations helped to forge her bond with her aunt Elena. She explained that her mother's sister took care of her grandparents:

> [My aunt] Elena became the only sibling to live with her parents. While all the other siblings moved on, getting married and starting a family, Elena stayed behind to take care of my grandparents. For this, I get to see her most because it's inevitable that when I go [to] visit my grandparents, Aunt Elena is there.

Family celebrations can also provide opportunities to reconnect with aunts with whom nieces or nephews have fallen out of touch.

> I went to a family gathering for my grandma's birthday. This was the first one I had gone to in a few years and it was certainly weird seeing all my relatives again. I got to talk to my aunt again and amazingly, we had a great conversation. (Asian American niece, college student)

This niece's enjoyment of her aunt's company highlights the significance of family rituals (such as celebrations marking milestone birthdays) for bringing family members together. While the niece and aunt may not maintain regular contact between family gatherings, the ritual space can provide an environment that facilitates the renewal of previous emotional connections.

One way our participants' aunts fostered a sense of cohesiveness among extended family was to organize and host (or help host) parties and other gatherings. These often occurred on major religious holidays (e.g., Passover), national holidays (e.g., Independence Day), or cultural holidays (e.g., Halloween). Often these traditions were repeated annually, imbuing them with more significance each time the ritual celebration was enacted. A nephew shared his aunt's Halloween tradition:

> The best part of [my aunt] is that every Halloween she always has a big party. She is a nurse and she would have [mannequins] and dress them up like scary looking doctors. I would go over to her house and have a great time with my little cousins.

Parties and special events are important to continuing a sense of family tradition and to maintaining kin networks and family ties, but they cannot be shared unless one or more family members commit to making them happen. Gretchen spoke of spending annual holidays at her aunt's house:

> We always went to her house on the Fourth of July. Because she lived right on the river. And we would all sit there in the yard, and have big cookouts, have hot dogs and baked beans. And we'd all sit and eat, and have a big family reunion with family and friends. And watch all the fireworks go off . . . After I got married and had children I even used to take our children there. Until we sold the house, it was a yearly event and tradition in the family—probably for thirty-some years or more.

While not substituting for daily care of children, special events organized by aunts clearly made nieces and nephews feel nurtured and connected to family.

Ritual celebrations also were frequently centered on neighborhoods and chosen family. Ella, a college student from Hawaii, spoke of one neighbor she called "aunty," who was particularly important to forging close connections among the families in her neighborhood:

> [My aunt] maintains very close relationships with all the kids in the cul-de-sac and is known as the "Party Coordinator." Ever since I can remember, Aunty has planned the neighborhood parties for Christmas, Easter, and summer. . . .

Sometimes families gather for sad reasons. Betty spoke of seeing her aunts and other relatives after more than a dozen years at the funeral of her great-aunt:

> I did get to see [my aunts] at the funeral which was unfortunate, but I did get to see all the kids there, and I got to see my uncle and aunt . . . so it was really nice, unfortunately under a sad circumstance . . . It was bittersweet.

Despite the sad occasion, Betty appreciated the opportunity to reconnect with her aunt and other relatives, and in doing so, she felt that her time at the funeral became both a celebration of her great-aunt's life and a way to foster continued relationships with other family members. The funeral ritual reminded extended family of their connections and obligations, as well as their shared love and loyalties. Being together—even under difficult circumstances—can reaffirm the care and kinship that bonds aunts and their nieces and nephews, along with other extended family members.

The importance of the aunt in narratives and memories of extended kinship and family gatherings was articulated by Elise as she reflected on treasured memories of her childhood that provide her a sense of identity and belonging:

> Every other month we'd see one side of the family or the other. One month we'd pack up for the weekend and go to Massachusetts, so I'd see my mother's younger sister. . . . And then the next month, we'd pack up and go to Canada, and then that was just, there was a lot more up there 'cause my father's family was all together pretty much

in the same town . . . and there was two, one of mom's sisters and one of her brother's there so, that was where you got to see most of the relatives anyways, and then at Christmas time, um, we'd all get together in Massachusetts at my grandparents' house, and there was usually, two or three of [my aunts] would come down . . . it was never about presents, you know, it was just a family thing. You would just sit around and talk and eat.

She added that her relationship with her aunts was bound up with her childhood experience of family: "It wasn't just the niece part, but it was more of the whole family thing that formed what I was when I was younger." She continues to enjoy her relationships with her aunts in the context of a boisterous and affectionate kinship network. "It just all goes back to the extended family, you know, knowing that there's somebody else out there that cares, whether you see them a lot or not, you know, they're still there." As an aunt herself, Elise now tries to ensure that her nieces and nephews (both biolegal and chosen) enjoy a similar sense of being grounded in an extended family. The web of relationships that Elise described—of relating to her aunts primarily within the context of her extended family network—was evident in many of our participants' narratives.

Kathleen, a Sister of the Presentation Order now in her seventies, articulated a responsibility as an aunt, godmother, and single adult to participate in family gatherings, and to alternate visits among family members who were geographically dispersed:

So, anyway I've always been on good terms [with family members], so I always get invited . . . [A]s a nun, I come kind of unencumbered with uncles and cousins, so that can be positive and negative, but as a result, I'm kind of the "floater" in the family too. So you know I get all these invitations, and I just float from one to the other. . . . In fact, [my niece] invited me [for Christmas] this year, but I think I'll go down to L.A. and be with my sister down there, so I kind of feel I have an obligation to float and, you know, cover all the bases. And maybe that's part of being the oldest too, you know; you take responsibility for everybody.

In this passage, Kathleen clearly acknowledges that her presence at family rituals is meaningful for both her and other family members. She notes that her single status (as a nun) offers a unique flexibility unavailable to aunts with spouses and children, and she consciously chooses to reaffirm her connections to a large number of relatives by alternating which gatherings she attends.

Aunts may foster a sense of togetherness within extended family networks through participating in ritual celebrations of nieces' and nephews' growth and accomplishments, hosting family gatherings that embody specific traditions and rituals, and enriching a sense of belonging within a kinship network. Such connections endure for many families despite significant geographic, generational, and circumstantial distances.

KEEPING IN TOUCH

In between or in place of family gatherings, our participants reported that aunts maintained communication with nieces and nephews and among other kin, often over significant geographic distance, primarily by phone and e-mail. While some scholars have warned that kinkeeping and extended family connections are declining in contemporary United States society, other scholars argue that these findings may focus too exclusively on face-to-face and sustained interactions and thus fail to take into consideration contemporary electronic means of maintaining close ties over large geographical distances as increased nuclear family mobility disperses family members.[5] Our findings support this methodological critique, as our participants clearly recognized and valued their aunts' participation in kinship rituals, gatherings, and long-distance communication (e.g., phone calls and e-mail). A niece described her situation as follows:

> I have never lived anywhere near my aunts. . . . I do, however, have what I would consider a good relationship with both of them. We have always communicated by the phone, mainly on holidays or special occasions. Even with the popular onset of the internet, we stayed true to the traditional phone. (22-year-old European American college student)

She also explained that she keeps track of her aunts' comings and goings by exchanging information with her mother. Another niece explained:

> I still keep in touch with my Aunt Cora through e-mail and occasional phone calls. I used to feel uncomfortable talking to her on the phone because we did not have much to say to each other. I feel closer to my Aunt Cora now because we can have real conversations without having to see each other. (21-year-old European American college student)

The ability to have "real" conversations marks this niece's coming of age; she is now an adult who has more in common with her aunt and hence feels more connected to her. E-mailing and calling aunts can also help preserve connections with a larger community, as another niece describes:

> Although I do not see [my aunt] as often anymore now that I am away at college, I still keep in touch with her via e-mail and letters. . . . I don't think that distance places a barrier on our relationship. With e-mail and cell phones, we are able to keep in touch pretty regularly. . . . She always makes it a point to include me in the e-mails and events that occur in the neighborhood, even when I am not at home to enjoy them. She keeps me updated and scans pictures to me so I can see what I missed. It is nice to know that I'm not being forgotten. (20-year-old Asian American college student)

Family e-mail lists help aunts and nieces/nephews to feel connected, to maintain links forged when the niece or nephew was geographically closer to an aunt, or to foster connections in between visits from kin who have always been geographically distant. Even transnational connections can be maintained electronically between nieces/nephews and aunts. Ahmed, a 21-year-old Kurdistani college student, described his connections with family members spread across several countries:

> In 1997 I moved to the United States and after I moved . . . I heard that my youngest aunt and my middle aunt have moved to Germany. Since they been in Germany I have talked to both of them couple of

times over the phone, they seemed to be doing very well, but I have not heard or talk to them for about two years now. I have my oldest aunt (mother's sister) that moved to Canada last year. I went and saw her last summer. She was very happy to see me and I was extremely excited to see one of my aunts for the first time in seven years. We had a great time with each other it was very fun. I am thinking about going to see her again. . . . I am also planning to save up some money and go see my other lovely aunts and family members back in my country and Germany.

Visits and phone calls provide a sufficient contact for Ahmed to feel a sense of connection to his aunts and other extended kin, despite huge geographic distances and dispersion across national and cultural borders. Our point is that electronic communication media facilitate aunting and can maintain connections despite little face-to-face contact. We shall have more to say about aunting across time and geographic distance in chapter 3.

INFORMING FAMILIES

Thus far in this chapter we have discussed aunts' communicative kinwork: connecting, networking, and perpetuating family traditions. These actions, choices, and interactions position aunts as "in the know" about other family members' lives, including their nieces and nephews. The knowledge acquired through maintaining kinwork connections may make aunts powerful within family networks, with both positive and negative consequences. While they can be invaluable resources, knowledgeable aunts can also spread damaging gossip or use information to manipulate other family members. To illustrate, we offer two contrasting narratives describing the central role of aunts as information repositories, disseminators, and critics.

Darla, who disliked her aunt's habit of gossiping, seemed concerned that negative gossip may be harmful:

Aunt Karina is my great-aunt who [sic] I love dearly but cannot stand to be around. This is because she is the worse [sic] gossip I know of. . . . I have two sister-in-law [sic] and they are both the best sister-in-law [sic] I have. But the thing is my Aunt Karina thinks that they are not good enough for my brothers, everyone else thinks otherwise . . . even know when I find my mister right she will say that he is not good enough for me. I hardly visit her but when I do I get questioned about everybody and then she tells me what everyone is up. I love her and care for her greatly but I do not like to hear about the gossip. (22-year-old European American college student)

Darla's suspicions that this aunt might gossip about her and that her aunt uses her to collect family information makes her wary of talking with her aunt at all. Clearly, Darla understood her aunt's gossip as a negative force. Yet she acknowledged that her aunt had "all the dirt" in the family, functioning as a resource for keeping up to date with family members' lives even though this meant listening to critical evaluations of her sisters-in-law, or other negative commentary.

In contrast, Kathleen held a much more positive view of aunts as working together to manage family information. For many of our participants whose families were similar to Kathleen's, aunts became the clearinghouse not just for information on family members, but for coordinating strategic (usually compassionate) responses by designated family members. Speaking of her father's family in Ireland, whom she met for the first time as an adult, Kathleen said:

[A]ll the aunts are called the "aunties," and one of my uncles had six daughters, so his children all refer to "the aunties" and it's like the aunties are a block, you know, and everything they do, they kind of contact one another or whatever on almost everything, and so it's like you have this formidable group. . . .

In her own life, Kathleen engages in the practice of organizing the aunties as a collective voice to help extended family members when they experience difficulties. Rather than make unilateral decisions, Kathleen reaches out and builds coalitions with other family members. She explained:

[I]n fact my sister and I are going to talk on Saturday about, not her children, but you know another mutual relation and ahh . . . it's a question of just knowing what your role is, knowing what you should and shouldn't do. . . . [M]y sisters and I talk among ourselves sometimes and then we say, "Well, what should we do," you know, and we do try to maybe err on the side of caution.

Kathleen explained that she felt it was a benefit to be outside the nuclear family at such times, and thus able to offer a concerned but more detached perspective on a problem, particularly in the lives of her nieces, nephews, great-nieces, and great-nephews:

> I think [aunts play] a lot of roles . . . I don't want to say there's a separation, but there's a sense of intimate family being the linear family line, and there's the lateral family and so, you're very close, but you're a little outside. You're one step removed from that box. . . . And I think as an aunt, I have to respect that, so in terms of what I can do and what I can't do, and what I can say and can't say—you've got to think about it.

Kathleen's comment illustrates the difficult process of negotiating boundaries between the aunt and the nuclear family. At the same time, she articulates a firm commitment to doing so in order to use her information and insights with the intention of nurturing individual family members and thus strengthening the extended family network.

Comparing Darla's and Kathleen's experiences illuminates the impossibility of labeling aunts' communicative kinwork—maintaining kin connections and managing family information—as simply helpful or harmful. Clearly, the communicative ties that bind can be used to support family members, to condemn them, or both, and aunts function as key players in the negotiation of these ties.

RECONFIGURING KINSHIP THROUGH CHOICE

> So, if someone asked me how many people were in my family, I would not be able to give them an exact number because my family extends beyond my Mom and Dad, it consists of other special people . . . [including] aunties like my Aunty. (Ella, 21-year-old Hawaiian college student)

Ella's words reflect the common practice in Hawaii of bestowing the title of "aunty" upon friends, neighbors, and community members who have established close ties with a family. The significance of such "othermothers" and "godmothers" in Black, Latino, and Native American child-rearing practices has been recognized and even celebrated.[6] In anthropologist Carol Stack's classic social ethnographic study of kinship ties and reciprocal support among poor and working-class urban African Americans, chosen sisters and aunts (called "fictive kin") featured prominently in narratives of creativity and resilience in the midst of hardship.[7] Such relationships hold similar rights and obligations as those expected of biolegal family members, but are constituted outside of marriage or hereditary ties.[8] A variety of communities invoke the term "aunt" and other familial titles for nonbiolegally constituted kin, as documented through research studying immigrants, older people, female prison inmates, homeless youths, lesbians and gay men, followers of the Yoruba religion, and Latina single mothers, all of whom are in socially and/or economically precarious positions where the construction of chosen kin is widely beneficial and even necessary.[9] Social commentators often promote such ties as models for mainstream American culture to foster nurturing communities that encourage reciprocity, compassion, and mutual responsibility.[10] At the same time, several prominent social trends support the creation of chosen kinship relations: people tend to delay marriage and child-bearing, remaining single until a much later age; geographic mobility of families is prevalent, often isolating them from extended family support; people enjoy longer average life span, creating a need for supportive relationships into old age; and displacement due to war and other political strife necessitates reformation of community bonds.[11]

The title of aunt may be given to a friend or community member in acknowledgement of a close tie, or alternatively, a friend's claim to the title that is subsequently acknowledged by members of a chosen family. Language is important to performances of self and to interpretation of one's relationships. The relative lack of terms for acknowledging meaningful bonds with people outside the immediate family is one reason why family terms such as aunt continue to be invoked so commonly across cultures.

The usage of family language reflects an underlying issue: There is no sufficient social script to guide or characterize nonbiolegal, platonic, emotionally intimate, and socially reliant relationships between close friends. Hence, some may have identified their significant friends as family *because such a bond is easily understood as being a meaningful connection.*[12]

The recognizable title thus serves as a symbol to others, in and outside of the social network, of a relationship's significance. It is no coincidence that a culture that idealizes the nuclear family as the unit of production, reproduction, and supportive relationships lacks a suitable vocabulary to express other types of relational commitments. The English language lags in this area because public discourse remains mired in the narrative of the intact nuclear family.

The power of naming is significant; many of our participants noted when describing a beloved aunt, "I call her my aunt even though she isn't really my aunt." We suggest that from a communication perspective, calling someone an aunt constitutes the relationship as such. In the same way that people are labeled "wife," "husband," or "spouse," the speaking or writing of "aunt," "niece," or "nephew" establishes the reality of that connection. Communication scholars point out that our talk not only expresses meanings but enacts relationships and commits social acts with real consequences (as when someone says "I do" in a wedding ceremony).[13] In this sense, calling someone an aunt not only names that person as an aunt but also mobilizes the personal, social, and cultural bonds of an aunting relationship.

In the remainder of this chapter, we discuss several common ways in which families invoke the title of aunt in different relational situations.

Creating Aunts with Distant or New Kin

Participants described chosen aunts who were drawn from among distant relatives or newly established relatives acquired through remarriage or blended families. These aunts were women related in some way by marriage or blood but not in typical aunt positions, that is, they were not the sisters or sisters-in-law of a child's parent, nor the aunts of a parent. In these cases some remote biolegal tie existed or family members formed a new relationship that they then reframed as an aunting relationship where none was expected or preordained. In this case, aunts, their nieces/nephews, and/or the nieces'/nephews' parents made active choices about building aunting relationships. Phrases such as, "Well, she's family but she's not really my aunt," recurred in such scenarios, followed by lengthy explanations of the official kinship ties that had been transformed into aunting relationships. For example, Laura's aunt Kay is actually her great-grandmother's (on her mother's side) uncle's granddaughter, or put another way, aunt Kay's grandfather was a brother of Laura's great-great-grandfather. The maintenance of this loose family tie was facilitated primarily by the fact that Kay resided in the same town as Laura's grandmother and great-grandmother. Among our participants, as in other kinship research, we found ample evidence that conferring the aunt designation upon women who are a generation or more older than the niece/nephew remains quite common. The aunt title was a sign of respect, an expression of affection, and an embodiment of (an expectation of) enduring ties.

Carolyn, a middle-aged child development professional, provides an illustrative example of reframing distant relations as aunts.

> My grandmother lived in a close-knit community that she had lived in all her life. . . . One of her closest friends was Susan, and I called her Aunt Susan. And then Abigail who is a cousin-in-law of my grandmother's, is Aunt Abigail, and then her children were aunts too . . . and Aunt May was [my grandmother's cousin], and [my grandmother] would wait on weekends for me to go see Aunt May, 'cause she knew I really liked going. I loved to go there [because] it was an adventure. And then my mother's cousin Katherine was my aunt Kathy. . . . I think we really are influenced by our family. My mother just thought the sun rose and shone with [Aunt Kathy], and I think that you kind of get that as a child, you pick up on how special this person is.

Both her grandmother's cousins and her mother's cousin thus became aunts who influenced Carolyn's sense of her family as embedded in a larger extended community. Interestingly, her friends and relatives were all part of a community within a small town, and the term "aunt" was given to those with marginal family status (e.g., cousin-in-law) and friends alike.

Another common designation of aunt occurred among people who adopted the practice of using the aunt title to refer to their spouse's aunts. Some married people chose not to do this, but others adopted the practice and were accepted as nieces or nephews by their in-law relatives. For example, Betty refers to her husband's aunts as aunts:

> I do have some aunts on [my husband] Mike's side, so, that I call aunt. So on that side he has three, on his mother's side . . . they're his aunts . . . I sure do [call them aunt]. That's what he's always called them, so that's what I call them—there's Aunt Elaine and Aunt Mary and then also Aunt Laurel is the other one, and so we call them all aunts.

Betty reported calling them aunts because she felt that her relationship to them was "niece-in-law" and that to address them by their first name or with a title other than aunt (such as Mrs.) would be both disrespectful and an indication that she did not feel that she was included within her husband's family. Interestingly, Betty was also open to being chosen as an aunt; her niece Heather's best friend Dawn, whom Betty had known for years, called her Aunt Betty too, reflecting a tradition of choosing aunts.

Blended Family Aunts

Aunts also may prove vital when families falter, fracture, or reconfigure over time. Given the frequency of divorce, blended families have become increasingly common, and these emergent configurations pose significant communicative challenges.[14] Kinwork and supportive communication from aunts can help with major disjunctures in familial life, such as incorporating stepparents, stepchildren, and half siblings into family units, and adjusting to and maintaining relationships with noncustodial parents. In such circumstances, aunts may be instrumental in building and managing familial ties. For example, Teresa explained that she chose to recognize the children of her brother's new wife and welcome them into their extended family network:

> I told my mom, "we have new nieces and nephews. You're going to
> be a grandma again." She goes, "what do you mean?" I go, "'cause
> they're not really our relatives, but they are going to be related to us."
> She goes, "yeah, if she marries your brother, they are [related]—
> they're my grandkids." And I go, "well, if they're your grandkids,
> I guess they are my nieces and nephews." . . . [Then] once I got to
> know [the kids] they wanted to be part of our family right away, and
> it remained that way. . . . They call me aunt, and I feel close to those
> kids, closer than my own nephew—my real, my blood nephew.

This aunt took it upon herself to set the stage for incorporating these children into their new family network by speaking to her own mother, the family matriarch, about their status as family members in order to ensure that the matriarch would welcome them to the large, extended Mexican American family. In this way, the aunt sent a clear message to the rest of the family that they would be expected to similarly accept the children. The aunt further validated her connection to her step-nieces/stepnephews by contrasting her affection for them with another one of her nephews who, while related by blood, did not maintain a close relationship with her. Plainly, this aunt made an active choice to accept the children and a flexible notion of family.

An aunting relationship also may be the basis for continuing familial ties even after a nuclear family dissolves.[15] For example, Rose, a 35-year-old Portuguese American, is the daughter of Portuguese immigrants; she is married with two young daughters. Rose maintains a warm relationship with her brother's ex-wife, who is her daughter's godmother: "We were very close when they were married, and so even though they got separated, we still wanted her to be part of the family," she explained. Her daughter remains very close to this aunt/godmother despite the divorce. Rose made a conscious effort to arrange visits and joint activities to have fun together, and always invited the ex-wife to family gatherings as her daughter's aunt.

Ellen was close to her mother's oldest brother's wife, the aunt mentioned in the kinwork chapter who reached out to Ellen when she was attending college. When this aunt and Ellen's uncle were going through a divorce, the uncle was killed in an accident. Ellen might have considered her tie to her aunt (related to her by marriage) severed.

Yet the bond between Ellen and her aunt has remained strong for over twenty years because of their commonalities and abiding affection. Ellen said, "I remember always thinking to myself, you know, if I could pick out the perfect mom she would be it; it's just, like, sometimes your relationships are *people*, are more important than blood, *your connections*." Such connections can be chosen or disregarded. Choice is key to the relationship's formation and to its character or substance. This aunt reached out to her first husband's niece and forged a connection based on their personal connection that persisted despite a pending divorce and the death of Ellen's biological uncle.

Neighbor and Community Aunts

Juanita, a young Latina woman, grew up on the West Coast of the United States in a diverse metropolitan area. Her views on chosen aunts were shaped by the neighborhood in which she lived, where she was a cultural minority but very much part of and connected to her neighbors.

> I've also grown up in a culture with a different view of the word aunt. I live in a largely Filipino neighborhood, and in fact, three households on the next street are all cousins. We used to joke that all Filipino people in town are related . . . [because] the terms cousin, aunt, and uncle are used much more freely. "Auntie" is the term given to another female adult, regardless of relation (unless there is another applicable one such as mother or grandmother). Older cousins can also be called auntie, as can people who are not related at all. A friend's mother hold [*sic*] the title auntie, followed by her first name. For example, one girl's mother is always Auntie Dara, never Mrs. Perez.

In Juanita's neighborhood, chosen kinship was common based on residential proximity and ongoing, friendly relationships, and not, as Juanita joked, because everyone was of the same ethnic background.

One of the most significant impetuses for constructing chosen kinship, including aunts, involves immigration.[16] To survive in a new, confusing, and sometimes hostile environment, people from the same or similar cultures often band together and create chosen kin networks to provide all forms of support. The functions of chosen kin among new immigrants "include assuring the spiritual development of the child and thereby reinforcing cultural continuity, exercising social control, providing material support, and assuring socioemotional support . . . [and serving] as an important buffer and resource."[17] Many of these kin are aunts.

Christine, the Thai niece who lived with her aunt throughout high school and college, is part of a large Thai immigrant and Thai American community on the West Coast.

> [My honorary aunts] they're actually other Thai people, some other Thai people who are my aunt's friends, who we're close to. For Thai Americans, um, we all call them aunts, because I guess, the Thai community is pretty closely knit; everyone's a family. Not, not really everyone's a family, but it's also a respectful thing. Um, because if you, if we call them the equivalent of Mrs. or Miss in Thai it would seem pretty distant, it's more like a formal thing. Yeah, so calling them aunt or uncle or grandma or mom, you wouldn't call them mom unless they were really close, but . . . if we consider them family also we would call them aunt.

Using the title "aunt" fosters a sense of closeness and a feeling of belonging to an extended family that is based on a shared cultural heritage and at least some shared experiences as an immigrant community.

Another cultural example of chosen aunts as a community or neighborhood practice is that of Hawaiian Islands natives[18] who construct chosen kin networks that extend beyond any given neighborhood and are an integral aspect of the traditional culture of these island communities. Tim, a nephew we discussed earlier, grew up on the Big Island of Hawaii, where dominant cultural norms of the United States are tempered by local island culture. There the practice of choosing aunts remains so much a part of their culture that they have a word for these chosen kin.

> [In Hawaii] you wouldn't distinguish among your blood aunties and what they call "calabash aunties." We're not actually legitimately

related, but we practically could be, you know, and it wouldn't make a difference in your interactions. In their own way they care about you like an auntie would.

A niece, also a Hawaiian student, concurred:

Being from Hawaii you definitely have a big family connection and network and even though they're not biological you would still call them your aunt. These aunts who I refer to, I see them every holiday because they join my biological aunt and like the whole family. We're a large family, and I would say there's about at least six or seven families or more. They come to our house every Christmas . . . And also I have a close friend who I've known since elementary school and [her] mom, I would call her aunt. I would call them auntie, like "Oh, hi auntie," it's like an informal thing. . . . The ones I'm really, really close to, it's a cultural thing, if you've known them for a long time.

The island culture supports a sense of everyone "practically" being family. The aunt is an integral figure in these community networks, a testament to the kinship-like bonds among the island residents.[19]

A final example of aunting as a feature of close communities is exemplified in an interview with Joshua, a young man raised in a Mennonite community. He explained:

Mennonite culture is extremely internal. There isn't much experienced with non-Mennonite people. . . . So, you know, they have their own schooling, they have their own way of life, they have their own economy almost. And because of that, since everyone is pretty much family as it is, there's this feeling of, "OK, you step in now." So people who'd be my grandmother's cousin's second nephew on the whatever, they would have some role in my family . . . [including] my aunts.

The voluntary segregation of the Mennonite community requires strong family and community support. The dense family networks that Joshua describes draw heavily on kinwork and kincare, and aunting is clearly a critical resource. Not coincidentally, this young man who articulated the insular nature of the community had chosen to move outside of the boundaries of this way of life because it did not suit him. We will return to his experiences in chapter 5, in our discussion of aunts as role models and mentors.

We have drawn on data from our participants to identify how choice, proximity, and relational practices constitute chosen aunting relationships. Our data confirm that some co-cultures take the creation of fictive kin as a way of life, such as gay communities in which the aunt identity shifts both female and familial kinships, African Americans living in urban settings, immigrant communities uniting to share support as newcomers to the United States, and members of small town communities. According to our participants, naming someone aunt (or auntie/aunty) is a way of honoring and formalizing connections in neighborhoods, in churches and other community groups, and among close family friends. Moreover, community aunting often manifests as organizing and hosting neighborhood gatherings or holiday parties and other special events, which over time become vital rituals of community and identity for our participants. In short, our analysis suggests the importance of aunting practices and choices as binding forces that constitute and perpetuate familial and community ties.

Family Friends as Family

Our participants spoke of friendships between families, particularly of mothers and their "best friends," that often included an emphasis on child rearing and aunting. For example, referring to her chosen niece, Elise explained:

> [H]er mother and I, and her father and my husband, we're just friends. We got married at the same time . . . and we had kids at the same time; my son was actually born a day before [my niece Madison]. . . . I didn't have any sisters and Sharon is probably the closest thing that I have to a sister, so she's always been Auntie Sharon to my kids and I've always been Aunt Elise to her daughter. So, it's been nice, you know, we do a lot of things together. The kids spend a lot of time together . . . I call and talk to Sharon on the phone, if Madison comes in I always talk to her, find out how she's doing,

what's going on in school. . . . Oh, we've gone out to lunch; it's usually the four of us—my daughter Kate and I, and Sharon and Madison, kinda like a little foursome, do lunch together, do shopping together. It's never, hasn't been a lot of one on one with just Madison, it's more her mother and I get together and the girls are there, that type of thing. Every Christmas, Madison's right up there with getting presents, on her birthday she gets presents. We've gone to school plays, you know, anytime we can make it, we go to her dance recitals. You know we actually interact more with Madison than we do with my biological nieces and nephews.

In this illustrative example, several dynamics are evident. First, the couple maintains a solid friendship with another couple that includes shared rituals and routines. From this foundation, Elise and Sharon became chosen sisters. Second, these two families encountered major milestones at the same time—marriage and the birth of their children. Hence, the families feel quite compatible. The proximity of age between the first child of Elise and the first child of Sharon, in addition to their each having a daughter (Elise's second child), meant that as the kids grew, they continued to have a lot in common. Third, Elise described the enactment of the relationship through giving gifts, attending special events, celebrating holiday rituals, and enjoying fun events with a foursome of the two women and their daughters.[20] Fourth, naming is part of the process; both women want their children to call the other by the title "aunt." Elise concludes by stating that she interacts more with her chosen niece than with the nieces and nephews with whom she has a biolegal connection. Also typically, the emphasis in Elise's story is on how she and her friend make this relationship real and perpetuate it, with far less emphasis on her and her friend's husbands, and on Elise's son.[21] All of these factors together combine to demonstrate that it is through communication and repeated performance of rituals and relational connections that a chosen aunt relationship is just as "real" as a biolegal aunt relationship, sometimes even more so, for, as Margery Williams said in the *Velveteen Rabbit* (1922), love makes even imaginary relationships "become real."

Indeed, chosen family bonds are often so durable that they persist in the face of negative, even painful interactions. One niece told a story of power abuse by a chosen aunt. In this story, the aunt arranged a job for her niece in her own office, where they worked together for two years. While the aunt was a source of assistance, she also subjected her niece to emotional abuse in the workplace.

> Sometimes it was hard because she treated me horrible, she could not separate family feuds and work. Several times she humiliated me by comparing me with the achievements of her sister. She always put herself as a role model and made me feel as if I was dumb. I have always taken her sermons and abuses because I can't disrespect her, she is older then I am. But, sometimes I really wanted to slap her. Sometimes, when I needed someone to talk to and I would go to her, I always ended up regretting it. She would turn it around and use it against me to humiliate me and talk behind my back. Needless to say that I quit last year, and that was the happiest day of my life. I still see her every weekend when I go back home. Sometimes I thought it was because she wasn't really related to me that she was so evil, but now that I've gotten to know her well, I understand that is just her personality because she does the same thing to her blood. (21-year-old Latina college student)

This story demonstrates the complexities of power and intimacy in the aunting relationship. While this is a chosen aunt relationship, the aunt and niece clearly shared an intimate relationship replete with shared confidences and a sense of family connection. Yet the potential for abuse in intimate relationships is demonstrated as well. The closing observations in this story suggest that the reason this aunt abused her niece was not because they were not really related; the aunt abused her niece because this relationship was real, as real as biolegal blood relationships in which apparently the aunt also was abusive.

WHY FICTIVE KIN REALLY MATTER

Some research shows that people are especially likely to turn to chosen kin when they are emotionally or geographically distant from biolegal kin.[22] However, other research found in contrast that people who form chosen kin networks for the most part did so for a variety of reasons, and having problems with their biolegal family members was not a common justification for doing so.[23] People come together to form mutually supportive networks under a wide variety of circumstances, and we promote valuing these relationships on their own terms rather than dismissing them as inferior because of their deviation from heteronormative, biolegal networks. Indeed, such views distort traditional biolegal family networks by romanticizing them as inherently good, ignoring or trivializing the fact that for many people, traditional kin networks are sites of physical, sexual, and/or emotional abuse, sexism, and other oppressions. For some, chosen kin "counter oppressive and abusive relational structures in those nonvoluntary communities by providing models of alternative social relationships as well as standpoints for critical reflection on self and community."[24]

Moreover, chosen aunting practices may become real aspects of our identities. Like any identity, the role of chosen aunt/niece/nephew is far less an interior aspect of an essential self and more productively thought of as a narrative of self. Scholars suggest that aspects of ourselves that we typically think of as fixed parts of ourselves are actually repeated narrative performances that we come to take for granted as natural and inevitable.[25] When the role of chosen aunt is adopted and performed repeatedly, it may become a valued enactment of a *relational* narrative of self. Likewise, becoming a chosen niece or nephew reflects a performance of self *in relation to others*—the chosen aunt, of course, but also others within the kin network, notably the parent with whom the chosen aunt has established a sibling-like relationship and any children of the chosen aunt who presumably would also fulfill the role of chosen cousins to the chosen niece or nephew. Thus, chosen aunts impact our sense of family, our beliefs about what families do, and our sense of who we are as part of a family configuration.

One might ask whether we are guilty of an overly optimistic or idealistic framing of the process of constructing fictive families as equal in value to the process of enacting "real" (i.e., biolegal, nuclear) ones. We argue that is not the case. Although one may choose how to enact biolegal relationships, they retain an external reality legitimated by law, ritual, and culture. In contrast, chosen families become "real" only through choice, communication, and action; that is, through *doing* them. Rather than an inferior or "pretend" form of family, chosen familial relationships are constituted actively, imaginatively, and reciprocally, constructing the reality of a voluntary commitment.

The examples in this chapter illustrate myriad ways in which aunts participate in the formation, maintenance, and endurance of family connections. Although the comfort, security, and sense of identity provided by being grounded within a network of family connections are inherently valuable, these networks also confer more concrete advantages on their members. Such networks of kin, chosen kin, and friends provide members with social capital. Social capital can be understood as "positions and relationships in groupings and social networks, including memberships, network ties, and social relations that can serve to enhance an individual's access to opportunities, information, material resources, and social status."[26] That is, our connections often provide us with the support we need to get along and conform within the status quo.

Yet such kinship connections—including chosen and biolegal kin—also contain the seeds for social transformation. Thus not only do such networks provide material assistance and emotional support, they also embody models for more compassionate, responsible, and creative ways to constitute and support families in today's society. Extended and chosen kinships can realize disruptive social capital in the sense that such relationships of choice model possibilities beyond the nuclear family and reject old definitions of what is "really" family or kinship or aunting in favor of creating new ones. Promoting extended family, chosen aunting, and unconventional family forms as we have done supports what feminist theorist Marilyn Friedman identifies as "socially disruptive possibilities, for out of the unconventional living which it helps to sustain there often arise influential forces for social change."[27] We maintain that encouraging a more expansive story of aunting can help to support all family forms by enriching nuclear family relationships and legitimizing nonnuclear families. The many variations on aunting in the stories our participants told encourage us to believe that aunting writ broadly may offer "disruptive possibilities" based on choice and flexibility for families, neighborhoods, communities, and even nations.

LOOKING AHEAD

Creating chosen family and creating connections may be enjoyable and beneficial, but like any relationship, aunting is fraught with challenges, distances, complexities, tensions, and negative emotions. All family relationships have painful elements—disturbing memories, difficult histories, hurtful experiences. In chapter 3, we will explore the damaging and yet surprisingly positive and meaningful aspects of problematic aunting relationships.

Aunts at a Distance

> When I think about my relationships with my aunts, I really don't
> feel close to any of them. Usually when I see them at a family gath-
> ering we just talk for a few minutes and then move on. (18-year-old
> European American nephew)

> I have no aunts on my father's side and one aunt on my mother's side
> whom I've never met because my whole family hates her. (18-year-
> old European American nephew)

Thus far, we have emphasized the importance of aunts in the lives of
their nieces and nephews and vice versa. In this chapter, we consider
aunts who are not close to their nieces and nephews. Why do these
distanced and sometimes unfriendly kinship relations still matter in
the lives of aunts, nieces, and nephews?

In talking with people about their aunting relationships, we found
that for some people, aunting was enacted as a strong emotional bond,
whereas for others, aunts were emotionally absent from their lives,
and for still others, family and personal animosities characterized the
aunting relationship. In short, there is no single emotional connection
that seems to characterize aunting relationships. Rather, the emotional
complexion of these relationships is created, maintained, and changed

in ongoing communicative interactions. Aunts may be the subjects of or participants in family rifts, tensions, and ongoing conflicts; they may offer closeness and affection or play a more distanced emotional role in a niece's or nephew's life. Yet across these variations, the aunt contributes significantly to our emotional experiences of family.

The premise of this chapter is that aunt/niece/nephew communication expands on the ways we think about family communication by including aspects we often do not acknowledge as critical to family life. Specifically, taking a close look at how people talk about their aunting relationships reveals that antagonisms may "bond" extended family together and that lack of involvement may be as important as close connections in mapping family relations. In short, this chapter illustrates that the complex emotional dynamics of aunting may include negative or uninvolved relational patterns that are just as important to our experience of family as the intimacies we explore in other chapters. We argue that there is emotional value in such distanced and unfriendly family relationships.

OPTING FOR NONINVOLVEMENT

Contented Noninvolvement

One finding that we find critically significant is what we call "contented noninvolvement." Many people reported that they have little contact with their aunts. And that seems to be just fine. We contend that noninvolvement is a form of interpersonal relationship that is undervalued both in daily life and in family communication scholarship. This is odd since it seems to be quite prevalent, given demographic, social, and cultural changes in family life over the past century. But the prevailing ideology of the family creates an expectation that all family relationships should be emotionally close. Further, the value of face-to-face interactions is assumed to be crucial in maintaining close intimate relationships. Family scholars incorporate these assumptions by presuming that infrequent contact, geographical distance, and a lack of in-depth interaction diminishes the quality of relationships.[1]

Yet these assumptions do not match contemporary experiences of family life that involve more complex relational dynamics. Significantly, many of our participants seemed content with infrequent contact and emotionally distant aunting relationships. They offered no explanations or apologies for noninvolvement—they accepted such a pattern as unremarkable and seemed unconcerned about the lack of interaction.

We argue that such contented noninvolvement is one way to continue a relationship in which partners are not often together. Scholars of long-distance relationships are studying how family relationships are maintained when there is infrequent contact and little face-to-face interaction.[2] According to communication theorist Stuart Sigman, interpersonal relationships "stretch" between moments of co-present interaction to continue and maintain the relationship.[3] That is, we are not always and everywhere in the presence of our relational partners. We maintain relationships across stretches of time when we are physically apart through our interactions with others, our memories and even idealizations of the other, and more and more, through mediated though often asynchronous contacts (e-mail, Facebook, blogs, and the like).

Communication scholar Erin Sahlstein, building on Sigman, argues that long-distance relationships negotiate multiple tensions as they navigate the differing experiences of being together and "being together apart."[4] Specifically, people in long-distance relationships reported both positive and negative aspects of being apart. Thus we need to question our "assumptions about the value of physical proximity and dissatisfaction with relational distance."[5] Notably, we found that nieces and nephews may express satisfaction with relational distance and noninvolvement with their aunts. In this chapter, we call attention to the multiple and flexible communicative patterns that maintain aunting relationships and family coherence across various forms of noninvolvement and relational distance—affective, geographic, and temporal.

While examples of noninvolvement recurred throughout the data, participants rarely stated that they perceived the lack of closeness as sad or as a loss. Most just did not think it was an important issue, nor did it seem to cause any appreciable concern. To understand the significance of contented noninvolvement, consider how much explanation is called for when one claims to be emotionally distant from one's mother. While the aunt is often equated with a mother ("she is like my second mother") and may even take on the role of mother—as we discussed in chapter 1—the fact that the aunt is relationally different from the mother is underscored by the taken-for-granted acceptability of noninvolvement among aunts and nieces/nephews.

We propose that this is an important difference between aunting and mothering—in the dominant United States culture, being uninvolved with your mother is simply not acceptable.[6] Consider the general dismay over the mother who is too busy or neglectful to be involved with her children and the regret, sadness, or anger we expect from the uninvolved child. Yet we do not look for the same explanations or render the same judgments on noninvolved aunts, nor do we worry about the well-being of the nieces or nephews who admit that they are not close or involved with their aunts. As one niece admitted without qualm:

> My aunts don't really play that big of a part in my life. Personally I think of them more as friends then [sic] of aunts. If I see them I'll have a quick conversation or two, nothing too deep, just enough to let them know I'm alive. (20-year-old European American)

Jack, a 24-year-old Native American nephew, said that he often saw his aunt and then upon reflection admitted, "Oh, not really even on holidays—just kinda—I don't know. Actually I guess I don't really see her. I just pretty much see her at weddings and funerals." Contact with his aunt simply did not register with Jack. Further, the contact that he could recall—if only vaguely—seems tied to family gatherings and rituals. In other words, communication with his aunt was bound up with ritualistic enactments of family more generally (see chapter 2 for our discussion of family celebrations and rituals). For this nephew and other nieces and nephews who participated in our study, noninvolvement with the aunt as a particular person in her own right was overshadowed by the family's enactment of family per se on holidays, in rituals, and simply as a lived fact of everyday life. Hence, despite infrequent contact and little in-depth knowledge of his aunt, Jack seemed to perceive his relationship with his aunt(s) as ongoing and familial.

As one niece explained, her uninvolved interactions with her aunts did not indicate that there was anything wrong with the relationships; rather, she found this lack of involvement unremarkable: "I am not really interested in talking with them . . . not because I have a bad relationship with them, but that tends to be how [it is]" (20-year-old Asian American niece). Nieces and nephews of all ages, genders, races, and ethnicities seemed to take contented noninvolvement as a self-evident feature of aunt/niece/nephew relationships. Importantly, these nieces and nephews reported that infrequent and fairly superficial interactions were acceptable ways of maintaining their relationships with their aunts.[7] As other research on family relationships has shown, perceptions of ongoing bonds and symbolic contact with family members may be more important than how frequently those members actually see each other.[8] Frequency of contact and degree of intimacy are not the only ways to assess how significant a kinship relationship is, or how satisfied those involved may be with it. Symbolic contact, kin-scripted roles, and the perception of a familial bond may be just as important in understanding the quality and significance of an aunt/niece/nephew relationship.

Among our participants, contented noninvolvement was often expressed as the norm, an unremarkable and completely acceptable feature of extended family communication patterns. They seemed to assume that minimal contact with their aunts was normal, and their descriptions of their aunts were often positive but quite generic ("nice"). For example, one nephew admitted that he saw his aunt "at least once a year" and she's "extremely nice" (20-year-old European American). A niece with eight aunts said, "I don't get to see them much but when I do see them, they're awful nice" (22-year-old Puerto Rican). A middle-aged niece said, "I just feel like it's a general aunt relationship. She's my aunt" (44-year-old European American). This generic relationship had become, in her words, "faded" over time because she and her aunt did not see each other; the implication was that generic noninvolvement simply continues over time. This niece had close relationships with two other aunts yet she offered no apologies or explanations for this more uninvolved yet ongoing aunt relationship.

Sometimes our participants offered explanations for their noninvolvement. For example, some felt that their nuclear family relationships were sufficient, and they had no need for more involvement with extended family members. A college-aged nephew expanded on this explanation by noting that the only reason he was involved at all with his aunts was because his parents had relationships with them:

> The depth of my relationship with my aunts is based solely on the depth of the relationship my parents have with my aunts . . . I was never in any need of emotional support from either aunt because I always received the support within my family at home. Since my parents do not see their sisters very often, I do not see them very often either. They are still family, but I do not view them as support givers or as very close relatives to me. (20-year-old European American)

The exclusive relationships of the nuclear family are part of the dominant U.S. cultural family portrait. The aunt/niece/nephew relationship is often overshadowed by the primacy of the nuclear family, and the passage above expresses the culturally prevalent sense that the nuclear family is emotionally self-supporting. For this participant, the aunt relationship was superfluous to the parent-child relationship. For others, the aunt relationship was characterized as merely an extension of the nuclear family. For example, one nephew recognized that his relationships with his aunts were based on their attachment to his parents:

> Both of my aunts live considerable distance from where I live. . . . I don't see my aunts very often, maybe once or twice a year. But when I do see them it seems like we live next door to each other. I think this is because they are family and that we are supposed to get along, but mostly because it is either my mom or my dad's sister so they grew up with this person. Therefore when my parents get along well with them, so do I just because they are family. I would say that I don't really know that much about my aunts. We exchange gifts at Christmas and we see each other maybe a couple times a year but I would say that our relationship is not that close. (18-year-old European American)

The proximity this nephew experienced—it is "like we live next door"—seemed to counter the geographic distance between him and his aunts. Yet this closeness was based on the centrality of his nuclear family relationships; his aunts entered into the nuclear family circle when they visited. He admitted that he did not know his aunts and was not personally close to them. Instead, the primacy of the nuclear family determined his affective investments in extended family relationships.

Contented noninvolvement can be seen as a response to the contingencies of family life in contemporary America. While many participants maintained a close and valued relationship despite geographical distance, busy schedules, changing life stages, and other obstacles, many others had little involvement with their aunts, a situation most of them found to be ordinary and untroubling, regardless of whether this lack of involvement happened by conscious choice or due to circumstances. The nonengagement of (some) aunts in (some of) their nieces' and nephews' lives should not be dismissed as a source of relational dissatisfaction nor as a failure to maintain kinship ties. Limited, infrequent, or even nonexistent contact between aunts, nieces, and nephews does not necessarily dissolve the aunt/niece/nephew relationship. Nieces and nephews stated their lack of involvement matter-of-factly, expressing no distress or self-consciousness about revealing the lack of a close tie with a given aunt.

Remorseful Noninvolvement

While the previous examples illustrated contented noninvolvement, some aunts, nieces, and nephews expressed remorse over their lack of relational involvement. Elise, a middle-aged aunt in rural Maine, expressed distress over her lack of involvement in the life of a young niece living in a different state: "She's only three, two, three, can't remember, I'm bad. . . . We've seen her twice . . . yeah twice since she's been born so, really not much interaction there at all." While she attributed some of this noninvolvement to geographic distance and to her husband's lack of closeness with his brother (the niece's father), she also expressed guilt: "I could make more of an effort, send her a card you know do things like that, but I haven't and . . . you know and it, unfortunately, I do, I feel guilty, I feel bad. . . . " Elise had nieces and nephews who lived in the same vicinity, but she admitted that she did not see them much either. Again, she expressed dismay, especially compared with more satisfying relationships with several unrelated children for whom she was a chosen aunt (see chapter 2). She argued that being an aunt was an important extended family role and confided that she tried to let her biolegal nieces and nephews know she wanted to be more involved in their lives: "You know, knowing that there's somebody else out there that cares, whether you see them a lot or not, you know, they're still there . . . and I try to get it across when I do see them."

Despite a lack of contact and little face-to-face interaction, Elise's affectionate interest in her nieces and nephews was ongoing. However, she made it clear that a more involved relationship had to be actively facilitated by all parties. She told us that despite asking her siblings to keep her in the loop, she rarely heard about her nieces' and nephews' lives:

> I don't know when their basketball games are, I don't know, you know, when Elicia's cheering or playing soccer or whatever and in a way I kind of resent my brothers for that 'cause you know, they are part of my family and it's like I haven't been given a fair chance to be a good aunt, you know, but then, I don't go out of my way to call them either so, you know, it works both ways. And I think it's the family relationship that really, really defines what aunting is and how much you actually can, how close you can get and how, what your role is gonna be in their life.

Elise's closing observation seems to confirm the flexibility of the aunt's role and the negotiable nature of kinscripts about aunting. Middle-class American culture does not closely script this role, and the ideological dominance of the independent nuclear family also makes the kinwork expected of aunts ambiguous. For Elise, relations among siblings as much as interactions between aunts and their nieces and nephews determined how involved she would be as an aunt. At the same time, she felt that she could have been a better aunt but was not "given a fair chance," suggesting that she has a different model of aunting in mind that entails more involvement.

Elise spoke from the perspective of an older woman who could look back on family connections and reflect on their value and the importance of making an effort to bridge emotional, geographic, and lifestyle gaps. Yet this same kind of remorse over lack of involvement with his aunt was expressed by Randy, a nephew of college age who admitted that although his aunt lived near him, they had had little contact, in part because this aunt was the sister of his father, with whom he had a "falling out." He said, "It really is sad because I would love to rekindle our relationship," and then reflected:

> One day we will look past all the mess and become friends again I know it. At least I hope [so]. Truly there really is no reason why we can't, it is not like we do not get along because we do. These family things take time and soon someone will be brave enough to take that step and begin what was lost years ago. (22-year-old European American)

Clearly, this nephew took his relationship with this estranged aunt as dormant not dead; in a sense, this was an ongoing family relationship awaiting the young man's decision to move beyond his aunt's loyalties to, and his own conflicts with, his father.

A college-aged niece expressed a similar desire to connect with her estranged aunt, but just as Elise and Randy suggested above, she emphasized that family kinscripts are critical in bridging gaps and rekindling familial connections:

> I would love for *everyone* to get along great and get together maybe once a year for a reunion. We have reunions with my mom's side of the family, just not my dad's. I think it depends a lot on how he was raised and how much his parents stressed the importance of family to him and his brothers, which obviously was not a whole lot. (22-year-old European American)

These examples of remorseful noninvolvement imply a cultural ideal of close connections that can inspire regret over such a gap.[9] Participants suggested that overcoming family hostilities in the aunt/niece/nephew relationship requires time, courage, and family scripts that emphasize the importance of family membership and kin connections. Whether noninvolvement is contented or remorseful, we find that nieces and nephews and their aunts are actively defining what it means to be a family member, as well as the obligations and responsibilities that attend to extended family relationships and how to enact them.

We turn now to antagonisms that separate and distance aunts from their nieces and nephews. These include family or personal conflicts as well as difficulties in making connections interpersonally and conversationally. For example, family conflicts may affect both physical and emotional distance among aunts, nieces, and nephews if the nieces and nephews mirror another family member's animosity toward an aunt. Thus, feuds among parents and their siblings may affect a niece's or nephew's feelings toward their aunts. Another form of family antagonism is a divorce situation in which a niece or nephew is left "in the gap" when a family separates. A third form of antagonism more directly involves the aunt with her niece or nephew, as when the niece or nephew actively dislikes the aunt, whether for perceived personality features—she is mean or strict or nosey—or because the niece or nephew feels a lack of emotional connection—she does not care about me. A final antagonism involves the conversational topics among aunts/nieces/nephews—the aunt introduces topics that are annoying or nagging, or the niece/nephew simply feels there is little common ground for conversing with an older aunt. We address each of these antagonisms in turn to explore these difficult communicative tensions in the aunting relationship.

Family Rifts

Antagonisms in the aunt/niece/nephew relationship often reflect the tensions in parent-sibling relationships or tensions in extended family relationships. Given that sibling relationships among parents affect children's perceptions of their relatives,[10] aunts who are emotionally distanced from a child's parents may be perceived as less integral in the child's experiences of family life.

The experience and meaning of an aunt's role are implied more than specified in research. Conflicts among adult siblings may obligate husbands and wives to distance themselves from their spouse's siblings, and such "family feuds" negatively impact their children's relationships with extended family members like aunts.[11] For example, June, a college-aged European American niece living in the South, who expressed remorse about her lack of involvement with one of her aunts, felt that her perceptions of her aunts had been wholly circumscribed by her parents and particularly her father's problems with his siblings:

> My parents' relationships with my aunts (and uncles) have been heavily affected by my dad's relationship with his brothers and how much he respects them more than anything. In turn, my sister's, brother's, and my own view of our aunts and uncles have been formed by what my parents think of them. We were never able to form our own view of these people. I wish my family was closer and we saw them more.

The importance of parents' relationships in shaping the relationships their children have with extended family members changes over time, as we will discuss below.[12] Yet as June observed, this is a central factor in the extent and quality of an aunt's involvement during her niece's or nephew's childhood. Rifts in sibling relationships among parents can create unbridgeable gaps in the aunt/niece/nephew relationship. This was affirmed by Muriel, a 60-year-old Finnish Canadian aunt who had several rewarding honorary aunt relationships but no involvement in the lives of her sisters' children:

> I do have two younger sisters with five children between them, but they've estranged themselves from me for their religious reasons and I have no connection with them or their children or grandchildren. Friends tell me it's their loss because I'm a really good auntie and they've chosen to miss the whole experience of my love and caring. But that's just how life goes; some folks love you and some folks hate you for assorted reasons. The challenge is to focus on the positive relationships that can be salvaged or forged.

Family rifts may strain or disrupt communication connections among extended family members. Family feuds may obstruct information sharing among close kin; for example, one study found that feuds hindered family members from sharing even critical health-related information about genetic risks like family propensities for cancer.[13] In this study, one woman reported that her maternal aunt was adamantly opposed to sharing the news of their genetic risk for breast cancer with children in the extended family, although her brother's wife, another aunt in this family network, wanted to share the news immediately. Given her maternal aunt's reaction, this woman chose not to continue passing along the information to family members.

Sometimes, despite family rifts separating members of the extended family, family traditions and histories may continue, maintaining a sense of family coherence. For example, aunts may play their roles as keepers of family traditions and histories despite bad feelings among family members. Rose, the Portuguese American aunt and niece whose close connections with her extended family we explored in chapter 2, noted that Portuguese traditions drew the extended family together even though her father and his brother had a falling out that created a "strained relationship" during these gatherings. Of her relationship with her aunt, her uncle's wife, she said that it had become superficial and polite: "Usually it's just 'How are you?' and 'How are the girls?' and just very kind of superficial. We don't get into anything . . . " Even as their personal relationships were strained, this niece and her aunts continued to carry on the family's ethnic and religious traditions. Hence, family rifts may strain or break personal communication connections but do not necessarily disrupt kinkeeping roles or the family's sense of continuity and tradition.

Emotional Distance

Emotionally distanced relationships may be painful and difficult to overcome. Feuds among family members can tear the extended family apart, yet there are always connections that can be taken up again, repaired, or made anew. As nieces and nephews grow into adulthood, they sometimes reevaluate their estrangement from their aunts when this distance was due to their parents' feuds. Some, like those we discussed as "remorseful" about their noninvolvement with their aunts, expressed a desire to bridge the gaps left by family rifts.[14] For example, one niece acted against her father's wishes to reestablish a relationship with her aunt, and she emphasized that the quality of this relationship was based on her own feelings and not her father's:

> My aunt lives in Florida so she is quite removed. I have fond memories about when I was young and how happy it was but when my grandparents passed away everything changed. My dad and aunt got into it about the money situation. Now, my dad will not allow me to see my aunt[,] talk to my aunt or talk about my aunt. . . . When I was a freshman in college I called her up for the first time in a very long time. She was shocked and thought I was rude and hated her. Which is not true at all. (22-year-old European American)

Clarice, a 20-year-old European American niece living on the West Coast, reported that her estranged aunt wanted to make contact with her, but she did not know how to respond. She was used to the lack of involvement, given that the relationship between her mother and her sisters, Clarice's aunts, was "not sound." Yet the aunt had not contacted her directly, and Clarice felt uncertain about how to understand or respond to this effort to bridge their relational gap:

> Recently, my grandfather told me that one of my aunts wants to get back in touch with me, but wants me to make the first move (which I find a little immature). I haven't had time to contact her yet but am thinking of writing her a letter this summer. I am not quite sure how to address the situation, as she has not made any effort to communicate with me her entire life and I am not sure where to begin.

Clarice's uncertainty suggests that she expected her aunt to be the "mature" one who initiated a relationship move. The aunt's apparent lack of communication with Clarice up until this point seemed to be a strong message that Clarice found difficult to address. Choosing to write a letter rather than speak with the aunt face-to-face, that is, choosing an asynchronous exchange through a medium that permits more control over presentation, strongly indicates that Clarice felt uncertain about the relationship with her aunt.

Jane, a 21-year-old Native American/European American student, told a story that began with her father's resentment over his father's second family and her parents' dislike for her aunt, her father's stepsister. While she admitted that she did not know this aunt very well, she found herself adopting her parents' attitude and looking down on her aunt, although initially she was not sure why. However, she found out for herself that her parents' dislike was justified when the aunt tried to get her to take sides against her mother.

> The more that I got to know her, the faker that I realized that she was, and the more I realized that my mom had a reason for not liking her. Then came the clincher. My brother had a baby out of wedlock, and the family was in an uproar. There was an incident between my aunt and my mom, and they decided not to talk to each other after that. Well, my nephew was born three months premature and my aunt decided to come and visit him at the hospital one time when I was also up there. I still had no problem with my aunt, the argument was between my aunt and my mother, but then Pam decided to start belittling my mom. This was the end to it all. I respect my aunt's opinions, but my nephew's hospital room is not the place to put my mother down. Especially considering that I am loyal to my mother above all others. Needless to say there was a little disagreement between us, and we haven't spoken since.

This niece was open to a different relationship with her aunt than her parents had but came to dislike her aunt based on her own experiences. These stories illustrate the way aunt relationships change through the life course of individuals and families, in this case, as nieces and nephews grow into adulthood and reassess their estrangement with aunts their parents dislike.

Finally, one nephew seemed to take the family rift between his parents and his aunt as an opportunity to assert a bit of rebellion and independence. Elise, the aunt we cited earlier who expressed remorse about her lack of involvement with some of her nieces and nephews, observed that her youngest nephew made use of her strained relationship with his parents:

> My youngest nephew likes to come over and it's kinda funny 'cause my brother and I don't get along very well so he kinda, it's almost

a throwback, where he thinks we're cool and fun, and this might aggravate his parents, so he likes to come over and play.

Elise's nephew seemed to be engaging in a subtle challenge to his parents' authority by using his father's strained relationship with Elise as a basis for expressing his autonomy from his parents and his ability to make his own choices. The emotional distance between Elise and her brother seemed to provide both material and emotional resources for her nephew to use in an intergenerational power struggle.[15]

We have shown how parents' relationships may estrange aunts from their nieces and nephews, cutting off communication within the extended family. This lack of communication can become a message in itself about the aunt relationship. Yet aunts continue to figure as kinkeepers of family traditions and continuity, leaving open the possibility for mending estranged relations. As nieces and nephews age and seek independence from their parents, they may revisit their relationships with their aunts and decide for themselves whether to initiate renewed connections, reaffirm their parents' animosities in their own experiences, or make use of family feuds as resources in asserting their own autonomy.

Divorced and Blended Families

Research suggests that divorced and blended families face complex communicative dilemmas in reconfiguring family relations.[16] While most of this research has focused on nuclear family and grandparent relations, there are important implications for extended family communication as well. Divorce may sever the aunt connection or create an emotional gap that makes estrangement the most obvious option. One nephew explained that his parents were divorced and he lived with his father and sister, so his contact with his aunts was minimal, especially with the aunt on his mother's side:

> With the exception of my Aunt Janie, the only time I see my aunts is on holidays. We have a family tradition on my father's side of having Thanksgiving together as a family. I have not seen my Aunt Janie in a couple of years, and she just passed away a few months ago. My parents are divorced and I live with my dad, since she is on my

mom's side that might go towards explaining why I never see her.
(20-year-old European American)

One issue in divorced and blended families is revising family boundaries and membership. For this nephew, the boundaries were clearly
delimited between his nuclear family and the extended family. His
maternal aunt's death was of little concern, given the rigid boundaries
that left her out of his family network. Another participant offered a
far more complicated portrait of estrangements in her extended family
relationships that she traced to her grandparents' multiple marriages:

> Both of my grandparents were married before they were together
> and I have contact with one of my aunts from my grandmother's
> marriage, but we don't have a close relationship. My grandfather's
> children from his first marriage are in their sixties and they didn't
> get along with my grandfather when they were younger, so only one
> of my aunts keeps in contact with us from his first marriage, and I
> am not close with her. (21-year-old European American)

This example suggests that reconfiguring the nuclear family may
have long-term repercussions, rendering family boundaries both more
ambiguous—who is in and who is out?—and. ironically, more rigid—
the nuclear family configuration is the entrenched cultural paradigm.

The ambiguities of family boundaries and relational obligations
after divorce can create considerable tension in aunt/niece/nephew relationships. For example, Elise, mentioned earlier in this chapter, spoke
of an awkward moment during a niece's wedding, when she encountered both her uncle's previous and current spouses. She implied that
emotionally the previous wife was still an aunt, while the status of the
new wife, although she could claim the title of aunt legally, was—for
Elise—emotionally ambiguous:

> And it was kinda weird, 'cause I saw, we went up to his daughter's
> wedding in Montreal and of course my mother's brother was there,
> plus his new, I don't know if he was remarried or just dating, I can't
> remember now, but she was there, and then my aunt was there, you
> know, 'cause this was the one I grew up with. . . . They didn't get
> divorced until I was about fifteen or so. . . .

Nieces and nephews may actively negotiate kin status and kinscripts for the aunting relationship in a divorce situation. Jeff, who had fourteen paternal aunts and three maternal aunts, spoke of his initial resistance to an aunt who came into the family as his uncle's second wife, although he later came to like her. But another uncle's second wife failed to negotiate an emotional connection, and her assumption of kinship privileges created considerable resistance among her new nephews.

> She came into the family after my uncle got divorced. However, his first wife was the one that was there since I was born until my junior year in high school. Then by the time I graduate he was remarried. The first marriage created a bond between that aunt, and me, which still is strong today. . . . The new wife came in to the family being forceful trying to make his three sons from the other marriage, my brother, and me all cooperate with her wishes. She had a controlling personality and just created a bad vibe that still creates an eerie feeling when she is around. So, I can say I like her but love would require some serious thought. (22-year-old African American)

We take this nephew's assessment of his second aunt's controlling behavior to suggest that aunting involves negotiating kinship privileges and expectations. Some of these may be granted during childhood on the basis of adult/child authority relations—the aunt as the adult has the presumption of authority and control—and on the basis of relationships with the child's parents. Yet, as the story above suggests, a new aunt must negotiate her place in the affections of nieces and nephews, as well as within their emotional/cognitive map of the family. In this sense, nieces and nephews are not passive observers but active participants in the relational choices and performances of their aunts, uncles, and parents.

Similarly, the aunt's role in maintaining, dissolving, and reconfiguring nuclear family relationships is often an active, even critical, one. As interpersonal scholars have pointed out, intimate relationships are social—our family and friends are always involved in our expectations, stories, and practices.[17] The story told by Jennifer, a 26-year-old Latina whose parents were divorced, showed the considerable influence of both her paternal and maternal aunts. As she explained, both her mother and father felt some animosity toward their respective sisters-in-law. Her mother, for instance, never got along with her aunt, her father's sister.

> My mother throughout the years always had some conflicting arguments with her at times even though I wasn't supposed to know about them. But I know like she [was] kind [of]—I'm not saying jealous, but wouldn't approve of some of the things that we've done together just because aunts let children do things that they're not supposed to anyways, but . . . I don't think since the divorce they have seen each other.

While the mother in this story is portrayed as jealous of the indulgences the aunt provided, and the relationship between mother and aunt was strained, the divorce aggravated those animosities.

Jennifer's relationship with her mother's sister was equally as strained, given her father's relationship to this maternal aunt; her perception was that this aunt had been an active participant in the unraveling of her parents' marriage and her mother began the divorce process while visiting with this aunt. "So," she explained, "there is a lot of tension" between her father and her maternal aunt. She concluded, "I'm not quite sure how my dad feels about her—since the divorce. There hasn't been anything between them since then. I'm sure if he did have to come together in a room with her that he would be polite and just say hi and be on his way."[18] For Jennifer, aunts on both sides of her family played active roles in the tensions that led to her parents' divorce, and she was aware of the residual antagonisms between each parent and the other parent's sister. This certainly colored the relationship between those aunts and this niece.

Finally, while the aunt may play the role of confidante or mediator in family rifts or divorce situations, the aunt's entanglement in divorce tensions may create added emotional difficulties for the children in a divorce situation. Heidi, a niece whose family origins were in Ecuador and Romania, felt that her place in her father's affections was compromised by the emotional manipulations of his sister: "I often get very angry with Janice because I feel that my father has less time for me during the brief moments that I have to spend with him during the holidays due to her constant need for his attention." Describing her aunt as "cunning and coy," Heidi explained that her aunt's subtly aggressive behavior often made her feel disempowered: "I do not put up fronts myself or deal with things in a backhanded way like she does. Thus, I would look like the irrational one when I would become visibly upset with her." It was not until age gave her equal footing that she came to terms with her aunt: "I think that I have an easier time getting along with Janice because I am older now and we can treat each other as equals." In the perceptions of this niece, her aunt had actively interfered in her relationship with her divorced father in ways that disempowered her. With age, this niece felt more empowered and yet the tension in this aunting relationship remained palpable.

Dissolving and recreating nuclear family relationships entails complex relational tensions that, as we have shown, have repercussions for extended family relationships as well. Significantly, aunts are not always passive bystanders but can play instrumental roles, facilitating dissolution or mediating reconciliation. Likewise, the aunt relationship is not always "collateral damage" in the collapse of a nuclear family. Instead, the aunting relationship may continue on the basis of emotional bonds that survive both the dissolution of one family unit and, in some cases, the creation of another family unit. At the same time, our participants indicated that in the context of family dissolution and recreation, the aunt relationship is a matter of emotional negotiation with new kinship relations haunted by prior aunting experiences.

DISLIKE AND DISCONNECTION

Communication among aunts, nieces, and nephews is marked by emotional intensity as much as by contented noninvolvement. While most of our chapters focus on positive emotional connections, participants reported negative emotional connections with aunts as well. Aunts may be perceived as mean, selfish, strict, or nosey; nieces and nephews may be perceived as spoiled, rude, or thoughtless. Our participants indicated that the relationship between aunt and niece or nephew is not merely a reflection of parents' relationships. Instead, aunts and nieces or nephews form their own affective bonds or, in this case, their own antagonisms. We highlight dislike and disconnection as two forms of personal antagonism among aunts, nieces, and nephews.

Taking a Dislike: Personality and Behavior

We begin with reports of personal dislike and animosity. Nieces and nephews may identify personality traits and behavioral patterns that they do not admire or that threaten their self-identity or the status of their family. In these reports, we found that among the most frequently reported personality attribute that nieces and nephews disliked was self-absorption—an aunt who thinks too much of herself, usually without warrant in the opinion of the niece or nephew, and to the neglect of others, especially her nieces and nephews and their parents. For example, Ahmed, the 21-year-old Kurdistani student we introduced in chapter 2, said he was close to all his mother's sisters except one. The reason was this aunt's elitist attitude toward the rest of the family.

> She thought too much of herself and acted like she was better than everybody else in the family. She bad mouthed a lot of people and never appreciates what other people did for her, always acted high above everybody else. For that reason I could not get along and it really bothered me when she thought she was always better than everybody so I stayed away from her.

Aunts who care more about themselves than their nieces and nephews may violate the implicit but prevalent cultural script for aunting that casts an aunt in the role of indulgent and affectionate kin member. One nephew described three of his aunts as very supportive but noted that a fourth aunt, his mother's older sister, made him feel as if he was a burden. In contrast with the others, she seemed to expect his family to oblige her and attend to her interests.

> She is very self-centered and thinks mainly of herself. When she wants to come and visit us in Miltonville, she expects us to drop everything and entertain her. On the other hand, when I have wanted to visit her in Atlanta, Georgia it has been a difficult task to

accomplish. I always feel as if I am taking up too much of her time. I have to beg her to stay at her house. She would rather me stay in a hotel so that I won't be in her way and regular schedule of things. My aunt makes me feel as if I am in the way and it would be a big deal for me to come and visit. (22-year-old European American)

His aunt's one-sided sense of obligation and stingy hospitality contrasted poorly with the support he felt from his other aunts. Ironically, the perception that aunts are too self-centered or wrapped up in their own lives to sufficiently attend to their nieces and nephews may draw on a culturally prevalent sense that the center of attention should be the niece or nephew.[19]

A final reason for dislike and disconnection was the perception that an aunt's personality or behavior was eccentric or deviant. These aunts were "othered" in the sense that they were described in terms—as "deadbeat" or "looney"—that reduced them to their differences against an implicit model of normalcy. One niece who has seven aunts mentioned only one specifically: "My Aunt Sally is the family deadbeat. She bums money from my grandma and drinks too much" (21-year-old European American). Another niece described her aunt as a "looney":

My mum's sister, is unfortunately, the looney of our family. I suppose every family has one, it is like the gay uncle. She has always been eccentric and a bit off her rocker and it shows in her behavior, what she talks about, and how she looks. (22-year-old European American)

This aunt, as it turns out, is mentally ill, and her niece was clearly comfortable with their disconnection:

Because of her weirdness, I never had any relation with her. She was never in the right mind to know my birthdays or send gifts to us, and she was pretty weird to be around so I haven't minded not knowing her.

Similarly, Ariana, a 21-year-old European American on the West Coast, gave a matter-of-fact reason for her disconnection from one of her maternal aunts: "The [sibling] immediately younger than [my mother] was born with muscular dystrophy and was sent away to a nursing home around the age of five. I have never met her." Othered as deadbeats, looneys, and institutionalized ghosts, these aunts are quite effectively cut off from their nieces and nephews.

Another way of othering the aunt involves negative comparisons and evaluations against familial or sociocultural standards. One niece, protesting her love for her aunt, nonetheless portrayed this aunt quite negatively:

> She had a successful job . . . a house, two kids, and no financial difficulties. Then one day . . . she divorced her husband . . . sold her house, got big on drugs . . . She lost her job and was in a long boat to nowhere. After all of this pain, being bankrupt, borrowing money, she decided to go back to school to become a nurse. She now attends [a state university] and is starting to get her life back on track, along with my sister. I am proud of her and I love her. (18-year-old European American)

Yet ambivalence marked this niece's sentiments, and through her use of negative evaluations, she cast her aunt as deviant:

> The only problem with her is that she is always talking about someone and is very green a lot of the time . . . Joy acts like a spoiled brat sometimes. A student with three kids and a rental house is not where I want to be, but I have to say that she has made the best of the situation and is turning her life around, living for God [like my aunt Caryn]. . . . To be as genuine as Caryn, Joy needs to work on her attitude and jealousy.

Aunt Joy in this story remains a figure of deviance; despite protesting her affection and support, the niece's story about her aunt emphasizes the contrast between the sincerity of Aunt Caryn and the failures of Aunt Joy. In the examples in this section, the aunt is constructed as "other": as a deviant or eccentric whose life performances do not accord with social norms and expectations.

Taking a Dislike: Insincere Affection

Along with unfavorable personality attributes, the most frequent reason given for disliking an aunt was the perception of insincere affection. Aunts are supposed to like nieces and nephews for themselves, not because of familial obligations or social pressure. As we have discussed in chapter 2, aunts often are expected to bring gifts, shower affection, and be genuinely interested in their nieces' and nephews' welfare. Perceptions to the contrary justify dislike and disconnection.[20] One niece offered her aunt's "inability to buy gifts" as justification for, in her words, a "less than perfect" relationship. She contrasted this aunt with another aunt whose behaviors seemed to her to exemplify sincere affection:

> While I have a really great relationship with Marnie I have a less than perfect relationship with my Aunty Penny. Penny only married last year . . . in Las Vegas at The Little White Chapel, she's never had kids and she's not very affectionate. Marnie is one of those women that forces you to hug them as soon as she can get close enough to grab you, Penny just kind of leans in and hugs the air. I'm not sure why, but it just seems that she's so wrapped up in her own life that she doesn't really have time for anyone that isn't named Penny. Aunty Penny is also the one relative that cannot buy presents for anyone; I remember receiving a Barbie Doll board game for my fifteenth birthday, I was expecting GAP jeans. I think the inability to shop for others is a reflection on the impact she has in her nieces and nephews [sic] lives. (21-year-old European American)

Aunty Penny fails on two counts of aunting: she is too wrapped up in herself to demonstrate more than superficial interest in her niece—even physical contact is superficial—and she does not make gift selections with the recipient in mind—a sign of relational carelessness. That this aunt only goes through the motions is all the more inadequate in comparison with an aunt who is genuinely involved with and cares for her niece.[21]

Another niece also made a distinction between sincere and insincere displays of affection and care, finding both her maternal aunts to be motivated not by genuine interest in her but for selfish reasons or out of obligation. She complained that one aunt, her mother's sister, tried too hard to be friendly but often did not seem to have time to really talk. In addition, this aunt "does what she tells me not to do"; and, as the niece observed, "It seems like she makes time to talk to me when there is something she wants to know or is trying to find out." Of her mother's other sister, this niece noted that obligation was her chief motivation:

> She hardly ever comes around. When she does it seems as though she shows interest only because she feels it the right thing to do. She doesn't offer any kind of support or advice about anything. You wouldn't even know that she was a part of our family.

Consequently, the niece did not send her aunt an invitation to her high school graduation.

> I knew that it was mean but she hadn't been coming to anything else I participated in at school. And she wasn't around during my high school years. When she saw me after graduation she acted to be very upset with me because I didn't invite her. I feel she didn't have the right to be mad. She does every one in the family this way. She lives her life on the other side of town and doesn't think of anyone else but when she misses something then she will be mad at any and everyone. (19-year-old African American)

While one aunt feigned friendship to get information from her niece and was a poor role model, the other aunt's lack of sustained sincere interest justified a negative sanction: being excluded from a major event in her niece's life. In both cases, an aunt's insincere affection was offered as reason in itself for dislike and disconnection.

A related reason for disliking an aunt was the perception of competition, jealousy, envy, and other negative emotions. For example, one niece gave several reasons for feeling emotionally disconnected from her paternal aunt, including the perception that her aunt's interest in her and her brother was based on a sense of familial competition and obligation, manifested in her aunt's tendency to focus their conversations on her sons:

> Each time we talk, she talks endlessly about their activities, accom-
> plishments, and achievements. While I understand that she is
> extremely proud of their success . . . she usually fails to ask about
> my life, my accomplishments, or my activities. And when she does,
> she usually compares them to that of her sons. Everything seems to
> be a competition with her.

Upon reflection, this niece added, "Sometimes I wonder if it is because she is insecure or jealous." These negative emotions were compounded by a sense that the aunt's interest in their relationship stemmed from obligation rather than any feelings of affection. Again, a telling piece of evidence was gift giving:

> In addition to this, she always sends me gifts for the holidays,
> but they always reflect the fact that she does not know—or try to
> know—me at all. They never speak to my interests or my personal-
> ity. I appreciate her kindness, but sometimes I wonder if she tries to
> maintain contact with my brother and I only because it's a familial
> obligation. (20-year-old European American)

All of these examples indicate that nieces and nephews expect the primary relational motivation in aunting to be affection, whether manifested through thoughtful gifts, attentive conversations, or supportive presence.

Taking a Dislike: Unfairness

The implicit evaluative contrast between sincere affection, insincere affection, and "mere" obligation is thus a critical measure of the quality of an aunting relationship. In addition, we found that participants evaluated their aunting relationships on perceptions of interpersonal fairness. For example, favoring one niece over another was the justification Ariana offered for disliking an aunt she sees "about one time a year":

> When I was younger we used to see her more often, and I did not
> like her because she has always favored my older sister. There is a
> story that my parents always tell me about what happened when I
> was young and she was visiting one time. We were all riding in a

car, and I asked my parents how far away from the airport we were. When they asked me why I said it was because I wanted to drop Jordan off there. My parents thought that it was really funny but I was dead serious. When she asked me if we could at least stop by the house and get her luggage, I replied, "we'll mail it to you." (21-year-old European American).

Favoring one niece or nephew over another violates a sense that an aunt should distribute her affections fairly and equally. Similarly, an aunt who favors her own children over a niece or nephew may be perceived as unfair and disliked. One nephew offered several examples of his aunt's favoritism toward her own children and the inequitable treatment he and his brother endured at her hands. This aunt once demanded that her nephew be punished for playing too roughly with his cousin.

Not to just be satisfied with herself yelling at me, she waited until my mother came back and tried to convince her to punish me to her fullest. My mother, always a bit more level-headed than anyone else in her family, opted to let me off with a mild discussion on how I shouldn't be openly aggressive.

In another incident, this aunt scolded her nephew and his brother for being noisy and disrupting an adult get-together:

This setting was in my own home, making it all the more unjustifiable. I mean, who comes into someone else's home just to scold their kids? . . . I mean, think of this injustice. . . . Anyway, she came upstairs and gave all three of us hell. . . .

Being treated unfairly, even in his own home, seemed to this nephew the height of injustice. These stories from his childhood not only suggest the assumption that children have a right to be treated fairly and in a nonarbitrary manner by adults who have legitimate authority over them (especially family members), but that in a boy's own home, he should be able to expect respectful treatment even when he has misbehaved.[22] For this nephew, his aunt acted unjustly; he conceded, "Really, she just isn't our favorite person" (18-year-old European

American). While these incidents seem trivial and are offered with no thought of the aunt's perspective, they serve as self-evident examples of unfairness justifying the nephew's dislike for his aunt.

These examples suggest that aunting entails moral and relational expectations and responsibilities.[23] As we have shown, nieces, nephews, and aunts themselves assess the quality of aunting on perceptions of sincere or insincere affection, altruism or instrumentalism, and fairness or unfairness.

CONVERSATIONAL DISTANCE

A final form of disconnection between aunts and their nieces and nephews, one particularly relevant to an understanding of the aunting relationship as communicative, is conversational distance. Having nothing to say, feeling uncomfortable, limiting conversation to small talk, or finding the typical topics to be annoying—especially when an aunt is nagging or being nosey about future plans or dating activities—are examples of conversational distance. Conversation can lead to those benefits of a close aunting relationship that we have spoken of in chapters 1 and 2; but some conversational patterns may inhibit closeness yet at the same time reproduce the personal and social significance of the aunting relationship. For example, aunts may be very familiar figures in our lives and yet we may fail to converse with them in ways that lead to closer relationships or deeper personal knowledge. As one niece reflected, "Now that I think more about it, I guess I've never really had a heart-to-heart with my Aunt Sylvia. I know her well, yet I don't. It's kind of strange" (18-year-old European American). Our data suggest that this experience is actually not strange but quite common.

Focusing on conversational distance helps us understand the distinction between interactional and social relational dynamics.[24] While the aunting relationship is most clearly enacted during conversational interactions, the relationship itself continues with or without such immediate, face-to-face interactions thanks to social rules, kin structures, personal and familial memories, rituals, shared knowledge, and even cultural stereotypes. These larger dynamics affirm the ongoing significance of the aunting relationship even as the frustrations, disappointments, and miscommunications of immediate conversational interactions may inhibit relationship development and intimacy. Our data suggest that conversational distance is evidenced in both the content and flow of conversations among aunts, nieces, and nephews. Even as participants characterize their interactions with aunts as difficult or unsatisfying, they acknowledge the ongoing reality—the "ongoingness"—and social significance of their aunting relationships.

Disconnected Content

Generational differences between an aunt's life perspective, experiences, and interests and the niece's or nephew's was a primary reason for conversational distance. As a Latina niece put it,

> We tend to discuss more general, "safe" topics rather than anything deeply personal. This is probably because I don't feel all that close to her and I don't particularly want her advice, as her life is not really a role model of mine.

Jack, the Native American nephew cited earlier, described his aunt as a "born-again Christian" whose husband behaved "like a psycho" and was often in trouble with the law. He found trying to talk with his aunt frustrating: "I can't talk to her anymore because everything comes back to God and no matter what you talk about. . . . Not in every conversation." Niece Jingfang suggested that language issues can contribute to conversational distance: "English is my first language, while they all learned to speak Mandarin first and learned English in their late teen years or early 20s." While all but one of her aunts spoke fluent English, their cultural perspectives were disconnected from Jingfang's and contributed to very different views.

Along with differing life perspectives, conversations among aunts and their nieces and nephews were difficult when aunts exercised their prerogative as older adults to press their nieces and nephews about uncomfortable topics. Despite an expressed and often sincere interest, aunts who focused their conversations on personal life choices in their conversations with nieces and nephews often increased relational distance rather than bridged it.[25] For example, because many of our participants were college students, aunts often focused on future plans; yet, as Rebecca observed, this topic made her feel more distanced from her aunts despite their interest in her life:

> All they do is ask me what I want to do after school, and say things like well when I was at Berkeley bla bla bla bla. Not only do I not know what I am going to do after I graduate but I don't want to have to think about it right that second. I get enough from my parents I don't need other people telling me I need to hurry up and pick a career. (21-year-old European American)

Similarly, Vicky expressed frustration over her aunts' preoccupation with her postcollege plans, finding this a poor substitute for more substantive talk about feelings, hopes, dreams, and desires:

> There is very little talk about feeling, hopes, dreams, desires, that sort of thing. The exception to this is that now that I am about to graduate college, I keep getting the question of "what do you want to do after college?" Since I have no concrete plans as of yet, I tell them what I want to do when I graduate, and then listen to the bombardment of who did that from the family, why that is good or not good for me, and how best I should go about living my life. (21-year-old European American)

In both examples, the conversational topics did meet the cultural expectation that aunts should express ongoing interest in their nieces' lives. Yet there seems to be little reciprocal engagement or attentive listening evident in these vignettes; instead, these nieces emphasize the perfunctory, familiar, and frustrating character of their conversations with their aunts.

Aunts who assumed familiarity and broached topics that their nephews and nieces found sensitive or embarrassing also risked creating, rather than bridging, conversational and relational distances. For example, sexuality and attractiveness may be uncomfortable topics for adolescents. As one niece admitted, boys and dating had not been comfortable topics for her, and her aunt's persistence made her feel badly about herself rather than more informed:

Once I hit middle school, she got on my nerves more, because of the way she talked to me. She always wanted to know who I liked at school, and wondered why I never had dates. I wanted dates, but there was not much I could do if no one asked. There were several times that she made me feel dumb about not dating, but she did not mean to make me feel that way. I simply did not want to share with her because she acted silly about it, and I was not around her as much to form that type of relationship with her. I only discussed my boy issues with those that I knew very well. (22-year-old European American)

In this case, the aunt seemed oblivious to her niece's discomfort and to the possibility that her probing might damage the girl's self-esteem. While insensitivity may not always characterize awkward interactions among aunts and their nieces and nephews, choice of topic seems to be an issue that can create as well as bridge conversational and relational distance.

Disjointed Flow

Another reason for conversational distance was the manner in which conversations were conducted. Aunts sometimes controlled conversational flow as well as topics. For example, Jingfang explained that conversations with her aunts tend to be one-sided: "Conversational control usually goes to my aunts, in part because they are older than me, in part because I am not really interested in talking to them." Gloria described her aunt's interruptions and conversational dominance as annoying:

She annoys me terribly in that she often interrupts what I am saying: When we sit around talking . . . I can be several words into a sentence and she'll cut me off and start talking. I bet if I did that to her, she'd get very annoyed. I find it rude, but the others [in my family] are somewhat used to it.

Aunts who thoughtlessly dominate a conversation with their nieces and nephews do not offer much opportunity for meaningful conversation. Nieces and nephews might cede conversational control on the basis of generational respect or simply to avoid confrontation, but they may feel a lack of relational engagement.

Some nieces and nephews found conversation difficult because their aunts dominated the flow of talk, others because their aunts brought up topics that were embarrassing or annoying. We note that while our participants expressed frustration or resignation over their conversational difficulties, they also reported that, for the most part, they attempted to accommodate their aunts. Communication researchers note that intergenerational conversations require mutual and complex accommodations; participants must meet each other's conversational styles, abilities, and interests as well as interpersonal needs for control and affection.[26] Failing to make adequate conversational accommodations seems to undermine relational development and keep aunts and their nieces and nephews from engaging in mutual dialogue and reciprocal disclosure. Nonetheless, even difficult interactions affirm the ongoing significance of the aunting relationship.

CONTENT AND DISCONTENT IN AUNTING

Communication about aunts reveals the complex emotional dynamics of relational communication in extended family relationships. In particular, we identified "contented noninvolvement" as a pattern that maintains connections among aunts, nieces, and nephews despite their lack of involvement in each other's lives. In addition, we found that various animosities may affect the aunt relationship but that such family antagonisms may be revisited as people age and families change. At the same time, we found that family traditions and rituals may hold aunts, nieces, and nephews together even when family antagonisms keep them apart. In considering personal dislike among aunts, nieces, and nephews, we found that, along with personal foibles and perceptions of deviance, nieces and nephews seemed to evaluate aunts' affection on the basis of informal ethical standards involving assessments of sincere affection and fairness. Finally, as we have noted before, the aunt relationship is constituted, changed, and continued through communication, and even conversational distance affirms the ongoing significance of aunting.

Taken together, these negative relational dynamics in the aunt/ niece/nephew relationship illustrate the importance of such tensions and antagonisms in understanding the value of the aunting relationship. Even though nieces and nephews may not feel close to their aunts, even though aunts may not be present in the daily lives of their nieces and nephews, and even though there may be family tensions that shape the affective relationship among aunts, nieces, and nephews, the aunt remains a significant figure in the experience of family life. Our participants identified multiple and flexible communicative patterns that maintain aunting relationships and family coherence across various forms of noninvolvement and relational distance.

LOOKING AHEAD

Whether they described them as close or distant, our participants expressed strong feelings about their aunting relationships. In the following chapter, we focus on the relational dynamics of aunting to explore how aunts, nieces, and nephews may develop a sense of self through or within an aunting relationship.

My Auntie, My Self

Renita is my mother's youngest sister. Renita was my "cool aunt" because she was young and hip and always knew what the trends were. She was in tune with style; I was always so excited to receive gifts from her because I know they'd be just what I wanted. I remember thinking, "Why doesn't my mom know me so well?" Because [my aunt] was far away . . . and yet she could read my mind. Without even chatting with her and explaining what was "in," I would get my birthday package in the mail and inside would be something I had wished for. Renita was my fairy godmother—the magical half-human, half-spirit that could think and speak at my level, could carry my dreams, and could really understand me. (Ruth, 21-year-old Latina college student)

The profound feeling of being understood and accepted for who she was by her aunt—indeed, having her sense of self enhanced because her "cool" aunt embraced who she was—had a significant, even "magical" impact on Ruth's life.

Aunts and their nieces/nephews may provide each other with important relational spaces in which to experiment with aspects of their selves that are new or that do not find support within other relationships (such as those with parents or spouses/partners). Interpersonal communication scholars teach us that selves develop within relationships; we become who we are through a continually evolving process of interacting with others who respond in confirming and/or disconfirming ways as we "try out" elements of our ever-changing selves.[1] Relational experiences shape who a person was, is, and will become, and the meaningfulness of such experiences is created through social interaction. So, for example, Renita's gifts were nonverbal reinforcements of Ruth's sense of herself as a young woman, as fashionable, and as having a caring relationship with her aunt.

In this chapter, we explore how aunts and their nieces/nephews co-construct spacious "selves-in-relation."[2] That is, the aunting relationship may not impose the constricting identities that sometimes shape nuclear family relationships, offering instead more open, less predetermined, and flexible possibilities with the potential for authentic encounters. Over and over again, participants said of certain aunts or nieces/nephews, "I can be myself with him" or "She really *gets* me" or "We really connect." We explore this expansive co-construction of selves between aunts and nieces/nephews as it relates to the giving and receiving of gifts, the special "savvy peer" relationship between youngest aunts and nieces/nephews, aunts/nieces/nephews as confidantes, the aunt as a mediator or bridge between children and their parents, and aunting as a nurturing space for women without children to experience the rewards of relationships with children.

ACKNOWLEDGING SELVES THROUGH GIFTS

Aunts may provide fun, joy, and treats that are not necessary for survival or even meeting basic needs, but that supplement the care of nuclear families. Even when small in scope, such acts of kindness and support were interpreted by participants as meaningful displays of affection and of recognition of their self-identity.[3] For the most part, aunts described giving gifts, while nieces and nephews described receiving them. Younger participants infrequently described giving to aunts, while aunts and older nieces/nephews described fond memories of receiving gifts along with stories of the enjoyment and satisfaction of giving to their nieces/nephews. Participants considered receiving age-appropriate holiday and birthday gifts that reflected their interests to be signs of a caring aunt. Explained one niece, "[My aunt] has always made an effort to honor my birthday and other holidays with gifts, homemade cards, and homemade cookies." Participants also valued an aunt's spontaneous gift giving and/or special meals, trips, entertainment, movies, or other activities that parents did not provide regularly. Another niece exclaimed, "Every time I go to visit, she cooks for me—anything I want. She spoils me rotten!"

Other aunts were prized because they gave gifts that made a child feel special, as in the following example from a nephew: "I remember going to a family Christmas party and she was so cool, she was the only relative that got my brother and I completely separate gifts." As a little boy, having his own gift was a meaningful symbol, and yet most relatives gave him one that he shared with his brother. The aunt who provided separate gifts was "cool" because she understood her nephew's need to be acknowledged as an individual and not regarded as just one of "the nephews" along with his brother. Nieces and nephews recalled many instances where an aunt identified and fulfilled a longing for a particular item that was significant in some way to the child. One aunt, according to her nephew, "was really nice. She would come to visit and she'd take me shopping and one particular time she bought me cowboy boots because I wanted them." He described how another aunt celebrated his twelfth birthday by getting him a special present:

> . . . [a] really really nice basketball hoop that we put up in my grandfather's yard. And it still stands there today. I shot the lights out of the thing; it's wore right out. By far that has to be one of the best presents I've ever had.

The basketball hoop was a special gift that acknowledged this boy's interests and remained central to his experiences and memories of being at his grandfather's house. Conversely, gifts that clearly reflected an aunt's failure to understand a niece's or nephew's personality or preferences were seen as signs that the aunt did not care enough to find out what her niece or nephew wanted or needed. One niece told us that her aunt gave her a Barbie doll for her sixteenth birthday, an act she offered as a self-evident example of her aunt's failure to care enough to select an age-appropriate gift.

In contrast, an aunt's gift was often deemed particularly special if it was chosen with a personal touch that reflected loving effort from the aunt to make or do something for the niece/nephew. Ellen, the office manger, spoke fondly of her aunt's special gifts:

> [She] cross-stitched me a beautiful picture . . . that was very special to me. And she cross-stitched me this beautiful Christmas Stocking 'cause that's what she makes for everybody—her grandkids and stuff—so I felt pretty special that I got one.

Being made to feel special was itself a gift from the aunt, above and beyond any particular gift. Rose, a bookkeeper, spoke of the importance of her large, extended Portuguese American family. She felt a close connection with one niece in particular, her brother's daughter, who lived with her divorced father and grandparents.

> Last year I actually helped her redo her bedroom and so it wasn't like a birthday thing. . . . I just thought it'd be a nice thing to do for her and so that was kind of fun. . . . My dad repainted it and I just helped with some of the accessories and stuff and bought her a new comforter set and curtains and just kind of neat stuff.

Aunt Rose made a concerted effort to consult with her 11-year-old niece about the girl's tastes and preferences before buying the bedding and other accessories in order to make sure her niece was happy with the colors and styles. Because a girl's bedroom is her own private place in the house, this aunt cared about making it a comfortable and attractive space for her niece as she grew into adolescence. Personal spaces like a child's bedroom tend to be decorated in highly gendered ways that shape and express the child's sense of identity, so the aunt's gift of furnishings and accessories likely had a significant impact on her niece's sense of self.[4]

Participants described special events provided by their aunts, like vacations, summer visits, and evenings out for movies, meals, shopping, and other special treats. One nephew told a story of his aunt's spontaneous generosity:

We went out to my cousin's wedding last November. And I was flip-
ping through her sports page one evening and I go, "Oh the Detroit
Redwings are in town." [My aunt] goes, "Oh they are!" She picked
up the phone and got us four tickets. Right there on the spot, lickety
split. Just took us right there!

Another nephew shared this memory of special outings with his aunt
when he was growing up:

My greatest memory of [my aunt] was when I was still a little boy
was when we went to [a local] park. It was this huge park where
they rented out bicycles, which we could ride. . . . We would all
bike around the park and then go to the museum. . . . My sister
and I would usually sleep over and she would cook breakfast for
us the next day. Then we would dread coming home to our house
the next day.

Sometimes aunts broadened the niece's or nephew's horizons through
their choice of outings. Betty, a medical transcriptionist, spoke of visiting her aunt: "I would see [my aunt] usually with my mom. We'd go
out and stay with her . . . for a few days and go to operas and sympho-
nies." Now that she has seven nieces and nephews of her own, Betty
endeavors to carry on the aunting tradition of expanding nieces'/neph-
ews' horizons. She explained that she paid for her nieces to fly from
their home to stay with her in a distant state so they could see a bit of
the world. "We paid for them to come out and we took them to do all
kinds of things, [local attractions] . . . so it was a lot of fun."

In other cases, aunting is less about expanding world views and
experiences than loving indulgence. A niece enthusiastically described
her favorite aunt's generosity:

[My aunt] often took us out to the movies or out to dinner . . . and
shopping for toys. We went to Lake Tahoe every summer together.
She would cook for us every night and let us eat junk food on
the beach.

Another college-aged niece said of her aunt who lived in another state
and visited periodically as she was growing up,

She would come and take me to do things, like go roller skating or go
sledding or stuff when I was a kid. . . . As soon as I got old enough,
we'd go out to a dance and we'd take trips to Mexico together, which
was really nice . . . [my mother] wouldn't approve of some of the
things we've done together because aunts let children do things that
they're not supposed to.

Clearly, these aunts afford the opportunity for their nieces and nephews
to be indulged, played with, and petted. They provide liminal spaces
in which mildly "naughty" behavior is tolerated or even encouraged,
as a way for nieces and nephews to enjoy special times outside of the
typically more rigid rules accorded in schools and the daily routines
of home life.

Giving gifts and treats has long been recognized as a key aspect
of kinwork.[5] Of course, nurturing nieces and nephews by bestowing
gifts and outings depends in part on economic resources, and illuminates the complexity of performing gendered roles at either end of
the economic spectrum. Paying for expensive items and opportunities reflects the generosity of an aunt, but it also may signify economic privilege. Homemade gifts such as special foods (e.g., cookies)
or crafts (e.g., cross-stitch picture), along with indulgences such as
allowing nieces/nephews to eat junk food or stay up later than normal,
rely less on financial resources than on aunts' time and labor. Nieces/
nephews appeared to appreciate the work involved in homemade gifts
and treats as well as the money spent on items such as event tickets,
and aunts reported feeling pleasure at being able to give meaningful gifts to their nieces and nephews. Thus, mediating the financial
value of aunts' gifts is the value of aunts' kinwork resources—time,
energy, and expertise/talents. That is, aunts' ability and willingness to
make nieces/nephews feel special through their purchase and/or production of treats are highly valued and not necessarily equated with
what things cost. Rather, the practice of aunts' gift giving affirmed
relational significance and personal identity, provided that the niece
or nephew perceived the gift as meaningful, chosen with care, and
appropriate for the recipient.

BEING COOL

Aunting can be a way of doing friendship; while the aunting relationship was often described as friendly, we focus here on those accounts that described an aunting friendship as a fulfilling intimate relationship based more in mutual identification than in crossgenerational kinwork. Participants used the terms "special," "fun," and "cool" consistently to describe this form of connection. Ahmed, the Kurdistani nephew we introduced in chapter 2, described his peerlike friendship with one of his aunts: "My youngest aunt (mother's sister) was my best friends [*sic*]. I liked her very much." Comments such as this suggest that nieces and nephews felt complimented when their cool aunt wanted to hang out with them; as we will show, this seemed to affirm their own sense of self-worth.

More often than not, it was the youngest aunt who was described as the "coolest." That is, the aunt who was closest in age to her nieces/nephews was most often the one who was described as being able to identify with the niece/nephew, being the most fun, giving the best gifts, and being the most able to understand the experiences of the niece/nephew. Age was often mentioned as the primary reason why this aunt shared many common interests. Presumably, aunts close in age share their nieces' and/or nephews' worldview, so they can talk with and more acutely understand their nieces/nephews. Two nephews described the nature of such conversations with their young aunts. One said,

> [My aunt] is quite a bit younger than my mother is and it seems like our conversations are more about the "cooler" stuff in my life. Like girls, or the clothes I'm wearing, or how many home runs I've hit this year. Let's just say she understands the vernacular of kids in their early twenties.

Another nephew explained,

> [My aunt] can talk to me more about girlfriends, jobs, and my social life than my mother . . . my aunt experienced the same things I did in college so she can relate. . . . My mom is the oldest in the family, and [my aunt] is about ten years younger, so I think her age has something to do with me talking to her about certain things.

For these nephews, their aunts actually speak a generational dialect that their mothers were unable or unwilling to speak. The men perceived that both the terms used and the topics raised were comprehensible to their aunts because of their biological age. This cross-sex relationship gave these young men the opportunity to be understood by someone old enough to provide some perspective but young enough to be in touch with the language and perspective of their generation.

For some nieces, a strong sense of identification with and similarity to the aunt underlies their closeness. One niece, Chandra, explained that her favorite aunt is very much like herself:

> The reason why I think my aunt is the coolest, is because she is not old fashion [sic] at all, she is out going [sic], loves shopping, likes to be in style with the young girls and she fits in well. I also like that she has a lot of energy to keep up with me, we would often go out on Friday and Saturday night every week, and we don't get home until 5 a.m. (22-year-old Guyanese/East Indian college student)

This woman and her favorite (and youngest) aunt shared common interests and activities, but just as importantly, the aunt reflected the niece's own values and qualities. Further, the niece used comparative terms to describe this aunt: coolest, not old fashion(ed); these terms imply a contrast with others—perhaps older aunts and parents—who do not share these qualities. Celia, the African American niece profiled in the introduction chapter, compared her "cool" Aunt Irene with the other aunts in her extended family and cast this aunt as the one she could most identify with:

> Aunt Irene, that's the cool Aunt right there. We get along real good, she listen to like, 50 Cent [pop music band], and all that stuff. She dress fly—she give me pointers! And she likes to hang out real late, she go partying. She told me, "When you're 21, I'm going to take you out!" I'm like, "OK!" So, you know, I can't wait! (19-year-old African American college student)

Celia "can't wait" to party with her aunt; more importantly, Celia already saw herself reflected in her aunt's character and activities and described a friendship as well as a kinship relationship with her aunt. Another niece also mentioned partying with her aunt and made a point to contrast this aunt with some of her other aunts who "are very old and very traditional and so they do not understand some of the things I do." She gave the following description of her "cool" aunt, one of her mother's sisters:

> [She] is the youngest of all the aunts. She's [sic] dresses very fashionably and loves to party. Now that I am 21, she takes me out with her to bars and clubs to hang out . . . I refer to her as my cool aunt who loves to have fun.

Such young aunts were seen as slightly older peers rather than as adults or parental figures, with whom they were often contrasted, and that perception appeared to be critical to nieces'/nephews' views of their relationships as friendships with these "cool" aunts. Aunts who were kind and nurturing but who did not understand youth culture were more likely to be described as second mothers. Christine, the young Thai immigrant woman who lived with an older maternal aunt, described her youngest aunt on her father's side:

> [She is] more like a friend than another aunt. She is an air stewardess, and so she travels a lot. She's into fashion, she's pretty trendy, things like that. Sometimes I would go places with her alone, I actually at one point thought she was more fun to hang out with than the other aunt, because she was more my style, she's very pretty too, and I don't know, it's fun.

The youngest cool aunt both shapes and reflects the self that these nieces enact; at the same time, they do not threaten the niece's own self-concept the way a mother might[6] but instead serve in friendship roles that contribute to a positive sense of self-worth and that support each other's interpretive frameworks. As Ruth put it in the opening passage, the "cool" aunt is young, hip, and knows the trends and her niece's style even better than a mom. In the passage that opened this chapter, Ruth described her cool aunt in magical terms: as a "fairy godmother—the magical half-human, half-spirit that could think and

speak at my level, could carry my dreams, and could really understand me." In Ruth's words, the aunt can carry nieces'/nephews'
dreams, becoming a critical part of their evolving selves. The cool
aunt not only shares interests and qualities with the niece or nephew
but can offer what interpersonal communication scholar Steve Duck
calls "thought-world-personality" support, a reassurance that what
we think, the realities we perceive, and the beliefs and behaviors and
even the dreams that make up our personalities are understandable and
acceptable.[7]

The close friendship relation with the youngest, coolest aunt was
sometimes described in family terms, putting the emphasis on kinship
rather than on friendship. For example, the peer relation between a
niece or nephew and a younger aunt sometimes seemed incongruous
with the adult status of an aunt, so the label "cousin" was used instead
to emphasize both the peer and kinship relations. Kathleen's explanation of her relationship with her aunt is one such story:

> Then, after the war [my father] brought his youngest sister over
> [from Ireland], so now by that time I was in high school, so we
> did have one aunt, but . . . she was just so young and kind of trying
> to find her own way, that she was more like maybe a cousin than
> maybe an aunt, I mean. She didn't have any experience of aunting, if
> you want to put it that way . . . and I don't think other than the word
> "aunt," I don't think she had a clue, you know.

A sister relation offered another option more intimate than cousin for
labeling a close relationship with an aunt near in age. For example,
Betty said of her niece Allie, "I'm like a sister to her so, yeah, instead
of an aunt, she [often] says 'My big sister' . . . so it's nice, since she
didn't have any siblings, so she thinks of me as an older sister." The
label "sister" conveys a close bond, one that Betty perceives as closer
than the label "aunt" might convey. At the same time, the analogy
"like a sister" demonstrates the same lack of relational vocabulary that
we observed with the analogy "like a mother" in chapter 1. Lacking a
language for aunting, our participants often resorted to the most available labels for intimate relationships in the dominant United States
culture, those of mothering and the nuclear family.[8]

In some cases, an aunt was no longer young and cool but was still perceived that way. These nieces/nephews perceived age more as a state of mind. In contrast to most cool aunts who tended to be ten to fifteen years older than their nieces/nephews, one cool aunt was described by Isabel, a young woman from a Mexican American family, in this way:

> My aunt's always been a real fun type. She's always been the wild one of the family, as I have perceived, which has probably has fell [*sic*] into me since I feel like I've kind of stepped into her footprints, you know. We're a lot alike. . . . Growing up I look a lot like her. . . . She likes to dance and have fun and she crochets and knits. She's only forty-two, I'm thinking, so she's still young.

Despite their age difference, this niece strongly identified with her aunt, an identification reinforced by physical and behavioral similarities.[9] Likewise, Margaret, the Portuguese American niece we described in chapter 1, named one of her great-aunts (whom she addresses using the Portuguese term "Tia") her "cool" aunt despite their almost sixty-year age difference:

> [My] younger aunt who I actually got on a whole lot better because she seemed to have—she understood, I think, the kids and understood that we just did not want to sit and crochet for hours. I mean as much as I loved and I loved my Tia Aelah, my Tia Lourdes was more—"let me cook for you, do you guys want cookies, I'm gonna make desserts and we're gonna run down to the store and get ice cream—you know I'm not gonna make you sit and pray the rosary. We're not gonna go sit in mass." Which I find so ironic, because they're all within the same age range. They're not that far apart, but she's the younger, cooler aunt. She's like eighty now, but she's still the younger, cooler aunt. And I still go spend weekends with her.

Tia Lourdes retained an ability to understand children's perspectives that her sisters did not, and Margaret appreciated her willingness to forgo religious instruction and substitute a child-focused activity for one favored by her elderly aunts. In both of these examples, the aunt is judged to be young in perspective, despite an advanced biological age. Thus, for some, age-based empathy is a state of mind, not an inherent biological reality. This suggests that what is often attributed to the youngest aunt may be more of a capacity and desire to meet nieces/ nephews where they are, to enter into their frame of reference, rather than a true designation of biologically determined connection based on similarity of age.

Our stories of ourselves are impacted by aunting as friendship based on shared life perspectives and interpretive frameworks. The "cool" aunt was one who could identify with the frustrations and challenges experienced by their nieces and nephews. Further, these special aunts performed the communicative friendship functions that scholars argue make friendships so important to personal well-being: emotional understanding and perceptual validation, intimate communication about personal concerns and beliefs, affirmation of self-worth, and thought-world-personality support.[10] Nieces and nephews reported of their younger, savvy aunts, "they *get* you," "they understand you," and "you can trust them." Through confirming a niece's or nephew's perceptions and the legitimacy of her or his dilemmas and concerns, aunts opened up a path for personal self-knowledge and development. Parents' love and close identification can lead to an inability to perceive and/or relate to some aspects of their children. Aunts as friends can be thought of as intimate mirrors, confirming who and where the niece/nephew is in a particular life moment, but also revealing a larger context beyond the moment that may open up space for them to imagine other ways of being, creating room for growth, change, and more mature decision making.

HOLDING SECRETS

Many aunts reported that they functioned as important confidantes and sources of advice to their nieces/nephews. Research indicates that both men and women prefer confiding in women, so perhaps it is not surprising that the aunt should play such a role.[11] Yet our participants emphasized certain qualities of the aunting relationship that they perceived as critical to sharing confidential messages. While not all aunts fulfilled the roles of confidante and advisor, aunts considered by nieces/nephews to be "favorite," "the best," or "the aunt I am closest to" tended to be described in this way. The terms "nonjudgmental" and "open-minded" were repeated across our participants' stories. An aunt often functioned as a safe person to turn to when a mistake had been made, or a tough decision needed to be faced and advice was needed. One nephew offered a description of his trusting relationship with his aunt: "My mom's other sister is the youngest and has a bond with me as a close friend. . . . We hold a connection like no other, but I can confide secrets with her." Along with a trusting bond, a niece said she valued her aunt's honesty. She described her aunt this way:

> I can trust her with my problems—that she'll be empathetic, loving, kind, non-judgmental, and usually positive about whatever I'm dealing with. . . . not only will she be wonderful at providing wisdom . . . but she'll also call it like she sees it, whether she thinks I'll like hearing it or not. She's honest.

For this niece, honesty was as important as attentive listening and kindness. The aunt's willingness to express an opinion whether she believed her niece would be receptive to it or not was taken by the niece as a sign of her aunt's love and respect.

Trust, honesty, empathy, and affection appear to characterize the aunt as a confidante. Yet a salient factor in the aunt's desirability as a confidante is the freedom of choice in trusting her with confidences. Gregory's story makes a poignant case for this factor:

> I have one small theory on why I'm so close to my aunt. She wasn't immediate family, so when I was introduced to her when I was 11 or so, I literally had a choice on how I wanted to except [sic] her. . . . Since I got to choose just how much I wanted to accept my aunt it sort of took the family part out of the equation. . . . I feel like I was introduced to a stranger and eventually became good friends with them. . . . I don't trust a lot of people, and I don't really have that many close friends. I have even less family that I can talk to . . . I mention this because what I share with my aunt is really special.

While the aunt is embedded in family relationships and thus shares a background understanding of the family, she also occupies a more peripheral position that makes disclosure a matter of choice rather than obligation and can even facilitate a sense of reduced personal risk. As another nephew explained, talking with his aunt was "almost like talking to a long distance friend, your [*sic*] not afraid to really tell them anything because they are not present in your life, yet you still feel comfortable with them when they are around." This observation might be likened to the "stranger on a train" phenomenon: people may tell a stranger more intimate information than they would share with those in their immediate social networks, in part because there is less likelihood that the stranger will interact with people in those networks, and thus less likelihood that potentially self-damaging confidences will become known.

Nieces and nephews reported that their aunts were not as closely tied to them as were their parents, and that this emotional distance enabled aunts to help them without the emotional upheaval, and inability to be reasonable, that the nieces/nephews anticipated from their parents. In this sense, the greater relational distance and a reduced sense of reciprocal obligation between the aunt and the niece/nephew actually enabled them to become more intimate. Sometimes this was because the problems with which a niece or nephew needed help actually involved one or more of the parents. For example, one niece explained, "I often talk to [my aunt] about problems that I have with my parents. She listens and offers a different perspective." Knowing both the niece/nephew and the parent, an aunt is in a good position to understand the nature of the problem, the personalities involved, and what steps would best address the problem. Similarly, a nephew observed, "When there is a huge family fight between my mother and I, would call [my aunt]."

Other times, the issues are not related to the parent, but they involve sensitive topics. A niece explained, "Oh, and if I need someone to talk to about taboo issues that my mom would slip into cardiac arrest over, I call auntie Pam" (22-year-old, European American niece). Another niece said,

> I know that even if I screw up and am unable to talk to my parents about something, I will always be able to talk to [my aunt]. She can

offer me a parent's spin on things, but has never reprimanded me, even when I do really stupid things. (21-year-old European American college student)

Aunts reported that they shared this same feeling. Elise explained:

Being an aunt . . . you don't have to worry about a lot of the things, you know, you can be more fun, you don't need to be as strict with them. And then also I feel like, if I'm not as strict, if they get in trouble, maybe they can, they'll have somebody to come to besides being on their own, you know, that's the kind of relationship I want. I want them to know that they can talk to me, and I'm not going to go tattle to their parents. I'm not gonna um, you know, criticize them or berate them or whatever. You know, I feel there are a lot of kids, when they turn into teenagers, don't feel they have anybody they can talk to. . . . I like to be there for them, let them know if they need to talk, if they can't talk to your mom and something comes up or whatever, you know, call me—don't get in worse trouble just because they're scared and lonely and don't know what to do. Call me!

By providing her nieces and nephews with an alternative to admitting to their parents that they were in trouble, Elise hoped to be able to keep them safer, healthier, and happier.

However, facilitating confidences is fraught with relational tension. The aunt is connected not only to the niece or nephew but to her or his parents, whether as a sibling, an in-law, or a friend. Further, confidences from a young niece or nephew may create a paradoxical choice between protecting confidences and thereby condoning undesirable behaviors and decisions, and betraying confidences in order to enforce personal, familial, and cultural sanctions. Carolyn expressed these tensions as she contemplated her relationship with her niece. She reflected,

[H]ow do I support Kayla and give her the kind of love that she needs and not betray my sister? And to let her know that she always had a place to come and to always talk to me so that she had somebody you could talk to. That was important to me. . . . I thought

the most important thing I could do for Kayla is to let her know that
she could talk to me about anything and always be there for her and
to try to never betray that trust.

Over time, the exchange of confidences between an aunt and a niece
or nephew may become reciprocal and shift aunting toward a more
mutually supportive relationship as the niece/nephew matures. Ruth,
whose description of her aunt opens this chapter, described the reciprocal confidences that characterized her relationship with her aunt:

> I loved talking to [my aunt] because she always seemed to have time
> to listen. More than my parents at times, Renita and I had long con-
> versations. About anything and everything seemed to be the topic
> of our call. We could laugh, we would cry. I could tell we were sup-
> port for each other. I realized then that I was just as much a nurturer
> for her as she was for me. Renita opened up to me and I would
> listen. . . . We could speak our minds and not worry about what the
> other would think. Renita was the older sister I never had, a second
> mother when my mother was too busy to keep in touch.

The responsiveness of aunting is well illustrated in Ruth's story.
Reciprocal self-disclosure may characterize aunting during certain life
moments and not others, just as caregiving may shift as some nieces
and nephews take on the role of caregiver to the aunts who once provided care and support to them (discussed in chapter 6).

MEDIATING BETWEEN PARENTS AND KIDS

Aunts may act as mediators or translators between parents and nieces/
nephews, and even as advocates for a niece/nephew at times. As a
generational peer of the parents with a direct relational connection to
the niece or nephew, the aunt brings a unique perspective to familial
decisions and conflicts and provides an emotionally invested type of
mediation. In these ways, aunting may support nuclear family relationships by intervening in parent-child relations.

Parent-Child Buffering

Some aunts functioned as a relational buffer between the niece/
nephew and one or both of his or her parents. As a buffer, an aunt

may circumvent bitter, painful, and/or fruitless conflicts in which she
and/or the niece/nephew wish to avoid engaging the parent.[12] Wilaluk,
the Thai aunt whose niece Christine was staying with her during college, said that when Christine asks if she can do something, she has to
decide whether or not to make a decision herself or to have her niece
call her mother in Thailand:

> [S]o those kind of stuff that I cannot make decision or I don't think
> is right then, you know, I'll tell her to talk to her mom. But sometime
> when she want to do something and she doesn't want her mom to
> know or if I think it's the right thing for her to do, then I tell her to do
> it, but don't tell [her] mom. . . . But I mean if I know if I tell my sister
> she probably say no, and I think, if it me it's OK, it's a good thing for
> her to do, so I just say go ahead and you know, do it, and I won't tell
> your mom, so don't tell your mom, OK? . . . And most of the time she
> always come and talk to me about some stuff that you know when
> she has a problem or when she want to talk, so I told her if you want
> to tell me anything, you can. . . . So when she came talk to me about
> a few things that important, that need decisions, then I feel kind of
> wow! That's great that she feels she can come talk to [me].

The decision of whether to keep something from her sister is complex,
because of the differences between Thailand and the U.S. concerning
cultural sanctions on young women's behavior. Deciding on a case-
by-case basis, Wilaluk would weigh the implications and sometimes
opted to give or deny permission herself, while at other times she
would require her niece to consult her mother for a decision.

Tim, a nephew from Hawaii we introduced in chapter 2, shared an
interesting culturally specific variation on the tension between allegiance to the parents and to the niece or nephew. He differentiated
between "calabash" (i.e., chosen, honorary) aunties and "blood" aunties, in terms of their loyalties to the niece's/nephew's parents:

> [I]f you did something bad and one of your blood aunties found
> out about it, it would get back to your parents. But, if one of your
> calabash aunties found out about it, you know, she would probably
> talk to you and tell you, "don't do whatever it is you did," but I don't

think she would rat you out basically. . . . It's different in respects and it's the same in a lot of respects . . . the whole aspect of being actually related throws in the family obligation factor, like she'd be obliged to your parents in a lot of ways as they are to you. [With calabash aunties] I was friends with their sons, so the relationship flows through me almost. . . . You wouldn't get ratted on [by calabash aunties] unless it was really bad.

Tim identified the allegiance of blood aunties as primarily to the parents. In contrast, calabash aunties engage in aunting by choice; the relationship is enacted primarily at the discretion of the niece or nephew and the aunt. Hence, loyalty to parents could be subordinated to the allegiance felt toward a chosen niece or nephew. Limits existed, however; Tim made it clear that calabash aunties would contact parents in the case of an incident that was deemed "really bad," presumably in order to ensure the safety and well-being of the niece or nephew.

Translating and Advocating

Some nieces, nephews, and aunts told of aunts who engaged in active mediation regarding a parent-child conflict in order to help a parent understand a child's point of view. One nephew, Juan, a Filipino American college student, described the helpful mediation of his aunt who lived in the Philippines. Despite the great distance, he considered this aunt a "second mother" with whom he felt very close. He explained:

Ako [Tagalog term for "aunt"] Jan and I call each other at least once a month. When there is a huge family fight between my mother and I, I would call Ako Jan. Ironically, my mother would also call Ako Jan. She would usually give her information on what I am doing. Sometimes, this information is extremely biased and usually wrong. But that's my mother and that's also another story. I would call [Ako Jan] and she would usually know that something is wrong. I do call her once in awhile just to say hello, but we usually chat via email.

Ako Jan would speak to both her nephew and her sister (Juan's mother) in turn, going back and forth between them to discern each person's perspective and to try to restore harmony between them. A 21-year-old niece from Oregon told a similar story of her chosen aunt (a longtime friend of her parents) who both assisted her niece in making a decision and assisted the niece's mother in understanding her daughter's perspective.

> She has very strong intuitions and insights that I find very valuable. . . . I was trying to make a big decision last spring about whether or not I should take an opportunity offered to me and live and work on a dude ranch in Montana for the summer, and [my aunt] made herself very available for consultation as well as worked with my mom to help her see what I was trying to say.

She used the term "work" to describe her aunt's efforts at translating or interpreting her thoughts and feelings, an acknowledgement of the emotional labor involved in mediating a conflict.[13] Likewise, an African American niece explained that "when no one [in] the family thought I should leave home and got [*sic*] to college, she supported the ideas of me living and recommended it as well. She [talked] with the rest of [my] family and gave them her thoughts on the situation." These examples illustrate how aunting may involve translating, and advocating for, a niece's or nephew's desires, choices, or behaviors in order to deflect or direct parental reactions.

While many aunts openly advocated on behalf of their nieces and nephews upon request, others provided this support more implicitly. Muriel, our Finnish Canadian participant, named her aunt as a valued role model for her own life and admitted that it was not until long after her childhood that she discovered her aunt had interceded on her behalf with her brother, Muriel's father.

> Aunt Ellen (b. 1914 in SK [Saskatchewan]) along with my father (b. 1913) were the two children who excelled in school and went on to university. Ellen was my academic model and, I learned only a few years ago, was the one who pressured my father to make sure I went to college.

An aunt's "insider/outsider" perspective on the nuclear family affords her a helpful point of view when intervening in parent-child conflicts

and in advocating for a niece's or nephew's case. An aunt may understand her sibling or sibling-in-law (i.e., the parent) as well as a niece
or nephew, and thus may bring a more empathetic understanding of
the complexities of a situation into consideration. In this way, aunts
use communicative practices to help nieces and nephews explore new
opportunities and to assist in their personal development.

Learning Civility

We would be remiss if we did not note that in addition to practices of
friendship, disclosure, and buffering, aunting also engages practices of
civility. Indeed, forced politeness to one's aunt is a dominant cultural
storyline. While we have concentrated on stories about favorite aunts,
many of our participants described their predominant experiences
with aunting as lessons in civility: nieces and nephews had to learn
to repress spontaneous thoughts and feelings about their aunts with a
mask of politeness. Scholars of communication and politeness point
out that civility often depends on superficial interactions and even
minor acts of deception.[14] Performing family relations requires politeness rituals such as kissing a disliked aunt when she arrives or leaves
or submitting to an aunt's scolding without rebuttal.[15] Such acts of
politeness socialize us to the need for civility and teach us to suppress
our private aversions and antagonisms for the sake of appearances and
family propriety.[16] One niece with many aunts and great-aunts on both
her mother's and her father's sides of the family affirmed the importance of politeness as a way to show proper generational respect and
good manners: "My relationships with my aunts are strictly based on
respect. When I see them, I acknowledge them because I was taught
that it was rude if I didn't." Another niece explained that being impo-
lite would reflect on her parents:

> I sometimes feel that my aunts have higher expectations of me than
> my parents do. In front of my aunts, I have to act and speak prop-
> erly because they are very critical. If I were to do anything that is
> out of place, meaning that something a woman is not supposed to
> do, or show disrespect in any way, my parents would be criticized
> for not teaching me what is right and wrong. (21-year-old Asian
> American niece)

Such observations certainly are not limited to the Asian American community. Deflecting an aunt's criticisms with politeness, protecting the nuclear family from criticism by showing proper respect for elders within the extended family, and submitting to criticism based on crossgenerational differences are dimensions of the power relations that characterize aunting relationships in the United States. Gregory, the nephew who felt so close to one of his aunts, pointed out that politeness was the initial default setting of their relationship as circumscribed by his parents: "My family introduced me and really from then on all I was responsible for was being cordial." Moving beyond polite exchanges was optional, and he felt empowered by that choice.

MOTIVATING

Some aunts actively motivate their nieces and nephews by recognizing achievements, encouraging behaviors and attitudes, and nurturing self-esteem. The aunt as a motivating agent and a source of support is emphasized in popular portraits of the aunting relationship.[17] Along with other kinkeepers, aunts were found by family communication researchers to engage in supportive communication, including esteem support and emotional support.[18]

We delineate motivation from other types of caretaking and social support. This is a focused form of encouragement, assistance, or self-esteem bolstering related to the niece's or nephew's accomplishments, goals, or personal development. In this sense, we look for communication activities that were perceived as motivating, or intended to motivate, the niece or nephew to take certain paths, or that were intended to reward certain accomplishments. We begin with the most overt and embodied practices—"being there" for nieces and nephews. By this we mean that aunts are there, sometimes physically, sometimes emotionally, to encourage and recognize the efforts and achievements of their nieces and nephews. Another form of aunting as motivating entails encouraging nieces and nephews to make preferred choices, most clearly by advocating and exhorting, but also by offering emotional support for difficult choices. Finally, aunts motivate their nieces and nephews by bolstering self-esteem.

Teresa expressed her determination to be involved in the special events in her nieces' and nephews' lives because they were grateful for her presence: "you know how they feel about it; they're happy because you did something for them." Another form that "being there" might take is in the aunt's economic and symbolic support for a niece's or nephew's causes and activities. For example, in high school, this might mean supporting all the fundraisers that schools are forced to do to raise monies for school activities like sports or music. One college student explained:

> They would help me the best way that they can. . . . They're very willing to help in every situation. Like, during high school or college, I'm like selling all these random things for fundraisers. They're always the first ones who I ask and always willing to buy like 10 different things . . . (Filipino/Caucasian niece)

The aunt who is "there for you" with a donation, who can be counted on to buy whatever one is selling for this month's fundraiser, provides considerable support beyond the cash contribution, both for her niece or nephew and for their experience of family as a network of support.

Along with actually "being there" to support their nieces and nephews, aunts provided verbal encouragement, described as "pushing" nieces and nephews in a desired direction. In our data, this was largely about getting an education, particularly a college education. Aunts can "be there" by promoting preferred life choices and directions explicitly and by exhorting their nieces and nephews to continue in those directions. Several participants specifically identified their aunts as motivators in this regard. Winston, a 20-year-old African American nephew, explained, "My aunts love to 'push' all of their nephews and nieces towards success by any means necessary. . . . They are also big advocates of higher education. They have pushed my whole life and constantly opened my awareness. . . ." Christine, the Thai student living with her aunt, told us that she did not see very much of one of her aunts but "when I was looking at colleges, she would come with me to look at the colleges and things like that, during the interviews, she actually sponsored one of our trips. She was helping me with the interviews and stuff. . . ." A final example of "pushing" comes from Margaret, whose family traditionally offered little encouragement for going to college, especially for women. But her mother, who had "almost a high school" education, encouraged her, and, as she explained, so did one of her great-aunts: "Tia Lesa, she actually promotes it . . . she actually says to me 'Stay in school.' She tells me not to get married too, which I find hugely ironic." Against cultural and some familial expectations, this aunt exhorted her niece to take a different path.

Aunts as motivators also contribute significantly to building self-esteem and self-respect in their nieces and nephews. For example, Roxanne, an African American niece, described how she was grateful to her aunts for instilling in her the drive to succeed in her education:

> Both of my aunts stress education. . . . They encourage me to be
> headstrong and assertive because black women are at the end of the
> social totem pole. . . . They want me to work hard and not depend on
> anyone else to obtain my success. [My aunts] have instilled in me
> that this success will not come easily and I must endure a struggle
> to appreciate it. This gives me confidence in myself to continue this
> difficult academic [path].

For this woman, her aunts offered an image of herself as a strong, independent woman who could succeed against the odds. She set their encouragement in the context of sociohistorical obstacles that make success for black women more difficult. In this sense, this story about her aunts affirms her self-confidence and self-image without denying the difficulties that their shared cultural identity might evoke. In other words, aunting in this case strengthens the niece's self-esteem both personally and culturally.

A striking aspect of the way nieces and nephews talked about their aunts was the focus on themselves, their childhood experiences, and their sense of who they are and want to be.[19] In this aspect of aunting as motivating, expressing care and concern contributes to a niece's or nephew's positive self-image. Winston put this succinctly:

> I think the characteristic that all my aunts have is that they all think
> highly of me. . . . They all seem to have a genuine interest in me. I

think that is the great things about aunts: they make you feel good about yourself.

Another nephew characterized his communication with his aunt in this way: "When I talk to Aunt Rena all she does is express her love for me." Another male student confided, "I love talking to [my aunt] because every time we talk she just makes you feel that she is truly interested in what you are saying." For these young men, the aunt's willingness to focus on them with genuine interest and care encouraged a sense of their own significance.

The most moving of these characterizations of the aunt imply a story of the niece or nephew as beloved. Regarding her great-aunt, one niece wrote,

> [She] was the only person who ever made me believe that I was beautiful. People told me that I was pretty, but everyone tells children that. The difference was that Aunt Irene said it in a way that made me assume it was true . . . my worth was never a question to her. Her confidence in me was the greatest source of confidence I still draw from today as a young adult. (19-year-old European American college student)

In another illustrative example, a niece remarked about one of her aunts, "I think what I like the most about our relationship is that she never speaks down to me as if I'm some naïve kid." Here the aunt's image of her niece as an "equal" motivated the niece to see herself as more mature. This aspect of the aunt's role as motivator indicates that such unconditional regard motivates increased self-regard and self-confidence.

An African American professor, Camille, explained how an aunt can inspire her nieces and nephews to become mature and responsible:

> [A]nd then yeah we just liked her so much. She was really easy and funny and she treated us like adults you know. She used to call me Miss Camille, so it was kind of like "Hmm . . . yes, I could be a Miss," you know. And I'm like five [years old], running around with my hair all over the place, and I'm like "I'm Miss Camille!" So she was pretty subtle in like getting us to become mature in some ways.

And she used to play cards all the time. And she always had ginger
ale and ham sandwiches and statues of Mary in her strawberry garden and stuff like that, and I was like "Oh, this is neat."

Notice how Camille's memories of her beloved chosen aunt as a motivator who influenced her sense of self as a mature child blend seam-
lessly with her memories of special details that made her aunt who she
was: cards, foods, religious icons. In this example, Camille's sense of
self and her sense of the uniqueness of her aunt's self come together.
Selves, memories, and the aunting relationship are mutually constitu-
tive in this example.

FULFILLING THE NEED TO NURTURE

Aunts similarly talked of creating meaningful relations with chosen
nieces and nephews for a myriad of reasons—affection, fun, common
interests, and satisfaction in being part of a younger person's life. Also
evident was a strong tendency among women who had chosen not to
have children to feel very connected to and appreciative of a family that "adopted" them as an aunt. Voluntarily childless or childfree
women and couples still face significant stigma within Western prona-
talist cultures, that is, in cultures in which the desire for child rearing
is considered not only normal but an indicator of a healthy, mature
adult.[20] Yet research on childless (or childfree) women supports the
idea that many women without children actively seek out opportunities to play supportive roles in the lives of children.[21] Muriel, whose
story about her own aunts was mentioned earlier, felt that her role as a
chosen aunt gave her a sense of groundedness.

Serving as Aunt Muriel in the Donovan clan has been a stabilizing
influence in my life. I've traveled widely, had two marriages, and
never had children. Ian, Sioban, and I are all the same age, they live
within ten miles of their birthplace, they've been married for over
thirty-five years, and they've had three children and remain a very
close family. I've provided the adventure (they visited me in Jamaica
when the kids were nine, eight, and seven) and a role model for
eldest daughter and cousin. They've provided home for me and con-
sistent love and support through some very rough times in my life.

Muriel presents the relationship as reciprocal and mutually enriching: the chosen nieces and nephews and their parents provide love and stability; Muriel provides adventure and an alternative role model for choosing and following a life path.

Many lesbian and gay couples also benefit from chosen relationships with children.[22] The couple we mentioned earlier, Janice and Chris, decided not to have children themselves, but enjoy being with kids. Spending time with their chosen nieces was a way for them to enjoy some of the benefits of parenthood without having to commit to raising children themselves. Through aunting, they crafted for themselves a space in which they could develop as caregivers to children. Moreover, they grew as a couple as they exercised distinct and complementary ways of relating to the children. We quote extensively from their joint interview to highlight the ways in they each expressed a sense of self in relationship to their chosen nieces, as well as to each other.

> Janice: I like being part of kids' lives in a way that is long-term. You know, it's a really different relationship than the drop-in one. . . . also like being needed, like sort of from a psychological standpoint. . . .
>
> Chris: Well and these girls love us.
>
> Janice: . . . It's really amazing, like this phone call. I can't tell you what these two phone calls the last two weekends on Saturday, like [imitates the kids' voices] "Are you coming over?" and "I miss you." And there's something very intoxicating about child love, you know, like this little kid love toward an adult who cares for them. That is pretty hard to match anywhere. . . . And [Chris] actually has more fun, even more fun playing than I. Like I like to do sort of art projects.
>
> Chris: . . . It feels wonderful to be liked by little kids.

That wonderful sense of being liked, needed, and enjoyed by children has become an important feature of these women's self-identities. Through their chosen nieces' love, they experienced themselves as family members, as nurturers, as caring adults who are influencing the next generation. Such feelings were significant, particularly given the couple's decision not to have their own kids.

> Chris: We, Janice and I, spent a good couple of years thinking really seriously about whether we wanted to have kids, and Janice was more interested in it than I was, but in the end we decided we were— in the true sense of the word—ambivalent. There were things that really attracted us and other things that we really weren't sure we wanted to take on, and we ultimately decided not to do it and you know this, as the sort of auntie, you get just the good stuff. . . .

> Janice: Well, that's not completely true. But, generally, you get a lot more of the good stuff than the bad stuff. . . .

> Chris: [The kids' mother] definitely calls me her weekend husband. . . . One time, I know I was fixing something, and she said, you know, "Thank you so much for all the stuff you do for us," and I said "Well, thank you for having babies for us!"

This couple exemplifies the benefits of aunting for people without children who find meaning in experimenting with, and developing nurturing selves in, close relationships with children.

BECOMING WHO WE ARE TOGETHER

Aunts and nieces/nephews who become friends, confidantes, and enjoy significant nurturing relationships do not just bring out the best in each other; in a very real sense, they co-construct the best in each other. The participants' voices in this chapter illustrate what we call a spacious way of relating to each other. As we mentioned earlier, selves develop in relation to others, and their communication with us shapes who we think we are. We see ourselves through what scholars call *reflected appraisal*, or the way we believe others see us.[23] The remarkable thing about nieces/nephews and their aunts is that these nonnuclear family members often become significant others, or people whose opinions are especially important to us. For many of the nieces and nephews in our study, one or more of their aunts became hugely significant at a time when their self-concepts were put to the test through life changes such as leaving home, attending college, and entering the work force. At the same time, each aunt's sense of self was impacted deeply through her relationships with one or more of her nieces or nephews. For women without children, the opportunity to provide nurture to a child and to receive love from a child was important. Moreover, for many aunts who mother their own children as well, there was still a special value to their bonds with other children and in the opportunity to be the adult who was cool, understanding, willing to listen without harsh judgment, able to keep confidences, and able to help in a crisis. Such relationships avoid the singular intensity of parent-child bonds, which generally involved deep identification that made achieving a more detached perspective difficult. In all of these ways, aunting accomplishes a much more spacious way of relating than other, more well-scripted family and friendship relationships; that is, the choices, responsiveness, and flexibility of aunting provide space for aunts, nieces, and nephews to affirm self-worth, develop relational identities, and explore opportunities for communicating with and for one another.

LOOKING AHEAD

In the next chapter, we expand on aunting in the context of generational relations and collective family identity as well as community and cultural traditions and practices. Aunting in these contexts contributes to the persistence and well-being of family and community.

MENTORING AND MODELING

[My aunt] has been one of my greatest role models. Her work has taken her to many exciting places, and she is now the CEO of a non profit [*sic*] charity that offers services to families and children. She has accomplished so much in her life . . . and she has set a great example for women. She has succeeded in business without conforming to any of the gendered workplace stereotypes. (22-year-old, European American niece)

Mentors and role models are figures of guidance and wisdom who speak of and for the implicit expectations, responsibilities, and opportunities that a novice needs to know in choosing and following a particular path. Our participants offered many stories of aunts who provided critical models, life lessons, and mentorship for them throughout their lives. These stories point to the aunt as a significant resource in family life and often an important influence in the lives of their nieces and nephews. The prevalence of the aunt as a role model or mentor in participants' stories suggests that aunts may implicitly or explicitly teach lessons beyond those learned from parents, friends, or teachers.

However, the portraits our participants shared of aunts as role models or mentors were complicated. As we shall see, nieces and nephews both applauded and criticized their aunts for following

traditional expectations about women's roles and place; they both celebrated their aunts for being independent or defiant and denigrated
them for being deviant or willful in pursuing alternative life paths.
We argue in this chapter that the life variations that aunts model can
either reinforce or expand on a niece's or nephew's perceptions of
what women can do and be. Further, the differences among aunts and
other female family figures—particularly mothers and grandmothers—offer lived lessons in variations on femininity within a family
and in the culture at large. Whether or not the aunt's choices are
approved of, she still offers a model of what else is possible. In this
sense, we contend that aunts model variations in femininity and multiple possibilities for women's life choices.

Significantly, our participants' stories about their aunts as role
models or mentors often turned out to be stories about their own life
journeys and choices. Clearly, telling us stories about their aunts provided our participants with opportunities to tell us about themselves.[1]
Because the aunt is a family relationship, her story is part of a niece's or
nephew's family story already. But when the story is about the aunt as
a model or mentor, the story becomes focused on the niece or nephew
against the background of the family story that encompasses both of
them. We have already observed that young adult nieces and nephews
seem to know their aunts largely in terms of their own interests and
experiences. This is even more the case when the stories characterize the aunt as a role model or mentor. The focus is on the niece's or
nephew's life and the way the aunt shaped particular understandings
or choices, whether intentionally or not. We argue that the stories that
nieces and nephews tell about life lessons they have learned from their
aunts are stories about their own lives.[2]

ROLE MODELING

Many stories of aunts as role models portrayed aunts as either positive or negative models, usually based on whether or not the aunt had
taken or resisted traditional feminine life paths. The stories ranged
from accolades to cautionary tales and often featured stereotypically
feminine characterizations of aunt figures, from the beneficent nurturer to the oppressed victim. We begin with those stories that feature

aunts who are lauded for modeling traditional or proper behavior for wives and mothers. Participants reported that they looked to their aunts as models of proper social behavior, religious devotion, motherhood, or career success. Next, we discuss stories about aunts who did not conform to traditional expectations of femininity or female behavior; these aunts provided models of eccentricities and lessons—positive and negative—about deviating from expected feminine identities. Other aunts were cast in stories as victims—as subjects of oppressive gender roles. Finally, aunts were sometimes models of the disastrous consequences of poor life choices; their stories were told by nieces and nephews as cautionary tales of what not to do. We conclude this section by considering stories that compare and contrast different aunts in a family, creating composite family portraits that show multiple enactments of aunting, variations on femininity, and a wide range of women's possibilities.

Even though each participant's story about her or his aunt was unique, all of these stories together demonstrate how our unique family stories incorporate culturally shared sanctions on women's roles and identities. Aunts as narrative characters often embody cultural stereotypes about women's nature, role, and place, and their nieces and nephews see in their aunts the consequences of living out these stereotypes, whether positive or negative. Once again, the specter of mothering haunts aunting in the sense that stories about aunts often confirm the value of mothering. Yet aunts are just as often credited with offering their nieces and nephews living examples of life views, behaviors, and choices that differ from what parents, particularly mothers, seem to offer. For example, the stereotype of maternal self-sacrifice was both affirmed and qualified in the comments of a 22-year-old African American man about his aunts. While he lauded his mother's self-sacrifice, he admitted that his aunts demonstrated the viability of other possibilities available to mothers:

> Both of my aunts are successful, well-groomed, and educated women. . . . They were the clear-cut evidence that women could be moms, full-time [*sic*] workers, and students. They never ceased to chase their dreams and I am confident that they have few regrets.

> Though I am thankful for my mom's sacrifice, I can see in many
> ways how her own desires have been sidetracked because of the fact
> that she has children. If it wasn't for my "crazy" aunts I probably
> would have went on believing that women "need" to be at home with
> the kids and that's "just the way it is."

This nephew recognized a contrast between the choices his aunts
made and those of his mother; by calling his successful aunts "crazy,"
he pointed out that women who have the gall to be more than just self-
sacrificing deviate from the conventional expectations. Thanks to his
aunts, he realized that both his mother's traditional "self-sacrifice"
and his aunts' successes are possibilities for women as mothers.

A 20-year-old Latina aunt reminded us that role modeling is
embodied; we often see ourselves through the physical family resemblances that are literally inscribed in the bodies of our kin. Unlike
features inherited from our parents, kin resemblances are enacted in
shared family observations; when everyone agrees that "she looks just
like Aunt Gert," that resemblance becomes visible, a shared family
"fact." Our Latina participant noted that her own deviance from the
conventions her sisters expected gave her look-alike niece a warrant
for similar behavior:

> My niece kinda doesn't wanna like listen to me sometimes because
> everybody has told her that she looks a lot like me and that she's just
> like me, and since I do stuff that, you know, really my sisters don't
> agree with me, she's trying to do it too, because she thinks that they
> won't say anything to her because she looks like me.

This aunt observed that her young niece identified with her on the basis
of perceived similarities that "everybody" affirmed. Further, the niece
was trying out behaviors her mother did not approve of on the basis
of this embodied identification. The aunt literally *performed* as a role
model, and her young niece mimicked her performances. This aunt
embodied for her niece an alternative performance of self that defied
the mother's preferences, and the description above demonstrates the
aunt's awareness that she was the model for the niece's resistance.

A very different example of the aunt as a role model occurs in narratives about aunts portrayed as strong women overcoming difficult life circumstances. Finding strength in the life trials overcome by strong women is a perennial theme in family stories.[3] For example, Betty told us that she had become very close to an elderly aunt and had learned the details of the hard times her aunt endured when the death of her husband left her a young widow with three children. The details of her aunt's struggle to overcome grief and raise her children alone seemed to provide a model of strength for Betty: "I kind of looked up to her. I just really enjoyed being around her and so we really kept close through the years."

We have discussed the ambiguity of aunting kinscripts in previous chapters. Playing a "loosely scripted" role like the aunt role offers considerable latitude for personal preferences; little wonder that we see so many variations on how to act as an aunt. At the same time, cultural prescriptions idealize the aunt role and set standards against which lived experiences of aunting may fall short. Such idealizations often circulate through popular culture, socializing us to canonical stories and scripts about family life and figures.[4] An aunt who explicitly provided her niece with an ideal kinscript for aunting was described on a recent National Public Radio broadcast titled, "An Expert's Lessons on Being an Aunt."[5] In response to her niece's question, "What are aunts for?" this aunt set a high standard:

> Aunts are to be a pattern and example to all aunts, to be a delight to boys and girls, and a comfort to their parents—and to show that at least one daughter in any generation, in every generation, ought to remain unmarried, and raise the profession of auntship to a fine art.

This idealization promotes a dominant cultural prescription for aunting—make children happy and support parents—but also casts the aunt in the stereotypic spinster role, devoting herself to the needs of her nieces and nephews.[6] As we have argued elsewhere, aunting kinscripts available in popular culture are often ambivalent, offering both an unrealistic standard and an often implicit alternative that casts this ideal into question.[7]

More prosaically, several participants commented on age differences as a reason that aunts might be seen as role models. Madeline,
a middle-aged Puerto Rican woman, observed that her older aunts
were role models but that such a role did not make sense for her as a
younger aunt:

> They [my aunts] have always been attentive towards me and I have
> always seen them, I think of them, like as a role model or big figure
> that I can look up on to. But being an aunt and being younger, that
> just didn't make me feel like I was supposed to be a role model for
> my nieces and nephews because they were older than me.

Madeline's assumption seems to be that the aunt should be in an adult
role in relation to the niece or nephew. Her discomfort as an aunt
and her explanation that an age difference is necessary for appropriate role modeling may seem like common sense; after all, America
is an age-conscious society in which ageism or discrimination on the
basis of chronological age is taken for granted.[8] Aunts should take on
an adult role in relation to nieces and nephews; those who do not or
cannot are seen as deviant. Sometimes this may be a matter of birth
order: aunts may be born after their nieces and nephews. But aside
from birth order, aunts who do not assume an adult role are subject
to criticism. For example, another participant, a European American
woman, explained how her aunt went from being a role model to being
a model of what not to be:

> My aunt was my idol. As a young girl . . . she represented everything
> I thought a woman should [be]; beauty and femininity. In my eyes
> she was kind, happy. . . . She was perfect. [After I grew up and dis-
> covered her tremendous irresponsibility] I truly have lost all respect
> for who she is. . . . It seems as though, when we talk, that I am the
> grown-up, that I am the mature adult . . . It's like a mother-child
> relationship where I am the mother.

This niece told a tale of personal enlightenment in which she grew out
of a naïve idolization of her aunt. The aunt in this story changed from
"perfect" in the eyes of a child to a child in the eyes of a young adult;

hence, the story criticizes the aunt for not being an adult and emphasizes the niece's growing social and ethical maturity.

Modeling Eccentricity

While we received many stories about aunts as exemplary role models, we also heard stories about aunts who functioned as models of deviance and eccentricity. These often humorous or tongue-in-cheek stories subtly questioned the traditional norms governing feminine conduct, appearance, and character. Some aunts were portrayed as violating cultural norms by engaging in eccentric behaviors, making public spectacles, or exhibiting unconventional tastes and styles. We were struck by the affection and laughter evoked by these stories. Eccentric aunts often seemed to be beloved figures through whom the dangers and pleasures of deviance and defiance were vicariously enjoyed. For example, Teresa, a 63-year-old Mexican American woman, told us of her great-aunt's obsession with new cars:

> A great aunt . . . that lady was such a joy. She was still driving when she was about seventy-something years old [laugh] . . . Every year she would trade her car, that's the funny part. . . . She never had an old car in her life. She was always owing because she'd trade it, and trade it, keep trade [sic] it every year. . . . I go, but Tia it's only been a year, she goes I know but I'm gonna get me another one.

One of Patty's family stories features an eccentric aunt as well, a beloved character in her extended family. We shared this story at a conference presentation about our work on aunts:

> Once my aunt took the extended family to see the Moscow Circus when it was traveling through the U.S. We all stood up to sing the "Star Spangled Banner." My aunt boomed out the anthem in her trained operatic voice, and everyone around us stopped singing and turned to watch her, silent and uncertain about why there was an opera singer in the upper tier of stadium seats. My siblings and cousins and I were mortified. We laugh about it now, all those people watching us while we stood, trapped, waiting for our aunt to stop singing.[9]

This aunt's status as an eccentric character in our larger family story was affirmed in an interview with one of her great-nieces, who described her in the following way:

> She's like the classic TV kind of aunt. With the really red lipstick and the frizzy red hair and she's really loud and likes to yell and jump around and kind of talk to everyone all the time.

However, this aunt does not have red hair; the misremembered detail clearly conveys the image of an eccentric woman. This is now a crossgenerational story that portrays this aunt as a model of feminine eccentricity. Yet the family narrative is ambivalent: our aunt models a defiant femininity that we appreciate, but the story of our embarrassment at the circus exerts pressure to conform to conventions. At the same time, this story is told with affection and laughter; through it, we perform familial connections and maintain crossgenerational memories.

A similar example comes from an interview with Robin, a middle-aged Native American/European American woman who offered a portrait of a beloved eccentric aunt, a Native American woman uninhibited by feminine and ethnic stereotypes who disregarded tribal cultural sanctions against garish colors, women's marital subordination, and public meekness:

> We always called her crazy Aunt Hazel. [laugh]. . . . She was just a free spirit. Very eccentric. And did whatever she wanted to do. She used to dress, as my other aunts would say, very inappropriately. She wore garish colors. . . . This was why she just didn't fit into the family. She was a very thin woman who really cared what she looked like. And these colors that she wore, and she was loud. And she would drink but not to excess. . . . So she was known as kind of a party girl. And she smoked. Which just wasn't normal in my family. The women may have smoked but they would never be in front of everybody smoking. . . . [S]he'd use those tips on the cigarettes . . . that you stick them in, those really long things. And her nails, I always remember really long red nails on her hands. So she was our crazy Aunt Hazel.

According to this niece, Aunt Hazel married twice but kicked both her husbands out, a very uncommon stand for Native American women: "Not many women would tell their husbands to leave, that they were finished with them. But that's literally what she did." Aunt Hazel violated both the conventional norms for feminine decorum and the strictures on Native American women—she stood up to men, wore loud colors, did her hair and nails, and smoked in public (with a cigarette holder!). The other aunts decried her example. She modeled female defiance, and Robin told us her story with affection and amusement. Even as Robin cautioned that this aunt "didn't fit into the family," her story claimed the aunt as a family member. Also, by telling us about Aunt Hazel's defiance of Native American conventions, Robin emphasized her family's Native American culture and identity. In addition, the story implied a more troubling side by subtly testifying to gender strictures and the prevalence of alcoholism within her family and the contemporary Native American culture.[10] Her story of Aunt Hazel's eccentricities is a story of conventions defied and upheld, of a family's cultural identity, and of personal memories and identity claims.

Embodying Victims and Cautionary Tales

The cultural model of woman as victim appeared in some of the stories our participants told us about their aunts' lives.[11] For the most part, these stories told of women living in difficult marriages, struggling to raise children, and oppressed by cultural and familial sanctions on women's possibilities. Often, nieces and nephews positioned themselves as outside observers, helpless to intervene, perhaps because they were children or because they were outside the immediate family circle. At the same time, they cast their aunts as women who failed to stand up for themselves, who were complicit in their own domestic oppression, in contrast to dominant cultural narratives of individualism and agency that urge us to "stand up for ourselves."

For example, one middle-aged European American woman poignantly described why she did not want to be like one of her aunts: "There was just always something missing—like she lacked a spirit, or vitality, that I seek in others." This niece went on to say that while she enjoyed her uncle, he dominated his wife: "It is very clear who wears the pants in that relationship. I guess I always knew that, even when young, and I have always preferred strong, independent women." Watching her aunt's submissiveness inspired this niece to think about the model of womanhood she preferred and, implicitly, the kind of woman she wanted to be and perhaps even the type of marriage or partnership she would want to have.

Jack, a 24-year-old Native American nephew, offered a disparaging portrait of his aunts as "unmotivated":

> [My aunt] was never really career-oriented. She was kind of like floating from job to job sometimes. She stayed at her mom's house. She was into fancy dancing. And she went all over and won a bunch of trophies, and this and that. But kinda, unmotivated. She seems like she knows what she wants, but then she doesn't. . . . No ambition. . . . Then my other aunt, she, I don't know, almost the same thing. If I could call it one word it would be "unmotivated." I don't know, she's been going to school for a while, just because it's free.

This nephew was attending college himself, so the lack of motivation and ambition he saw in his aunts was perhaps more unsettling because their situations were more salient for him; they provided models of willful failure at a time when his own will and ambition were being tested. As role models, these aunts may have served to inspire him to defy their lack of ambition, or they may have offered self-fulfilling justifications if he failed to live up to his own ambitions. His story and the others we have introduced in this section illustrate that our aunts become narrative resources for stories about ourselves.

Modeling Multiplicity

One of the most powerful ways that aunts model alternative life paths is in the comparisons and contrasts that their nieces and nephews draw among them. Putting together characterizations of different aunts demonstrates that multiplicity and difference are inherent in family narratives about aunts. We asked our participants to give us descriptive adjectives for each of their aunts, and the contrasts among these labels demonstrated considerable variability. For example, a 20-year-old European/African American female living in a Southern state observed, "I have one uppity aunt Alisha, one eccentric aunt Marnie, one fun aunt Sarie, and one goody goody Candy." Clearly, these different aunts offered, in her view, four very different versions of feminine identity.

The stories told to us by nieces and nephews often portrayed their aunts as living out the consequences of choices culturally available to women. In the differences among them, these descriptions narratively modeled different possibilities. Ellen, the office manager we have cited in previous chapters, portrayed her aunts as contrasting models of women's life paths—the victim, the secret alcoholic, and the energetic caterer with the happy family. Ellen's narrative contrasts aunts who made self-limiting choices with an aunt whose choices—marriage, career, and outlook—were productive; the consequences of poor choices were sad families and blighted lives in contrast to a happy family and fulfilling life.

Ellen's story of her Aunt Wanda focused on this aunt's undeveloped artistic talent and the choices that ultimately restricted her. Aunt Wanda married before she graduated from high school and struggled with her husband's and children's problems—they were the "dark sheep of the family." Although she was a talented painter, she could not realize her ambitions because of her family responsibilities. Yet she recognized her niece Ellen's literary talent, buying her classic books and a subscription to *Writer's Digest*, encouraging her to write and eventually to go to college. Ellen characterized her aunt as "codependent," unable to leave her husband and children to pursue her dreams, and told us that her aunt lived her thwarted college ambitions "vicariously through me." While Aunt Wanda eventually began painting and opened her own gift shop, Ellen explained that she held her aunt responsible for the difficulties that hindered Wanda: "I mean she's let it happen to her. Do you know what I mean? She's allowed it but at the same time it's just like, give the woman a break. Let her live her life and enjoy her life." Clearly, Aunt Wanda's story was a cautionary tale about poor life choices and their consequences.

Another aunt, Sue, was the mother of Ellen's four favorite cousins. Ellen admitted that although she spent considerable time with her cousins during childhood, she did not realize that her aunt was a closet alcoholic until Sue went through detox. Ellen described her aunt as "very hyper," "very skinny," a small-town housewife who "knows everybody and knows all the gossip."

In contrast to her aunts Wanda and Sue, Ellen described a third aunt, Barb, as a "go getter," "a woman who could do anything." Aunt Barb worked in her family's catering business and helped her husband run their farm. Ellen described her aunt with a list of desirable qualities:

> She's a good person and she's very religious, loves her kids, great mom and she's one of those people that will just take on anything but doesn't ever get stressed out about it. . . . I wouldn't say I know her well you know what I mean? I just admire her because it's just you can tell her kids are well loved and well adjusted and she loves her grandkids . . . they're a happy family.

Ellen's stories cast two of her aunts as negative role models. Notably, Aunt Wanda did not earn any kudos for strength or for reaching out to encourage her niece's literary ambitions. Instead, Ellen portrayed her aunt as weak, a codependent living vicariously through her niece, a woman who was to be pitied for constructing limits to her own life. Aunt Sue's alcoholism overshadowed her story. In contrast, Aunt Barb's story was offered at face value as a positive model. Across all three stories, the features of conventional femininity play out as the basis for both positive and negative life choices. The lesson in these juxtapositions seems quite clear: women's choices can realize more or less out of the conditions of their lives.

Madeline's description of her aunts offers another example of how different aunts provide alternative models of life as a woman and of family life. Her characterizations were rich in understated details:

> I'll start with Adeline. From my mom's side, she's the oldest of my aunts. She's a very conservative person. She's not a very social type of person. She usually stays in the house and takes care of her only daughter. Serena, on the other hand, is the youngest from my mom's side. So she's a bit immature. She went through a lot of hard times during her teenage life. She got married at thirteen and had three

children. So pretty much that's what she has been doing with her life. The next up is Nadine. She's single. She lives with her brother and she's a very religious type of person. She goes to lots of church. From my dad's side, Esmeralda, she used to be a teacher in this military school back in Puerto Rico. She met this Air Force military man and they got married. And currently she lives in Texas. The other one is Camila. She's the oldest from my dad's side. She pretty much left school when she was nine because she had to take care of her younger brothers and sisters. She doesn't have any education at all but she's very very sweet. And you know, very into her house type of person. The other one would be Amaya. She's, I would say she's probably one of the craziest and most outgoing out of all my aunts. She is very very honest. She would speak her mind and she does not care who gets hurt.

Madeline located each of her aunts within the family configuration by maternal or paternal lineage and birth order. She distinguished one from another by highlighting a social trait, for example, "conservative," "immature," "religious." She also provided a concise characterization of each woman's place in the world: "married at thirteen and had three children," "single and goes to lots of church," "has personal problems," and so on. Religion, taking care of one's family, and speaking your mind stand out as valued attributes in this family portrait. Madeline also alludes to family history, for example, the various turning points in each aunt's life and the family's relocation to the United States, noted explicitly in Aunt Esmeralda's immigration. Finally, a sociocultural context is suggested in the family conditions that limited the life options for some of these aunts.

Madeline's descriptions suggested that these aunts embody family values and history. Describing the aunts together gave a sense of the similarities and differences across the women in this family and the attributes that the niece deemed important in explaining who they were. Through their juxtaposed descriptions, Madeline and Ellen each wove a textured family narrative in which their aunts modeled differences, choices, and constraints regarding women's roles and possibilities.

MENTORING IN MYRIAD WAYS

While aunts may serve as life models unintentionally, mentoring involves deliberate guidance and learning. The value of aunts as mentors can be set within the recent popularity of workplace mentoring.[12] Mentoring as a corporate practice is a mutual exchange in which the mentor and protégée both use the relation for advancing their separate interests.[13] Where the protégée gains access, connections, status, and protection, the mentor gains political and social support. However, the stories we heard about aunts as mentors differed from this model of self-interested exchange, often showing the promotion of the relationship itself over specific ends. In our participants' stories, aunting as mentoring appeared as a form of role/life guidance that enabled personal growth and supplemented parental and formal sources of learning. Aunts as mentors were characterized as sources of care and advice who taught practical skills, facilitated social and communicative competencies, and encouraged self-knowledge.

The definition of aunting as mentoring that emerged from our data entails both personal and relational growth and care. This emergent definition holds characteristics in common with definitions of mentoring that emphasize relational quality and learning. For example, the following definition of a mentor focused on personal growth seems apt: a mentor is "a person who achieves a one-to-one developmental relationship with a learner, and one whom the learner identified as having enabled personal growth to take place."[14] There are commonalities as well with feminist models of mentoring (sometimes referred to as "wo-mentoring") that emphasize mutual growth, relational development, and a multidimensional sense of care—caring for, caring about, and taking care of—in which the quality of the relationship is an end in itself.[15] While aunting as mentoring is not necessarily a feminist practice, we find resonance between these models and the descriptions our participants provided.[16]

Nieces and nephews credited their aunts with guiding their development of practical skills, social competencies, cultural understandings, and self-knowledge. Some aunts mentored their nieces and nephews in practical know-how, that is, everyday skills acquired through practice. Aunting also facilitated communicative competencies, largely through the quality of interaction among aunts and their nieces and nephews. Some aunts enculturated nieces and nephews to the tastes, habits, and comportment that mark class and gender distinctions. Other aunts, by providing "auntly advice" or life lessons acquired through experience, made explicit the usually implicit rules that govern how we get along in social life. Finally, aunting as mentoring enabled the development of personal identity and self-knowledge.

Across these examples, aunting as mentoring took place through commonsense understandings and everyday practices; the stories we heard were about learning to get along in the social world rather than learning to question, critique, or change that world. In offering stories about the value of aunting as mentoring, our participants seemed to emphasize learning to conform within dominant cultural conventions, and we found little evidence of the deviance or defiance evident in stories about aunts as role models.[17]

Instructing Practical Know-How

Many participants told us that their aunts taught them a wide range of practical skills and knowledge, from how to ride a bike, knit, and cook special meals, to how to run a successful business. For example, Amy, an Asian American student, depicted learning to bake with her aunt as relationally rewarding for both of them: "The reason why [my aunt] and I became more communicative was because she'd show me how to bake cakes and cookies. And I loved cooking, so this was a fun and good thing for us both." A European American woman remembered her aunt teaching her games when she was a small child: "She was a physical education teacher for an elementary school and was always teaching me how to play various games." A 20-year-old Hispanic aunt fondly recalled her 4-year-old nephew's plea to let him help her make his lunch; imitating a young child's voice, she entoned,

> "Please, can I help you make the soup for me? 'cause I love you." He kept on telling me that he loved me so much. And then I go like, "Yeah, O.K., you can help me" He got really happy, you know, because he was helping me.

For this aunt, giving her young nephew a lesson in making soup was one of her favorite memories and while he may not have remembered how to make soup, this early lesson in cooking was a positive one.

Coaching Communication Skills

Communication skills were often evident in the stories about aunting as mentoring. Among the skills most commonly mentioned were listening skills. As one 22-year-old Puerto Rican niece described her aunt, "She likes to have fun but at the same time, she's the type of person that can also hear you out and give you a motherly, or an auntly advice." Another communication skill was keeping confidences; Kathleen, a nun and teacher, stressed the importance of respecting her nieces's and nephews' wishes to keep some things to herself: "I've tried to maintain a pretty fast rule about security and privacy, so that what we discuss I don't share." Both accounts characterize the aunt as someone who will listen and take the speaker's perspective seriously. We suggest that these aunts are mentoring not only by providing "auntly advice" but by engaging their nieces and nephews in practices of active listening and perspective taking. Hence, these aunts can be said to mentor communicative skills as well as provide guidance on the issue at hand.

Aunts as mentor-guides may also foster social and communicative skills of empathy and mutuality. Several participants commented on the closeness they felt with a favorite aunt, but for some, this closeness entailed experiences in developing openness, empathy, and mutual understanding. One 44-year-old European American niece explained that she and her aunt have become closer over the years: "I've learned to understand her situation family-wise of what she went through, not being able to have children. And we've become closer because of that, because I haven't been able to have children—with my husband." She named as the best part of this relationship the "openness" they shared with each other, allowing them to empathize over this painful void in their lives. The ability to empathize and to come to a mutual understanding with another about emotional experiences is an invaluable social and communicative skill.

Schooling in Social Comportment

Families are primary sites of socialization, and the stories of aunts as mentors clearly evidenced their contribution to this critical social function. For example, some stories depicted aunts as schooling nieces and nephews in the rules of comportment and social discipline. Celia, a 19-year-old African American niece, described one of her aunts as a "disciplinarian":

> Aunt Lanae, she's like, she act real ritzy, or something. She funny. "OK, make those beds. Come on, be on time. Come on that's not appropriate. Sit up straight! Tuck in your shirt! Stop talking so loud."

Celia perceptively identified Aunt Lanae as acting "ritzy"; this aunt disciplined Celia and her siblings in habits associated with a particular class status.[18] A 20-year-old European American woman acknowledged the role that her aunt played in encouraging cultural sensibilities and a sense of cultural distinction:

> As I got older she gave me a chance to experience things that weren't possible in [my area] like going to museums, gardens, plays, and concerts. When she came to visit us we would always take time out to do all of the tourist things that we never did unless we had company.

A 35-year-old Portuguese/Argentinian woman told a story about learning how to wear high heels and use makeup:

> I remember she bought me my first pair of high heels and I went to her house and she had me put the book on my head and walk in them and practice and my mom thought it was kind of funny 'cause she didn't do anything like that so that was kind of neat. . . . She would take me to like Long's or something and she was the one that kind of started with giving me a little bit of makeup and stuff. . . .

Indoctrinating young girls into the mysteries of feminine beauty culture and shopping supplements more formal schooling, but these are ideologically critical lessons just the same.

Another aunt inspired her niece to reflect on the gendered inequities inherent in her own cultural community. Margaret's great-aunt, Tia Linda, exhorted her to stay in school and also warned her against getting married, despite the strong cultural and familial expectations that women would marry young.

> She just . . . not that she tells me that love's a crock, but it's almost in so many words I get that impression from her, but she tells me "Don't get married. You'll only end up hurt. Be strong. Be yourself. Be an individual" and it's interesting.

In part, Margaret understood her great-aunt's advice to be a comment on the double standard in Portuguese marriages—men can philander but women are expected to remain steadfast. She reflected:

> I wonder if people knew. . . . not even just our family, but our community in general. If they knew that my Tia Linda was telling her great niece that, I wonder what they would say. She's sort of unconventional and cool in that way. I like that.

Margaret's critical self-reflection is another skill that contributes to social and communicative competence. Hence, along with her aunt's sage guidance, this niece was offered an opportunity to reconsider her family's and community's standards.

Imparting Cultural and Spiritual Knowledge

Finally, aunts are integrally involved in preserving family memories, telling family stories, and situating the family within cultural traditions, customs, and narratives. A 20-year-old East Indian/American woman who visits her aunts in India observed:

> Generally when we go to India we go because there's a wedding going on and so those are like week-long processes . . . so generally there's like always festivities that we need to dress for that they'll [her aunts] help us with the outfit or go shopping for the outfit that we need and then kind of explain what's going on . . . .

Several participants mentioned that their aunts taught them particular family recipes or customs. For example, Gretchen, a Polish/Irish woman in her fifties, recalled that her aunt would make traditional Polish dishes for the whole family: "She would cook us meals and one time she taught me to make something called *kluski*, those are potato dumplings." Beyond a cooking lesson, this is a matter of preserving and passing along the family's stake in a cultural heritage.

Aunts also appeared as spiritual guides, as one European American female student explained: "When I was confused about the Lord and my beliefs [my aunt] took the time to explain things to me, and why faith is important." Margaret, a Portuguese American niece, told us that her great-aunt taught her both how to crochet and about spirituality:

> My Tia Helena used to bring me over and teach me how to crochet.
> . . . [I was about four or five] and I laughed because I did not pick
> it up and she just tried so hard to teach me. . . . I still have my little
> box at home with all my little utensils and yarn. . . . She would
> often take me and my cousins to church or give us religious books
> or pray the rosary with us and so that was another thing aside from
> crocheting and knitting. Trying to instill religious . . . just the whole
> spirituality . . . .

Aunting as mentoring in these stories served as a socializing agency, facilitating personal growth in accord with cultural conventions.

Fostering Self-Knowledge

One model of mentoring we find particularly appealing holds that mentoring "has to do with discernment of [life] choices rather than with self-advancement in choices already made."[19] We suggest that mentoring individuals in a way that helps them to discern their life choices involves enabling self-knowledge. Perhaps one of the most stirring stories we heard came from Joshua, a young Mennonite man who had recently come out as gay. He credited his aunt for fostering a sense of his own uniqueness from an early age and for encouraging him to be true to himself against his family's designs. Looking back on his childhood, he mused,

I sort of see my aunt as going, "Hmmm, hmmm, hmmm, hmmm, I'm not going to let you raise Joshua the way that I know you want to." So when I was very young, I was raised to be the farm boy. I was raised to be Daddy's little helper, and, you know, to put the work in, feed those cows . . . stuff like that. And then for my birthday, my aunt would buy me a gyroscope. Or she would get me like, a photo book about animals or something. And I loved 'em! . . . And it never really hit me until my freshman year in college. When I got here and I was disconnected from the farm lifestyle and I went, "Oh! That's why she instilled this love of science and mathematics and this other part of my life."

Describing his aunt's influence on him as small but persistent, Joshua nonetheless found his aunt to be a strong mentor for a very important life lesson. He observed, "She's got this aspect of her where she's longing to learn new things, constantly educating herself, takes things to the next level." Just as importantly, she showed him how to care for another without imposing standards or destinies. He talked about coming out to his family and their fear that the neighbors would find out. But he explained that he felt sure that his aunt's reaction would be different:

She's probably had me pegged since I was five. And she's just been saying these little hints of, going, "I know, I'm ok with this." And from my standpoint, that was very comforting. To know that at least someone in my family was ok with me the way I am. And wasn't trying to change me. Trying to give me all of these choices. And saying, "Hey, what fits for you? Where do you find your passion?" And I've sort of continued to cling to that glimmer of hope going, "All is not lost. There are people within this family that are on my side."

This story shows the aunt as a mentor whose support enabled her nephew to develop a sense of his own worth and to claim his identity against the sanctions of his family and community.

MUTUAL BENEFITS OF MENTORING

What do aunts as mentors gain from these relationships? Community mentors, discussed in a previous chapter, have proven to be quite vital in guiding at-risk youth on to productive life paths.[20] As community mentors enjoy reciprocal benefits, so do aunt mentors realize connections with a younger generation, thus satisfying the desire to contribute to the continuation of families and communities.[21] Aunting as mentoring offers reciprocal relational benefits: for the niece or nephew, the mentor can provide critical life lessons and facilitate access to social and material resources; for the aunt as mentor, the benefit may be a sense of contribution to the family's well-being and to the unfolding lives of her nieces and nephews. These are not the instrumental benefits of corporate styles of mentoring; rather, the quality of the aunting relationship itself is enhanced.

Ellen, the West Coast office manager who is an honorary aunt to her friends' kids, described the benefits of an aunting relationship in terms that attest to its reciprocal benefits:

> I want to have kids and I also just love how kids look at the world and their perspective and they're so present in the moment. . . . A lot of it just has to do with how they see the world and everything's new and I think it makes me feel like everything's new too because I can show them things and teach them things and I enjoy that.

Among the things she does with her honorary nieces are reading to them and teaching them to write, ice skating (a pleasure from her own childhood), picnics, and educational excursions (e.g., the library, the museum). For this woman, spending time with these girls is not a way of helping their parents out; rather, this is a relationship distinct from her friendship with the parents. She noted,

> Sometimes I'll take the kids you know like if I baby-sit like the girls or something or I'll do it to help them out but I also enjoy it. . . . I look at it you know I enjoy it . . . they always look at "Oh well we don't want you to . . ." and I was like "But you don't understand. I want to."

In this example, mentoring offers the aunt deeply personal benefits and cannot be reduced to an instrumental exchange. Unlike workplace mentoring models, the benefits of aunting as mentoring may be realized in the quality of personal and family well-being, connection, and continuation.

AUNTING AS MODELING AND MENTORING

Aunts as role models and mentors fill the gaps where formal schooling, family and peer socialization, and personal experience fall short. Our participants told us stories about the importance of aunts in their lives and the life lessons they learned. In depicting a variety of life choices—some lauded and others denigrated—stories of aunts as mentors and role models complicate the narrative construction of both family identity and the narrator's own sense of identity. Further, these stories invite us to reflect on the gendered expectations and opportunities of familial roles and life trajectories and to attend to the constructedness of family coherence, continuity, and solidarity. As we have shown, aunts' influence is double-edged, always constrained by the limits of traditional femininity and subject to condemnation as well as celebration. As mentors, aunts may teach practical skills, facilitate social and communicative competencies, prepare nieces and nephews for adulthood, or foster self-knowledge and faith. Mentoring offers aunts enjoyment and a sense of contributing to family well-being. Across these examples, aunting enacts flexibility, multiplicity, and responsiveness—critical resources for contemporary family life.

Our discussion of aunts as models and mentors illustrates the variations on femininity that aunts enact. An aunt may play traditional feminine roles—a wife and mother, for example—or unconventional roles that break with traditional feminine and family patterns—a successful business woman or a woman whose choices defy family expectations. Taken altogether, these variations show us the importance of aunts as alternative feminine figures and role models—both positive and cautionary—in family life. In highlighting the different feminine roles enacted by aunts, this chapter reclaims the value of different femininities.

The stories and descriptions of aunts in this chapter show how personal and family experiences, memories, and bonds are created and maintained through stories. In telling us stories about their aunts, our participants often portrayed their aunts as figures whose lives illustrated the opportunities and costs of critical life choices. Family researcher Elizabeth Stone holds that family stories define the family—providing rules for living as a family, identities for its members, and a shared memory and view of the family and the world. So perhaps it is not surprising that aunts are quite visible in family celebrations and stories, orchestrating family togetherness, actualizing family memories, and embodying lessons about what is and is not acceptable, possible, and desirable.[22]

We are especially aware in this chapter of the point made by family communication scholars who remind us that research is a collaborative project "in which participants interpret and give meaning to their experience and researchers represent those meanings."[23] This chapter shows our collaboration with our participants on stories about aunting that expand on our understandings of mentoring and extended family connections. In listening to these stories, we heard our participants interpret the consequences of conforming or not conforming to dominant cultural norms and familial expectations.[24] We contend that these stories of aunts as role models and mentors resist the cultural ideals of a self-sufficient nuclear family and a privatized model of parenting, by attesting to the need for—and value of—extended kinship in socializing us to our sense of self, place, and possibilities in the family, in the world, and as individuals in ourselves.[25]

Looking Ahead

In the next chapter, we turn from the relation of self and world developed in the mentoring relationship to aunting across generations as families pass along meaning, identity, and culture. Chapter 6 takes a long-term view, focusing on the ways in which aunting enacts the interests of future generations and expands our purview from selves and families to continuities and communities.

CARRYING ON THE FAMILY

> I admire [my aunt] the more I get to know her, and I learn about
> her life. She grew up in a completely different era, and through her
> I have learned a new appreciation for my family. . . . Now I really
> understand what it means to have history. (Jane, a 21-year-old Native
> American/European American niece)

Families persist. That is, even as families grow and change, family relationships continue. This is the case even when particular family members leave the family. They remain part of the family, if only as a memory or a story. The family also persists as a social institution. That is, the family as a legal, political, and cultural entity is a feature of our collective social life. Every society tells stories about what the family is and does, and how and why the family is necessary for the well-being of its members and productive for society overall.[1] In contemporary U.S. society, many differing stories circulate about whether and how families are adapting to new social relations, communication technologies, economic realities, and political attitudes. While some argue that the family is in crisis,[2] we hold that aunting is an important communicative strategy helping the contemporary U.S. family persist under changing demands and conditions.

In this chapter, we take a more explicit narrative focus to highlight the work of aunts as kinkeepers by considering the family as a story-telling system in which family histories, myths, and intergenerational connections are woven through stories told by and about aunts. The stories our participants tell feature the aunt as an agent of continuity and connection in extended family networks. We contend that it is not only the content of stories but the act of sharing stories that connects extended family members across time and place and contributes to the survival and well-being of individual families past, present, and future. Stories by and about aunts contribute to the continuity of family life and kin relations across generations as well as to a family's or community's narrative of its history and legacies.[3] This aspect of aunting entails what has been referred to as "generativity," or the "concern for and commitment to promoting the well-being of future generations."[4] Generativity expands the horizon of aunting communication from individual relationships and particular family experiences to communities and generational continuities. Accordingly, we focus on communicative practices of aunting that contribute to the family's ongoing narrative: aunts as family memory-keepers; aunts as subjects of family memories; "paying forward" on the legacies of aunting; and aunts as godmothers who maintain the presence of larger cultural and religious narratives in family life.

STORY-TELLING AND HISTORY-MAKING

Kinwork entails the tasks and roles that enable families to survive from one generation to the next in the face of economic, social, and psychological needs.[5] Family storytelling is critical to the maintenance and persistence of family life; stories give families a sense of their own identity, values, history, and direction.[6] Whether as family lore or gossip, this storytelling helps to extend family networks historically through the spoken word. As communication scholars Langellier and Peterson put it, "As surely as we are born into genes, genealogy, and a body of relatives by blood, marriage, and bonds, we are 'born into' family stories and histories, family myths and metaphors, family rituals and routines, family language and secrets."[7] It is often through ordinary conversations, bits of memory, and snatches of stories intertwined in the daily tasks and interactions of family life that family storytelling takes place.[8] Studies indicate that women often take on these mundane storytelling tasks that give individual members a sense of the family's identity and legacies and that maintain the family's sense of continuity and persistence.[9]

One common, and often overlooked, form of family storytelling is gossip. Family gossip offers one way in which family stories are passed within extended family networks and across generations. Gossip is a denigrated, feminine-identified form of talk.[10] Vicky, a niece mentioned in chapter 1 because of her close relationship with one of her aunts, dismissed her older aunts as "the gossip queens of the family." Far from valuing their perspective on the family's past, she reported that she found their stories to be dull and uninteresting:

> They always have all the dirt on who is getting married, who is pregnant, who is fighting with who and why, and how the older family members are doing in terms of health. They usually have stories that they find to be really funny, but I usually find very dull because I don't know half the people that are in them, nor do I care about things that happened ten or fifteen years ago at Thanksgiving dinner that is comparable to what happened twenty minutes ago. . . .

Not only did she resist participating in this type of talk, but Vicky felt that the stories did not relate to her and that they emphasized the gap between her life and her aunts' lives. This example may seem to contradict our claims that aunting is a form of family kinkeeping and historymaking. After all, Vicky ended up feeling estranged rather than enmeshed in her family's stories. Yet this example shows us that family storytelling forms and patterns may be just as important as the content of family stories. Who tells stories and in what form, who listens and who finds the stories interesting or uninteresting, matters in the work of kinkeeping. Family storytellers adopt certain narrative forms and patterns to make their stories more entertaining and "habitable."[11] Gossip, given its denigrated cultural status, may package family lore and history in a form that some family members find "unhabitable," that is, not readily adoptable as a source of useful information for understanding their lives and contexts. On the other hand, Vicky's aunts clearly found gossip to be a communicative practice that connected extended family members and provided a sense of the family's continuity. Even Vicky recalled their storytelling as a way of linking current interactions and identities with previous moments of family life.

While our participants viewed some aunts as family gossips, other aunts were viewed as valuable sources of family information. For example, Jingfang (mentioned in chapter 3) confided that she did not like talking with her aunts and did so "mostly for practical reasons or to be sociable." Yet she valued those conversations with her aunts that filled in the gaps in her knowledge of her mother's past.

> The kinds of conversations I enjoy most with my aunts are when they tell me about life when they were kids, especially when they talk about my mother. My mother rarely talks about herself, so any anecdotes I get from my aunts are really cool. This also consists of me listening while they talk.

For Jingfang, the stories of her mother's childhood and the experiences of her parents' generation built on her curiosity about her mother's past and created linkages that connected her to, and gave her a sense of, emotional investment in her family's past. In this way, her aunts served as family memory-keepers and contributed to Jingfang's sense of connection with her mother's generation and past family experiences and contexts.

We often listen to favorite family tales as children and pursue more coherent family histories as we become older. Indeed, people seem to develop more intense interest in their family relations and histories as they mature.[12] A recent study of popular historymaking found that many people have made an effort to investigate their family history, often by speaking about it with extended family.[13] The researchers attributed this interest to the importance of narratively "mapping" the family. That is, family members search for stories of their family's past in order to locate themselves and their families within larger narratives; they use family history "to define themselves, their place in their families, and their families' place in the world."[14] This desire for family stories was expressed by one of our participants, a middle-aged nephew who told us that he had become more interested in hearing his elderly aunt's stories as both of them aged. He related a story about taking his aunt to her childhood neighborhood, where the sight of the homes inspired her to tell stories of their family's history.[15] Her memories gave her nephew a deeply felt appreciation for the places and circumstances of his father's childhood and his family's history.

The generative kinwork of aunting involves multigenerational interactions and investments that enmesh each generation in family histories and cultural contexts.[16] One aspect of generativity in such kinwork is the explicit effort to teach nieces and nephews about their ethnic or cultural legacies. This is not only a problem of cultural transmission and the socialization of children but of creating and maintaining family and community identities.[17] For example, Jane, whose appreciation for her aunt's past opened this chapter, explained how her aunt had given her a new appreciation for her family's Native American history:

> I always took for granted the fact that I knew the entire history of my family back to the Indians, but now I really understand what it means to have history. I am learning all the stories that have been passed down through the generations, and I am eager to continue on with the stories. I am not sure if I will ever be completely comfortable with my aunt, but I am glad that I have been given this chance to get closer to her. (21-year-old Native American/European American)

Such family stories are critically important in conveying a sense of the family's longevity, legacies, and directions.[18] As both examples above suggest, stories of family history bind aunts, nieces, and nephews together through a shared past contextualized by historic events and conditions, and constitute the family as a "community of memory" where tales of earlier generations form communal bonds and a historical heritage among extended kin.[19]

Stories by and about aunts may contribute to family continuity and persistence by highlighting the continuity of certain personality traits and characteristics that are passed along through generations and that give a family a sense of genetic specificity.[20] Often we find the source of our own characteristics and predilections—both valued and regrettable—in stories about family members. For example, Muriel, a 60-year-old Canadian American introduced in earlier chapters as a chosen aunt, found the qualities in herself that she valued were evident in stories about her pioneering Canadian aunts.

> Aunt Linda (b. 1896 in Finland) was a hearty soul and I prize a photo of her WWI vintage in Saskatchewan standing next to her husband at the plow and a team of oxen and with a child in her arms and one tugging at her skirt. That's my hardy pioneer heritage. She also wrote for one of the Communist newspapers published on the prairies after the Russian Revolution. She was also my activist model. Aunt Siiri (b. 1911 in SK [Saskatchewan]) was an earthy woman with big hips and an even bigger laugh. One of my earliest childhood memories is being bounced along on her wide shoulders from the sauna to the farmhouse in Ontario. She was my model of a loving and physically strong woman.

Upon reflection, Muriel added, "Until this exercise, I've never realized that each of these aunts is, in part, embodied in me." As she recognized, Muriel's embodied story of her aunts depicts a family legacy of female strength, pioneering spirit, and feminine care, legacies that shape the ongoing narrative of Muriel's family and her own identity. In this way, the perspectives of our ancestors "may echo across the generations" in stories that shape the character and commitments of both families and individuals.[21]

HONORING HER LEGACY: REFUSING TO FORGET

Remembering deceased family members not only acknowledges and respects their memory but also verifies the continuity and persistence of family and community life. Past generations and absent kin can be very much alive and present in current family identities and traditions. A popular tool of family therapy is the genogram, an exercise in mapping kinship connections that can depict affective relations as familial relationships.[22] Genograms include absent kin, those who have left through divorce or alienation or those who have died, because these absences may exert considerable influence on family memories, identities, and relationships. So we were not surprised that some of our participants spoke of the ongoing presence of favorite aunts in their hearts. For example, a nephew spoke reverently of his favorite aunt even though she had been dead for five years:

> My favorite aunt would definitely have to be my Aunt Annie. She died about five years ago . . . She was definitely one of the kindest people ever. This is not another one of those cases however where someone is glorified after death. I felt the same way about her while she was alive. (19-year-old European American)

Similarly, a niece spoke fondly of an honorary aunt who had been dead for ten years:

> Although she passed away when I was twelve, my favorite and closest aunt was my mom's best friend. Aunt Jessica lived an hour and a half away from us and we only saw her every two months or so. But since her daughter was only four months older than me and since she and my mom were so close, I never felt that we weren't family—I could talk to her about anything. (22-year-old European American)

Most poignantly, one niece spoke of refusing to forget her aunt even though her aunt was suffering from memory loss and could no longer remember her. She shared these memories of this aunt's kindness and care for her and her brother:

> My memories of Auntie Rose are simple: she was almost always sitting in her rocker with a basket full of yarn and knitting needles at her feet. When my mother, brother, and I would arrive, she would drop every thing, hugs would be doled out all around and we kids would have to endure a cheek pinch or two. . . . It was always an enjoyable time sitting with Auntie Rose. (22-year-old European American)

This niece noted how the contrast between the aunt she had known and her aunt as she was now was emotionally painful:

As much as I would like to keep in touch with her, she no longer
remembers who I am. She seems to suffer from something akin to
Alzheimer's, but does not show all of the symptoms of the disease.
She has good days, now, as well as her bad days, and my mother's
brother checks up on her every weekend. It is extremely painful
not to be recognized by someone who has played such a role in my
younger life.

For this niece, honoring her aunt's legacy of care and kindness involved
not only confronting the realities of her aunt's mental deterioration but
also holding tight to happier memories. Across these examples, stories
memorializing aunts tell us as much about family patterns, relationships, and generational continuities as they do about particular aunts.
Notably, they suggest a larger cultural narrative about the ongoing
significance of the deceased and infirm and the cultural maxim that
"love endures beyond the grave."[23] In this sense, these stories attest to
our collective faith in the strength and durability of affective kinship
bonds and the strong social and narrative networks created through
the aunting relationship. They complement the stories of adult nieces
and nephews caring for elderly aunts in our discussion of kinkeeping
and caregiving in chapter 1. We turn now to another way in which
nieces and nephews reciprocate the care they received from their aunts
by extending affective and material support to the next generation of
nieces and nephews.

HONORING HER LEGACY: PAYING FORWARD

In extended family networks, intergenerational relations of trust and
reciprocal care may be inspired by the memories and legacies of particular family members. Specifically, many of our participants expressed
a desire to "pay forward," that is, to give the kind of support they
received from a favored aunt to their own nieces and nephews once
they themselves became aunts or uncles.[24] We contend that "paying
forward" embodies a critical mode of kincare and familial continuity
involving intergenerational giving within networks of affective and
symbolic obligation and caring. Reciprocating intergenerational love
and care is generative kinwork that clearly contributes to the family's
ability to survive both emotionally and materially.

Generativity is associated with parenthood and later life, but studies indicate that generativity may develop in the transition into adulthood from adolescence, although young adults may not have the opportunities and resources to realize generative impulses until they are older. The nieces and nephews whose stories expressed motivations to pay forward demonstrate the themes of generativity and contribute to research on generativity through the life course. This is of particular interest given the cultural emphasis in the U.S. on ego development and autonomy in late adolescence and early adulthood. That is, college-aged adults are expected to develop coherent life stories that emphasize their emerging identity beyond the primary family and anticipate a future path on their own.[25] Yet many of the young adults with whom we talked expressed a concern to continue a legacy of caring, a concern that expresses generativity and attests to the role of aunting as an agency of intergenerational connection and care.[26]

The values learned through such generative kinwork may contribute to the well-being of society more generally. Generativity is associated with a wide range of prosocial behaviors and attributes including strong social networks, community and civic voluntarism, and involvement in religious/spiritual communities.[27] Feminist economist Nancy Folbre argues that caring for each other pays larger social dividends.[28] When we learn to enact and value affective bonds, the responsibilities of care, and reciprocal giving as family practices, we socialize family members to these ways of living, and they in turn practice and value prosocial behaviors and altruistic relations as the basis for public and civic life. We take heart that among our participants, repaying the nurturing of their aunts by paying forward was a strong theme, evincing the trust, mutual responsibility, and reciprocal giving that are hallmarks of strong social networks. Hence, we suggest that paying the aunting relation forward benefits both families and the larger communities and social networks of which they are a part.

Our first example begins by illustrating the way that nieces and nephews honor a favorite aunt's legacy by keeping fond memories alive as part of their own identities and their family's story. Susan, a European American 21-year-old niece, confided, "I have recently lost an Aunt that meant a lot to me and have since become an Aunt of the most precious little girl." She went on to describe the close relationship that she had with her aunt and the sorrow she and her family felt when her aunt died of cancer:

> My Aunt Phoebe meant the world to me. She was married to my dad's brother and was definitely a loved relative by all. I loved her because she was so real. She was incredibly down to earth and never treated me like I was a little girl. That was my biggest problem growing up the youngest. However my Auntie Phoebe made me feel like the queen of the world. I remember when she gave birth to my cousin Katie. I was only eight and she let me hold her.
>
> It was six years ago when my mom told me that my Auntie Phoebe had cancer and they did not expect her to live more than five years. I could do nothing but cry.

Aunt Phoebe has remained in Susan's life, and Susan's story reveals that these memories maintain a permanent place for Aunt Phoebe in the family narrative. At the same time, Susan expressed a desire to pay forward the gift of her aunt's care and memory in her role as godmother to her sister's baby:

> My sister had asked me to be Eliza's Godmother. I have decided that I am going to be the best Aunt to that little girl. I hope that I can be as good of an Aunt to her as Auntie Phoebe was to me. Sometimes, kids need that. It can be hard to confide information in your parents. Having an Aunt around that you respect can make growing up so much easier. I was very lucky!

We will soon return to the significance of the aunt as godmother, below. Susan's story brings together past and future generations and depicts aunting as a generative relational practice focused on the well-being of younger generations. At the same time, this idea of bestowing a quality of aunting on the next generation as a way of honoring an aunt who is gone is a way of paying forward that enacts generativity through women's relational carework.

Another niece expressed a similar commitment to paying forward on the legacy of a deceased aunt. This niece never met her aunt;

rather, the aunt was a central character in her father's life story. The niece explained that through his story, she felt that she had learned an invaluable lesson from her aunt:

> I never met my father's sister, Aunt Diane. She has taught me some-thing that no one else ever could. She taught me that God has a plan for all of us and we have to trust Him even when we do not understand why things happen. My Aunt Diane died of pneumonia when she was thirteen. My grandmother was extremely devastated, so a doctor told my grandfather that they should try to have another child. These events led to the birth of my father. I am sad that Aunt Diane died, but I am also thankful. My father might not have been born if she had lived. (21-year-old European American)

This story clearly situates the niece's life—her very existence—in the context of an ongoing family narrative that depicts the family's trag-edy as generative. Later, she described how she is paying forward by investing her affection and care in the life of her niece: "I try to cherish every moment I spend with my niece. . . . I hope that I am giv-ing her wonderful memories that she can cherish forever." This niece honored her aunt's ultimate gift by creating "cherishable" memories, in other words, by paying forward on her aunt's contribution to the family's existence and continuation by making her own contribution to the family's next generation.

Many nieces and nephews shared their desire to pay forward by becoming as supportive and loving with their future nieces and neph-ews as their own aunts had been with them.[29] This is an example of how generativity in one generation can inspire generativity in the next. Jen-nifer described with fondness the adventures she had as a child with a favorite aunt. Then she expressed her desire to step into her aunt's shoes and reciprocate this special relationship with her nephew: "Nowadays her visits seem shorter and we are getting older but the conversations are endless. She has always been a creative thinker. We have many years ahead of us but now I can step into her shoes and be that favorite aunt to my nephew" (26-year-old Latina). Similarly, a niece who spoke of her "cool" younger aunt expressed her intention to become a "cool" aunt for her niece or nephew who was soon to be born: "In June I'll

be an aunt and I already want to be the 'cool' aunt. I want my niece/
nephew to look forward to spending time with me. I want them to know
who Auntie Janelle is" (18-year-old European American). One nephew
characterized his relationships with his cousins as mentoring relationships inspired by his close relationship with his aunt:

> My relationship with my Aunt Caroline consists of more of being
> friends and me acting as a mentor for my twin cousins Alan and
> Andy. She views me as almost a big brother figure for them, and due
> to this, she treats me with a lot of respect. There is a very deep sense
> of respect and overall friendship in our relationship with each other
> and this continues to last. (21-year-old European American)

For this nephew, mutual respect, friendship, and responsibility formed
the basis for paying forward what he had received from his aunt by
being a mentor to her children. Across these examples, nephews and
nieces found, in their valued relationships with their aunts, models of
the aunting relationship that they wished to reenact as they paid forward to the next generation of their kin.

Joleen, a 19-year-old European American niece, recalled her anxieties over losing her place in a favorite great-aunt's affections when the
great-aunt's first grandchild was born. Joleen had visited her aunt in
Florida every summer as she grew up.

> You can imagine my heartbreak as I returned to Florida for the sum-
> mer and saw her hold that baby with the same affection she had
> always held me. I remember thinking that I was never going to be
> as important to her because I was her great-niece and now she had a
> granddaughter. Why would she love me when she had someone who
> really belonged with her to love?

Instead of being relegated to second place, Joleen learned a valuable
lesson in the expansiveness of love. As it turned out, the love, trust,
and care in her relationship with her aunt came to include her new
cousin too.

> Our relationship didn't change with the addition of a new baby, except
> to include that child who [sic] I have grown to love as intensely as

I believe Pam loves me. I learned to love with abandon, fiercely and protectively from the way I was loved and protected by Pam. I learned that everyone needs someone in their life who thinks that they are the greatest thing since electricity and that making investments in the lives of people can change the course of lives. Pam's love for me put me on a path I would never have thought possible without her and I owe much of who I am today to the experiences and encouragement she gave me.

The love Joleen felt toward her great-aunt was being paid forward in her love for her young cousin, an intergenerational bridging through aunting. This story about aunting emphasizes how the aunt relationship shaped the niece's sense of her own identity and her possibilities; but it is also a story about unflagging love and the support of family caregivers, the lessons this niece learned about family and self from her aunt Pam that she intended to pass on to her young cousin.

A different basis for paying forward was described by two nieces who felt that their experiences with their aunts modeled what *not* to do; both held an ideal model of aunting in mind that they intended to enact if and when they became aunts. These examples suggest that generativity is an attribute of aunting in cultural kinscripts. Clarice, a niece we mentioned in chapter 3 because she did not have much contact with her aunts as a child, drew from that experience to express her commitment to pay forward by being a better aunt to any future nieces and nephews:

> Unfortunately, my relationships with my aunts have been anything but gratifying. My parents feel horrible about it, but as I have never really experienced close relations with them, I do not feel as though I am missing anything. I just know that the experiences I have had with them makes me want to be very involved if my brother has children someday. (20-year-old European American)

Corinna, a Latina niece introduced in chapter 4, contrasted her own experiences with her aunts and her sister-in-law with the way she interacted with her nephews and niece; she was glad to be the "loving" aunt and implied that her relationship was closer to the ideal:

I have three nephews and a niece and I love them with all of my heart. I spoil them to no end. I play with them and I hug them and kiss them and constantly tell them that I love them. I am not like the way any of my aunts were, and maybe that's because I don't have kids myself. I am the way I always wanted my aunts to be—the way I always thought aunts were supposed to be. And then I think about my sister-in-law. She's always been motherly and she treats my niece and nephews very differently. She is very authoritative, very controlling, always telling them what to do, always warping into the mom when the mom is not around. She is like my aunts. I am glad I can be the fun one, the loving one, the one who's not afraid to get down to their level and talk to them like they are normal human beings. As an aunt, I will make that my job.

For this niece, paying forward involves being the way "aunts are sup-posed to be" in contrast to aunts who confused their role with the authority and control of a mom. The ideal aunt in her view is loving and fun, and respects her nieces and nephews. As an aunt, this niece intends to pay forward the love, fun, and respect she desired from her aunt relationships, rather than what she experienced. In this sense, she is revising her story of family relationships to create a more positive relationship script for the next generation of her kin.[30]

We have emphasized the way nieces and nephews pay forward the intangible benefits of love and care they receive from their aunts, but paying forward can also involve the more tangible benefits of generat-ing and circulating social capital. Amy, a niece from an extended Viet-namese family, described paying forward in terms that made this idea of generating social capital within the extended family network quite tangible. She told a story about her newly immigrated aunt teaching her to cook, and in exchange, she taught her aunt to speak English, and both taught the other about their native cultures:

> As she taught me how to cook, I taught her how to speak English. As more time progressed we grew closer and closer as we taught each other about each culture. . . . We grew pretty close. That was I think when I was twelve years old. But she soon moved out of my home to live with the rest of her family because the rest of them had just

come over from Vietnam. I felt like she and I traded places, because now she was showing her family how to speak English and all. (21-year-old Asian American)

Sharing their skills with each other brought this aunt and niece close. By teaching her aunt English, the niece provided her aunt with a valuable skill that the aunt passed along to improve the family's ability to manage in the United States. In this sense, there was not only a reciprocal exchange of skills and knowledge—cooking for English and vice versa—but the aunt also paid forward on this exchange by teaching the rest of her family to speak English. This example of generativity shows how the aunting relationship can generate and circulate social capital for the benefit of the extended family.

Our participants illustrated that nieces and nephews may pay forward to honor a deceased aunt's love and care, to enact valued attributes or a desired ideal of aunting for the benefit of the next generation, or to effect an exchange of resources contributing to the family's social capital. In a variety of ways, paying forward illustrates how aunts contribute to the intergenerational connections and exchanges that preserve family life. In the next section, we consider the generative contributions of aunts within religious traditions.

SUSTAINING RELIGIOUS TRADITIONS

Churches and other religious organizations provide material and symbolic resources that keep families and communities together.[31] The role of religion in family life can be critical not only in shaping individual family identities, roles, practices, and possibilities, but also in setting the family within larger cultural, spiritual, and historical narratives. Religious rituals, ceremonies, and roles entail a sense of generativity as well. For many families, core religious beliefs, rituals, and affiliations function as key points of connection to other families within religious communities and among members of extended family networks; they "reunite families in time and space, reestablish and reinforce family bonds, and help to construct autobiographical family memory."[32] Bar mitzvahs and bat mitzvahs, bris observances, first communions, confirmations, baptisms, weddings, funerals, and other religious ceremonies are often occasions that bring families together. At such times, the women in the family typically are expected to organize and carry out the details (e.g., food, dress, setting) for the celebration. As we noted in chapters 1 and 2, aunts figured prominently in participants' memories of such important occasions. A majority of our participants mentioned religious holidays as occasions for family gatherings when their aunts were expected to perform the kinwork that sustained family bonds, memories, rituals, and traditions. We have documented the kinwork of aunts on such occasions in several earlier chapters.

In this section, we focus on a particular aunting role that is formally designated within certain religious and cultural traditions: the godmother. Generativity is inherent in this spiritual mother figure charged with guiding a child's religious education and growth, and with seeing to the child's spiritual well-being as a member of the historical church and the immediate religious community. The godmother's role is historically well established in Anglican and Catholic churches, and in Judaic communities whose members choose a godparent for their child in keeping with religious and cultural dictates.[33] Many culturally specific variations exist on the godmother role; for example, in the Latin American system of *compadrazgo*, chosen kin are created through participation in a Catholic baptism ritual and expected to fulfill a parental role in a child's life.[34] Just as importantly, commonalities cross cultural systems, emphasizing spiritual, emotional, economic, social, and ritual ties between the godchild and godparent.[35]

Parents often choose aunts as godmothers, a practice that recognizes existing family ties and can enhance generational connections. Many of our participants reported that an aunt served as their godmother and/or that they served as both an aunt and a godmother to one or more of their nieces and nephews.[36] Aunts as godmothers embody material and spiritual commitments to the well-being of individual children and their families within extended kin, community, and religious networks. We draw on our interviews to illustrate the multidimensional generativity of the aunt as godmother in assuring the future well-being of individual godchildren, the continuity of the family, and the family's place within larger religious communities and narratives.

Naming someone a godparent bestows both honor and responsibility on an aunt. In this way, parents can strengthen familial bonds and create a sense of connection and continuity in the extended family network. For example, Margaret, the daughter of Portuguese immigrants, explained that her father's sister was given the honor of being her godmother as a way of thanking her and of affirming this family connection, since the sister had brought the young woman's father to the U.S. from Portugal. Another participant, Ellen, also described godmothering as a way to acknowledge and strengthen generational connections within the family: "My aunt who is my godmother, she was the mother of my four favorite cousins. . . . I think [the baptism] was probably done more for the sake of my mom's parents, or my mom's mom, than any other reason." This woman was not raised in the church, but the baptism was a way of honoring her grandmother's religious beliefs and of reaffirming family ties both to the grandmother and to the aunt chosen to be her godmother. In this sense, choosing an aunt as a godmother may have less to do with a family's religious commitments and more to do with generativity; bestowing this honor may be a strategy aimed at maintaining and strengthening family connections within and across generations.

Another generative aspect of godmothering by aunts is that this role builds on women's relationships within the family. Specifically, long-term connections between women and their sisters, sisters-in-law, and often friends, cousins, and other close female friendships create established bonds and obligations between these women that spill over into a godmothering role. It is little surprise that aunts, who function as kinkeepers, are at the center of godmothering and other nurturing relationships. For example, Teresa, a Mexican American woman, said of her aunt, "I was real, real close to my Aunt Juanita because she baptized me." She also spoke of a great-aunt, her mother's aunt, who inspired her to have faith in God. Teresa's stories of her aunts suggest that these women bring each other into religious faith and that their religion provides a strong basis for the intergenerational connections and commitments that bind the women of this extended family together. Similarly, Rose, the 35-year-old Portuguese bookkeeper whose relationship with her niece was noted in chapter 4, described the web of godmothering that binds the women of her family together across generations:

> Typically, we have a close relationship with our godparents and so, like my Aunt Lissette was my godmother when I was baptized and then my Aunt Sarah, 'cause her husband was my godfather . . . she's kind of my godmother as well, and she would always refer to herself as my godmother, like when she'd sign a birthday card or whatever. And then later on we go through confirmation—we're just confirming our faith—and so my Aunt Lourdes . . . she was my godmother for that, or sponsor.

In turn, Rose chose her daughters' godmothers from among their aunts, and she acts as a godmother to her niece (her brother's daughter) as well, continuing the tradition: "I'm her godmother so I've always tried to be there for her."

Rose's role as godmother included helping her mother with the care of this goddaughter after the girl's parents divorced. This parenting role can be a spiritual role, but it often carries more explicit obligations to "step in" for a child's parents. For example, one of Margaret's aunts asked her to be godmother to her baby son Allen, and Margaret understood the acceptance of this role as a promise to become her nephew's parent if necessary.

> If they're to pass away then I'm to become Allen's mom. That's the end of it, you know. My cousin Dave is Allen's godfather and we step in as parents, so when they asked me at 17, it was a huge honor because they thought that I was mature enough that if they were to die the next day you know I would step in. I mean like I'm sure that my parents and other people would have been "OK we're gonna help too," if that were to happen at the time, but it was a huge honor and I was really touched and it was probably maybe a few weeks after Allen was born that they asked me and I was very involved. . . . He calls me Medlina, which is godmother [in Portuguese]. Well he can't pronounce it quite yet.

For Kathleen, a Presentation Order nun in the Catholic Church who was mentioned in chapters 2 and 5, who is godmother to two of her nieces, being a godmother means parenting the child's spiritual development. She seemed to take this responsibility as seriously as did Margaret, and she made clear the godmother's central role in the baby's initiation into the church and the importance of stepping in for the parents if necessary:

> In fact, you [the godmother] hold the baby, you hold the candle, you make the promise, because you're the parent in loco parentis, so if they supposedly don't uphold their task of parenting well, you're supposed to step in you know so, you promise. . . . as Catholics or maybe as Christians, because many faiths have baptisms, this is an important faith step for the child and for the family, but also as a result of that all the family gets invited [to the baptism].

Kathleen's observations emphasize the family's place in the faith community as well as the godmother's role in engendering that faith in her godchild.[37]

Finally, some of our participants highlighted the special bond that the godmother role added to their relationship with their aunt. After all, the analogy of the aunt as mother is suggested in the title "godmother" itself. While naming an aunt a godmother cannot assure this special bond, for some participants, this designation seemed apt. As one of our participants said, "Auntie Sarah is my godmother, and in a lot of ways, my mother." Similarly, Emily shared her story about the special name that identified her special bond with her aunt/ godmother:

> Ever since I can remember, my mother's sister has played an important part in my life. My mom has told me countless times the story of how I gave my aunt the pet name that I still use. I was a baby (not sure how old) and I could say "momma," my aunt's name is Lee and I just put the two together and her new name was "Momma Lee." Once I started calling her this I just couldn't stop. The fact that I refer to her directly as one of my "mothers" demonstrates the strong impact she has on my life. She is my godmother, and one of my most favorite people in the world.

The pervasiveness of cultural expectations that a special bond and parenting responsibilities attend the aunt-godmother and niece/nephew-godchild relationship was affirmed conversely by one aunt who expressed her reluctance to be named a godmother. Carolyn and her husband Rick were asked to be godparents to one of Rick's sister's daughters. Carolyn explained why they refused to be godparents:

> We didn't really want to be godparents to the kids because we wanted to treat them all equally and then if you were a godmother or godfather for one of the children, they were supposed to be more special than the rest, so I remember talking with them about that and then I remember doing a lot with them in the every day, day-to-day thing.

Carolyn made it a point to spend a lot of time with all of her nieces, but her refusal to take on a godmothering role attests to the expectation that an aunt will take on more special responsibilities and connections with her godnieces or godnephews.

Looking Ahead

We have explored four communicative practices of aunting: aunts as family memory-keepers; aunts as subjects of family memories; vows to "pay aunting forward," thereby linking generations through aunting; and aunts as godmothers who maintain the presence of larger cultural and religious narratives in family life. These aunting practices contribute to continuity and connection in extended family networks, community relations, and cultural histories. Hence, we contend that the horizon of aunting communication extends beyond individual aunt/niece/nephew relationships and particular family experiences to the life and well-being of communities and generations. In the conclusion, we connect these ideas to social and research implications.

Aunting
in the 21st Century

I feel aunting helps fill in many of the cracks and fissures that
inevitably occur in everybody's lives. When standard relationships
defined by Western family norms and marital situations crumble, it's
aunting that often supplies healing love and connectedness. For me,
aunting also helps remind us to stretch our love and caring, our time
and financial contributions to not just those immediately genetically
linked to us, but to stretch forth to the family of humankind. Sometimes families, communities, religious or political units, and nations
are too self-contained and self-serving. Aunting is embracing and,
writ large, may well be a model for healing our damaged world at
all levels. (Muriel, Finnish Canadian)

Muriel's testament to the power of aunting offers a perfect coda to
our analysis of aunting. As family communication researchers, we tell
stories about what families are like and how aunting relationships are
lived. The story we have told about aunting is both a representation of
our participants' characterizations and memories and a construction
of possibility. We encourage a more expansive appreciation for the
significance of aunting practices and their adoption for enacting all
sorts of relationships. As a story about doing kinship, our rendition of
aunting offers an alternative model to those grounded exclusively on

169

the nuclear family—for example, stepmothering is fraught with uncertainties and tensions; enacting this often difficult relationship as an aunting relationship offers an alternative that recognizes new kin connections even as it honors a stepchild's prior familial loyalties. Because our story about aunting emphasizes multiple, flexible, and adaptive relational connections, we see aunting as a powerful response to the need for ongoing but nonnuclear kinships in contemporary social life, where careerism, social narcissism, and individualism make it increasingly difficult to move beyond superficial relationships.[1] E-mail and social networking sites such as Facebook give us the appearance that we are all connected these days, sharing our intimate secrets with strangers and living out our relationships as serial encounters. However, the longing for meaningful connections persists.

As we have shown, aunting resists idealized versions of family solidarity and shared identities; instead, aunts, nieces, and nephews expect differences, discontinuities, and connections that change over time and periodically require renewal. Aunting, we maintain, is a story that meets the challenges of contemporary social and familial life. Our hope is that this book will call attention to the multiple ways that aunts contribute to family well-being and persistence. Most importantly, we hope we have made a convincing case for the mode of relational work we call "aunting" drawn on the aunt/niece/nephew relationship. Aunting is both a flexible and responsive relational dynamic and a repertoire of relational identities, skills, resources, and possibilities that can be mobilized to meet family crises and opportunities. Aunting in this sense is a verb, a relational practice that most of us experience firsthand in small but crucial ways as we reach out to others and as we accept the material and emotional support of those around us.

As a relational practice responsive within and to changing contexts, aunting allows for considerable choice. Compared with other family roles like mother, father, child, or even grandparent, aunting is loosely scripted. That is, our cultural stories don't "fill in" what aunts should be like or what makes a good or bad aunt quite as clearly as the stories about what makes, for example, a good or bad mother. One must choose how to enact the aunt role because there is no normative definition. As our participants described, the aunting relationship is what we make of it. While some people make this a very intimate and closely connected relationship, others find little contact or intimacy to be just as acceptable. Perhaps the element of choice is most evident in the practice of chosen aunts. Aunting as invitational and voluntary and the created kin relations that extend family networks and reconfigure family relationships demonstrate the power of choice in contemporary family life. Aunting experiences and practices offer creative possibilities for changing social patterns and configurations of family. By focusing on aunting rather than nuclear family figures, we have offered an alternative story of family life that encompasses chosen families, caring communities, dispersed families, and the changing demographics of familial networks and generational legacies.

We also called attention to the flexibility of aunting in relation to cultural norms of femininity. The aunt as a feminized familial figure is both bound by and enjoys considerable latitude within cultural norms of femininity. Different aunts embody different possibilities for what women can be and do. As a relational practice, aunting may be enacted through feminine nurturing or as noninvolvement. Compared with mothering, aunting is less culturally prescribed and more flexible as a feminized role and relational dynamic. The flexibility of the aunt in becoming "like a mother," a friend, or a stranger opens possibilities for thinking about our selves in relation beyond traditional family roles and for exploring more expansive connections among self, family, community, and culture.

Finally, we have adopted a narrative perspective because it offers a way of understanding how people make sense of their own lives. In this perspective, we take the family as a storytelling system creating, changing, and sustaining the identities, trajectories, and histories of families and family members: the stories our participants told us about their aunts or their nieces and nephews turned out to be stories about themselves and their families. In a sense, we have created a composite family portrait through the stories of different aunts as those stories create and enforce or alter kinship connections. Aunts themselves may serve as knowledge-keepers, family storytellers, or characters in family narratives. They may be the gossip queens or the memory-holders who sustain family histories. Chosen aunting is also a narrative construction that depends on ongoing stories of connection, affection, and mutual obligation. Finally, stories by and about aunts contribute to the continuity of family life and kin relations across generations as well as to a family's or community's narrative of its history and legacies. In this sense, stories of aunts are embedded in and draw on larger family dramas, cultural scripts, and historical narratives.

In the remainder of this chapter, we explore the social implications of our analysis and offer some suggestions for future research.

SOCIAL IMPLICATIONS: WHY DOES AUNTING MATTER?

Doing Families and Communities Differently

Throughout this book, we have suggested that aunting is a practice, something we can do, not just a role that some people are assigned within kin networks. We understand aunting as a communicative practice that enlarges the way that we think about doing family. Thus, we propose aunting not as a new metaphor for being a family, but as a way of conceptualizing flexible, choice-driven practices for doing family and for enacting community connections in ways that maximize the supportive benefits of traditional family structures while decreasing the powerful constraints that have always been a part of family life. Rather than arguing for or against particular configurations of family as valid or invalid, morally superior or suspect, functional or dysfunctional, we instead passionately advocate for the adoption of aunting practices in all families and community networks, and even in other social contexts such as workplaces and schools. The aunting ideals we have reported on here—flexibility, choice, and an emphasis on doing rather than being—are expressed in the form of a variety of behaviors: mentoring, listening, nurturing, challenging, distancing. None of these practices are inherently tied to nuclear families, or to traditional gender roles for nurturing and caretaking. In each chapter, we highlighted practices that contribute to healthy relationships. We urge readers to adopt the practices that would enhance their relationships—mentoring, perhaps, or maintaining long-distance connections. In thinking of these practices as aunting, we can stop participating in the limiting nostalgia for "the way we never were" and instead embrace and develop the many ways in which we live today.

Beyond Feminine Stereotypes

A second vital implication of our analysis of aunting lies in its simultaneous connection to and resistance of traditional femininity within the family. The second mother or other mother enactment of maternal nurturing fits comfortably within some aunt/niece and aunt/nephew relationships. At the same time, other aunts connect through fun, friendship, or role modeling, or shape nieces' and nephews' evolving selves through judgment, rejection, or distance. That the aunt can do all of these and still be thought of as caring challenges the good mother/bad mother dichotomy in which much of our cultural conceptualizations of family remain mired, and which underlies our good nuclear family/bad nonnuclear family dichotomy. In embodying such diverse practices as evidence of successful aunting—especially those practices that would render one a failed mother, such as noninvolvement—aunting counters the cultural assumption that mothering is the paradigmatic model of family nurturing. Instead, the various and flexible modes of aunting suggest that familial care can be a shared relational enterprise across extensive networks of chosen as well as biolegal kin.

Crucially, aunting need not be female identified. Indeed, we suggest that aunting is more usefully understood as a set of relational practices rather than activities associated with a female- or feminine-identified role. This suggestion undoes (or at least presents a strong challenge to) the feminine/masculine dichotomy that continues to influence our ways of understanding ourselves and our cultures. Specifically, nurturing, kinwork, caregiving, and caretaking are traditionally marked as feminine activities and responsibilities. Yet dividing relational care into masculine/feminine or male/female responsibilities severely limits our relational responsiveness. Such dichotomies, or mutually exclusive, paired opposites, restrict our ability to perceive and reflect upon the complexities of our experiences.[2] The good mother is still described in terms of her feminine traits and the good father in terms of his masculinity, de-emphasizing the ways in which their successful enactment of parenting necessitates a flexible blend of gendered behaviors and reinforcing our cultural obsession with traditional gender roles. Through aunting, we can break open this either/or thinking. Aunting lets us think less of being either feminine or masculine and more about choosing and doing a range of masculine and feminine behaviors. Using the language of aunting complexifies the enactment of nurturing, denies kinwork or care as the exclusive domain of women or as being inherently feminine in nature, and resists the nuclear family imperative.

We need a new language to express the evolution of our society's family configurations. Language is not static; it changes constantly as we strive to express our lived experiences. One area in which language desperately needs to catch up is in describing the realities of blended families, single-parent families, and lesbian/gay families in terms richer than those labels can convey.[3] Aunting is a socially subversive term; simply using it as a verb makes it impossible for people to take for granted their traditional views of family. At the same time, it resonates with the familiar—aunt is certainly a well-known form of address—providing a linguistic link to tradition. We are hopeful that aunting articulates new possibilities for familial, feminine, and relational practices.

Celebrating Aunting

Finally, we urge readers to honor and celebrate aunting. We are not alone in our recognition of the centrality of aunts; an emergent trend signifies their growing cultural significance. Several popular books have appeared in the past few years celebrating the aunt. Infant clothing manufacturers now market "my aunt loves me" outfits to complement those referencing mothers, fathers, and grandparents. Cards appear on the racks each Mother's Day that pay tribute to aunts because they are "like a mother" to us, and birthday cards for nieces and nephews abound. While we appreciate these capitalist odes to the significance of aunts, we urge people to honor connections with chosen and biolegal aunts through rituals and other ways of celebrating the strength of their connections. One possibility is to pattern a secular ritual after the baptismal ceremonies through which godparents are created in order to name and honor chosen aunts. Another model is the Australian practice of hosting a "wet the baby's head" party within a couple months of an infant's birth to introduce the baby to her or his extended family and community. The name refers to the practice of clinking cold beverages together in toasts to the baby, during which a few drops of condensation could possibly land on the baby's head. The celebration reaffirms existing ties and may create new ones as neighbors or new colleagues are invited to share in the celebration. Likewise, we could mark the addition of an aunt or the evolution of a relationship into an aunting one through a celebration or a toast. In the same way that aunting is a communicative practice, recognizing its value to us can become something that we express through personal, family, or community practices.

RESEARCH IMPLICATIONS: STUDYING FAMILIES AND AUNTING

Our research on aunting has several implications for family communication research. First, family research remains too narrowly focused on the nuclear family (despite some notable exceptions), obscuring the significance of extended families and kinship networks. While some researchers have argued for biolegal definitions of family,[4] our study of aunting evidences the value of more inclusive definitions. Similarly, we should refine our understanding of the particular practices associated with various extended family members—we applaud research that sorts out the practices constituting grandparenting, uncling, and cousining, as well as aunting.[5] By homogenizing these relationships, scholars contribute to the illusion of nuclear family autonomy and insulation.

Second, research often assumes the primacy of motherhood and parenting in accounts of family life. Privileging motherhood limits perceptions of nurturing; yet over and over, our participants attested to the care and influence of aunts. Further, all women are not mothers, and this narrow model of nurturing in family life leaves little room for childless or childfree women and couples. In addition, the importance of aunts in our participants' accounts indicates that studies of childhood development and well-being must consider the role of caring adults beyond parents. Finally, research on alternative relational dynamics like aunting offers a more robust account of gendered family relations than the model of the heterosexual parenting couple and the traditionally gendered dynamics of the nuclear family.

Third, there is need to parse the particularities of aunting across the variants of family life in the United States. Our work in this book has been to develop a composite portrait of contemporary U.S. aunting from a wide variety of narrative "snapshots" drawn from many different perspectives. Our concern was to highlight the practices of this relational dynamic rather than drawing out the particularities of aunting as a raced, classed, regional, and otherwise culturally variable dynamic. Yet these contexts are critical to understanding contemporary aunting. After all, the particular choices and responses of aunting are always embedded in these larger relational politics. It remains for future studies to parse out how social differences matter in aunting. Our effort offers evidence of the significance of aunting as a robust set of relational practices that contributes vitally to family life and well-being in the contemporary U.S. Similarly, we argued for the significance of aunting across generations and ages. At the same time, we do not mean to homogenize the experiences and practices of aunting. For example, age matters: the aunting relationship changes in response to the ages of aunts, nieces, and nephews; age-related passages and stages catalyze different aunting responses and relational shifts; and age-related crises and capacities affect how aunting is done and experienced, developed, and understood. Again, we encourage further research into the specificities of aunting in context. At the same time, we hold that aunting operates as a critical dynamic of contemporary family life across these differences.

Fourth, family research must reconsider the nature of intimacy and closeness in family relationships, particularly the privileging of face-to-face interactions and the equation of relationship quality with frequency of contact. We urge more research attention to the ways that intimate relationships may develop strategies for remaining close though distant, such as the "contented noninvolvement" we document in aunting relationships. We advocate that family researchers reclaim the value of distanced and unfriendly family relationships. Our findings that antagonisms may bond extended family just as more affectionate relations do contribute to research into the "shadow side" of intimacy. Researchers adopting a model of dialectic tensions in family relationships might explore the tensions of continuity and disintegration and bonding and estrangement as relational dynamics of aunting.

Our study also points tentatively to the role of contemporary communication technologies in maintaining family connections across time and space distances. Research into aunting online can contribute to the growing literature on mediated family communication and on mediated interpersonal communication more broadly.

GO FORTH AND AUNT!

In closing, we urge readers to reflect upon evidence of aunting practices in their own lives, and to celebrate these practices as useful in close relationships of many types. Aunting and being aunted continue to provide joy and challenge within our lives and those of our participants. Muriel's testament to the power of aunting in the world, which began this chapter, pointed to the way that aunting may "fill in many of the cracks and fissures that inevitably occur in everybody's lives." Aunting as a vibrant and varied relational practice has the potential to respond to these exigencies of our personal and community lives. At the same time, aunting has a subversive potential for creating new fissures that disrupt the traditional ideas and practices of family and femininity and encourage us to practice a more inclusive and expansive kinship—to "aunt" one another.

METHODOLOGY

This appendix elaborates on the details of data collection and analysis provided in the book's introduction. For scholars, students, and others interested in understanding the methodology behind our study, we review our data collection strategies and further explicate both our theoretical approach and our analytical methods.

DATA COLLECTION

From March 2003 through June 2005 we collected 40 interviews and 138 written narratives as our primary data. During this time, we immersed ourselves in the research literature on kinship, family composition, and communication within families. We further collected a huge volume of popular cultural artifacts that featured aunts to provide a larger cultural context for our analyses.[1]

Participants

From the very beginning of this study, we intentionally sought a broad and varied sample that would give us examples of aunting from across racial and ethnic groups; age cohorts; sexual orientations; citizen and immigrant communities; socioeconomic classes; rural, suburban, and urban populations; and geographic regions. While we did not attempt to meet the standards of a statistically random sample, we used our networks of connections to reach people whose experiences of aunting illuminated the tremendous variety of co-cultures within the United States today. The demographic characteristics of our participants included people ranging in age from 18 to 74; females and males (with slightly more female participants); participants from small towns and large cities across the Northeast, Midwest, Southeast, and West Coast regions of the United States; and representatives of a range of ethnicities including African American, Asian American, Native American/American Indian, Latino/a, East Indian American, and European American. In addition, we included immigrants from Mexico, Iraq, Thailand, Canada, and Portugal. Participants' religious affiliations included Judaism, Islam, Mennonitism, Catholicism, Hinduism, Buddhism, and several Christian Protestant denominations. We collected data from a number of lesbians and gay men, as well as single, married, and divorced heterosexuals, some of whom had children and others who did not. Thus our rich and varied group of participants aptly fulfilled the demands of "theoretic" or purposive sampling, which focuses on gathering participants well suited to the particular research objective.[2]

Interviews

Our interviews were all conducted in private settings, audio recorded, and transcribed. The authors conducted the vast majority of the interviews, but three research assistants also participated in conducting several of the interviews. Interviews ranged in length from about twenty minutes to two hours, with most averaging approximately one hour. Prior to the beginning of interviews, participants completed informed consent forms approved by the Human Subjects Board and brief questionnaires regarding demographic information.

Our careful review of the research on family communication, particularly among extended families, provided us with very little direction on soliciting data regarding aunt roles and aunting practices. Thus, we consciously chose to begin all interviews with a very open prompt that invited interviewees to "tell me about your aunts." In this way, we avoided limiting our participants' responses to only predetermined topic areas and enabled participants to explore a range of subjects of interest to them. Following our opening gambit, we utilized a "semistructured" interviewing style in which we followed a standard set of questions but freely followed up on any issues brought up by the participant, encouraging her or him to elaborate. All interviewers paid particular attention to stories of time spent with aunts, eliciting as many details of these interactions as possible. No topic introduced by a participant was off-limits, and we frankly were amazed at the wealth of stories we heard regarding parenting styles, sexuality, drug use, religion, career decisions, politics, and other highly charged subjects.

With the exception of the Thai immigrant aunt and her Thai American niece, we interviewed aunts (all of whom were also nieces), nieces, and nephews as singular representatives of their families. While this is an accepted, commonly used approach in family research, it admittedly does not engage the relational nature of aunting, since only one member of the aunt/niece or aunt/nephew pair was given the opportunity to represent this relationship.[3] At the same time, our diverse sample ensured that many different perspectives manifested in our data and provided evidence of aunting practices.

College Student Narratives

At three universities—one on the West Coast, one in the Midwest, and another in the Southeast—instructors in four courses offered students extra credit points to write a narrative in response to the statement, "Please describe communicating with one or more of your aunts." Participants also were asked to provide their age, sex, and ethnic/racial group. In most cases, responses were written outside of class over a one- to two-week span and returned to the course instructor. A smaller number of responses were collected in class. All students provided informed consent, following Human Subjects Board guidelines. Written narratives ranged in length from half a page to four pages, with the average length being approximately two typed pages.

While we were careful to solicit interviews from a wide variety of age cohorts, the vast majority of the participants who provided written accounts were traditional-age college students who are in the "emerging adulthood" period of their lives, and thus were uniquely suited to telling their stories.[4] Narrative identity theory suggests that adolescence is the time in which " 'personal event memories' become organized into a coherent life story."[5] Adolescents simultaneously strive for independence and autonomy while maintaining connections to their families.[6] In order to deal with such tensions, young adults actively construct meaningful life narratives, including their family histories and their own projected futures. Hence, eliciting written narratives from a large number of college students afforded us insights into the meaning of aunts to young adults for whom family relationships have a particular salience.

DATA ANALYSIS

Theoretical and Epistemological Perspective

We have adopted a relational communication approach informed by an understanding of communication as social construction. Our understanding is that we co-create worlds of meaning through collaborative and mutually responsive interactions with others.[7] In addition, a feminist theoretical perspective informed our analyses as we sought to address the aunt relationship as a gendered relationship, subject to conventional expectations for feminine identities and roles. Our concern in such analyses is to address implicit relations of power and disempowerment, notably the dominance of mothering as a paradigm for close relationships culturally defined as feminine or female, such as the aunt relationship. In developing a feminist critique of such simplistic understandings, we seek to intervene in the gendered structures of contemporary cultural life. That is, we intended to question the prevailing norms and narratives of how family life is or should be experienced, rather than taking for granted that existing structures are necessarily good or inevitable.[8]

Grounded Theory Analysis

We conducted a constructivist grounded theory analysis of interview transcripts and written narratives. Our inductive, analytic approach included a "revised, more open-ended practice of grounded theory that stresses its emergent, constructivist elements" and eschews positivist claims of objectivity.[9] While paying attention to the ongoing construction of meaning, we nonetheless followed the steps of traditional grounded theory research: coding data, developing inductive

categories, revising the categories, writing memos to explore prelimi-
nary ideas, continually comparing parts of the data to other parts and
to literature, collecting more data, fitting data into categories, noting
where it did not fit, and revising the categories using constant comparative analysis.[10] Moreover, as collaborators, we engaged in extensive
deliberation and negotiation over our interpretation of participants'
words and meanings. We engaged in reflexive consideration of our
own roles in data gathering and analysis to enhance "theoretical sensi-
tivity" or "an awareness of the subtleties of meaning of data."[11]

Eventually we developed the six categories of "doing aunting"
upon which this book is organized. We derived these categories induc-
tively, that is, as emergent groupings within our data rather than as pre-
existing roles based upon previous research. We deliberately sought to
resist previous emphasis on static familial roles and instead focused on
deriving practices or modes of enacting the aunt. At the same time, the
categories were not constructed in a vacuum; all of our previous experience as researchers, knowledge of theory and research literature, and
ideological commitments inevitably formed elements of the landscape
in which we constructed this approach to understanding aunting.[12]

As we finalized our analyses, we selected exemplars to illustrate
each of the categories and subcategories of aunting from all of our participants. In writing this book, however, we sought to balance the need
to include representations from all of our participants, necessarily brief
and scattered through the chapters, with the appearance across chapters of a smaller number of main participants, some introduced in the
introduction and others in the chapters. Through these participants, we
offer readers a richer, more complex rendering of the meaning of aunting in practice that helps to balance the decontextualized fragments of
multiple participants' stories by letting readers get to know a smaller
number of aunts, nieces, and nephews more intimately. In the end, our
goal was to provide a readable text that highlights the value of aunting
in everyday family life.

NOTES

Preface

1   Milardo, 2010.

Introduction

1   See, e.g., Bould, 2003; Edwards, 2004.
2   The National Center for Children in Poverty estimates:
    Over 13 million American children live in families with incomes
    below the federal poverty level, which is $21,200 a year for a family
    of four in 2008. The number of children living in poverty increased
    by 15 percent between 2000 and 2007. There are 1.7 million more
    children living in poverty today than in 2000. (Fass & Cauthen,
    2008, ¶1)
3   Clinton, 1996.
4   Hansen & Garey, 1998.
5   Coontz, 2000; Coontz, Parson, and Raley, 1999; Hansen & Garey,
    1998.
6   Floyd & Morman, 2006.
7   Johnson, 2000.
8   Johnson, 2000.
9   E.g., Christiansen & Brophy, 2007; Sturgis, 2004; Traeder & Bennett,
    1998.
10 Milardo's study (2010) was published as this book went to press. His
    interviews with 104 aunts, uncles, nieces, and nephews were designed

185

"to recover what aunts and uncles do, how they think about their positions, and how they are consequential" (p. 29). His analysis revealed that aunting and uncling may involve a wide range of relational roles and responsibilities, among them second parenting, mentoring, befriending, buffering, kinkeeping, and caregiving. See also O'Reilly & Abbey, 2000; Peington, 2004; Rich, 1976.

11 Turner & West, 2006.
12 Fictive kin (Stack, 1974); quasi-kin (Furstenberg & Cherlin, 1991); chosen family (Weston, 1991); pseudo-family, ritual kin (Ebaugh & Curry, 2000); intentional family (Muraco, 2006); constructed kin ties (Rubenstein, Alexander, & Goodman, 1991).
13 Ellingson & Sotirin, 2008.
14 Coontz, 2000.
15 Jago, 1996, p. 497.
16 E. Stone, 2000, p. x; Langellier & Peterson, 2004.
17 Koerner & Fitzpatrick, 2002.
18 Coontz, 2000.
19 Wood, 2002; Ferguson, 2001.
20 As Jorgenson and Bochner (2004) remind us, both researchers and participants tell narratives of family that do not merely reflect but shape the experiences and possibilities of family life.
21 Berger & Luckmann, 1966; Gergen, 1994, 1999; Hacking, 1999.
22 Ellingson & Sotirin, 2006, 2008; Sotirin & Ellingson, 2006, 2007.
23 Fox & Murry, 2000; Osmond & Thorne, 1993; Thompson & Walker, 1995; Thorne, 1992.

Chapter 1

1 E.g., Wellman (1998) argues that the increased mobility of families and the prevalence of divorced, single-parent, blended, and isolated families affords individuals and families less social capital, or relational resources that they can draw upon to help them to cope in times of need or transition and to lend a sense of security all the time.
2 See Coontz (2000) for a discussion of the fallacy of the nuclear family's functional independence.
3 See Leach & Braithwaite, 1996; see also Albrecht & Goldsmith, 2003.
4 Hochschild (2001) coined the concept of the "time bind" to explain the challenges faced by parents whose careers demand increasing numbers of hours spent at work, while at the same time they struggle to provide care for children.
5 Stack & Burton, 1998, p. 408.
6 di Leonardo, 1998, p. 420.

7 E.g., Stewart, Witteborn, & Zediker, 2004. This axiom was advanced by Watzlawick, Beavin, and Jackson in their classic work published in 1967, *Pragmatics of Human Communication*.

8 Psychologist Alvin Rosenfeld, as quoted in Trestrail, 2001. On the frenetic schedule of contemporary families, see Warner, 2005; for commentary, see Sotirin, Buzzanell, & Turner, 2007.

9 The idea of motherhood is readily available to us culturally, and we tend to reach for it to describe many types of relational activities and roles (Hayes, 1996).

10 For a discussion of the feminized, unpaid "reproductive" labor that the production of capitalism takes for granted and does not consider to actually be labor, see, e.g., Riley & Kiger, 1999; also Jackson, 1992.

11 Stack's classic study of an urban African American community illuminated the complexities of bartering and sharing resources among those struggling in the working class and those on the fringes of poverty (Stack, 1974). In a more contemporary case study of the "time bind" experienced by children whose parents both work full time outside of the home, Hochschild explored two girls' diverging experiences with day care. A working-class girl was cared for by an aunt and felt no resentment against her mother for working, while the daughter of a professional woman manager expressed anger and resentment about being left with a series of paid caregivers. The author speculated that the normalizing of kincare in the working-class girl's family network eased the transition between home and her time with a caregiver (Hochschild, 2003).

12 E.g., Bould, 2003; Putnam, 2001.

13 One study found evidence of "caring neighborhoods" in which White, middle-class women supported each other as chosen kin, functioning as aunts to each others' children, such that

> the aid and assistance given was of a profound nature. It was part of a sense of shared social duties . . . the reciprocal exchange of child care was common [and] . . . the neighborhood replaces kin in terms of close-at-hand helping networks and immediate supervision of children and teens . . . [respondents reported] "I call my neighbors aunts and uncles." (Bould, 2003, p. 435)

14 According to the U.S. Census, 25.8% of all U.S. children lived with a single parent in 2007, or a little over 18.9 million children under 18 years of age. The 2007 report is significant for the following change in tabulating the number of single parent families: "Before 2007, a child living with two unmarried parents was tabulated as a child living with a single parent" (U.S. Census Bureau, 2008).

15 E.g., Lehr, 1999; Roseneil, 2000; Weston, 1995.

16 Weston, 1991, 1995.

17 Muraco, 2006, p. 1314.
18 Muraco, 2006; Tillmann-Healy, 2001.
19 The need for positive adult community support and nurturers is reflected in programs such as the LGBT Aunts and Uncles Program in Massachusetts.

> This program creates a way for LGBT parents to augment their children's network of caring adults, capitalizes on the LGBT community's rich, untapped resource of LGBT persons who don't want to be parents but desire a meaningful relationship with a child, and provides children with a greater sense of connection and belonging to, as well as support from, the LGBT community. . . The program was founded: To actualize the much-touted ethic, "It takes a village to raise a child" (http://www.alternativefamilies.org/auntsanduncles.html. Accessed March 3, 2003).

This now defunct program is an excellent example of a community acknowledging the need of children and adults alike to have positive relationships across generations; it offered a formal channel to enhance opportunities for such connections, which may be difficult to forge for today's busy families. In the case of lesbian and gay families, bigotry is also an obstacle that may prevent them from being integrated into some community networks and may even lead to them being barred from their own extended family on the basis of their sexual orientation, a barrier not faced by heterosexual families. Clearly, this model of aunting (and uncling) could be applied to a wide variety of families in need of opportunities both for positive, fun relationships and for support.

The former Massachusetts program was administered by the Alternative Family Matters organization (http://alternativefamilies.org/) and the Justice Resource Institute (http://www.jri.org/index.php).

20 For more on college-aged children going off to college and still communicating with family, see Graber & Dubas (1996).
21 Davis-Sowers, 2006.
22 Davidson, 1997; Thorton, 1991.
23 Davis-Sowers, 2006.
24 Wellman, 1998.
25 One aunt, who reported being able to "barely support [her]self," took in her immigrant niece because "*family is family*. Could I have turned down my niece? Not at that moment, no way" (Bastida, 2001, p. 556; emphasis in original). See also Pozzetta, 1991.
26 Falicov & Karrer, 1980. A lyrical example comes from writer Sande Bortiz Berger's story of her aunt Irene, a poor immigrant from Lithuania, who cooked and cleaned in her brother's house, caring for his children after he brought her to live in the U.S. Years later, while visiting her grandniece, Aunt Irene immediately got to work:

It's only a few hours since her arrival, and already she's emptied the refrigerator of unrecognizable objects, polished the flatware, and refolded every towel in the linen closet. . . . My aunt has the soul of an immigrant, always anxious to earn her keep. (Berger, 2004, p. 4) This niece honors and appreciates the labor of her great-aunt, telling with great affection of her aunts' restlessness and eagerness to help with domestic work.

27 Brody, 2004; Roots, 1997.
28 Sotirin & Ellingson, 2006.
29 Feld, Dunkler, & Schroepfer, 2004; Johnson & Barer, 1995.
30 Hobbs, 2005.
31 Leach & Braithwaite, 1996. Of course, the mothers and grandmothers to one person are also aunts to other members of the kinship network, a fact which is ignored or deemphasized in most research on kinkeeping.
32 Coontz, 2000.
33 Cheal, 1988; di Leonardo, 1998; Dill, 1998; Johnson, 2000; Leach & Braithwaite, 1996; Rosenthal, 1985; Stack & Burton, 1998.
34 Hochschild, 2003.
35 di Leonardo, 1998, pp. 424–25.
36 Wood, 2008.
37 Gerstel & Gallagher, 1993.
38 di Leonardo, 1998; Gerstel & Gallagher, 1993.
39 Turner & West, 2006.

Chapter 2

1 Gerstel & Gallagher, 1993, p. 598.
2 Leeds-Hurwitz, 2002, p. 87.
3 Leach & Braithwaite, 1996. See also Fiese, Tomcho, Douglas, Josephs, Poltrock & Baker, 2002.
4 Cheal, 1988, pp. 638–39.
5 Johnson, 2000.
6 Collins, 2000.
7 Stack, 1974.
8 E.g., Weston, 1991.
9 Immigrants (Pei-Chia, 2002); older people (Johnson, 1999; Karner, 1998; Mac Rae, 1992; Rubenstein, Alexander, & Goodman, 1991); female prison inmates (Owen, 1998); homeless youths (McCarthy, Hagan, & Martin, 2002; Smith, 2008); lesbians and gays (Weston, 1995); members of the Yoruba religion (Ebaugh & Curry, 2000); Latina single mothers (López, 1999).
10 Clinton, 1996.
11 Turner & West, 2005.

12 Muraco, 2006, p. 1320.

13 Speech act theory suggests that in conferring a title, an act is committed, not simply an utterance. Conferring the title of aunt is an act; in speaking, something comes into being, in this case, that the person is now an aunt. See Austin's (1962) classic work, *How to Do Things with Words.*

14 Braithwaite, Olson, Golish, Soukup, & Turman, 2001.

15 Teresa spoke of how she tried to help one of her nieces when Teresa's ex-sister-in-law (the niece's mother) died. Teresa honored the family relationship even after the mother had abandoned her kids and Teresa's brother. She told her niece,

> You can't hate your mom. Your mother was a beautiful person; she loved you guys very much. You don't know what went wrong, you don't know. Yeah, she shouldn't have walked out on us, but we don't know what was going through her mind, we don't know whether she had problems.

She tried to reassure the kids that they had not caused their mother to leave and to make sure they understood how much love she and other members of the family had for them. This aunt performed kinwork that sought to repair a broken family tie by creating a sympathetic story of caring and forgiveness to replace a negative and potentially damaging story of maternal abandonment.

16 Bastida, 2001.

17 Ebaugh & Curry, 2000, p. 199.

18 Natives of the Hawaiian Islands are not necessarily of native Hawaiian ancestry, but commonly reflect a blend of Pacific Islander, Asian, Anglo, and other cultures.

19 There are various reasons why the Hawaiian practice of inclusive aunting may have emerged; we can only speculate as to its origins. Perhaps the practice emerged because of the native Hawaiian people's isolation from mainland culture, the traditions of the native Hawaiian people, and the relatively small population of people who make their permanent home on the Hawaiian Islands. Additionally, the heavy development of the islands as a tourist destination may provoke a need to reinforce signs of belonging for local community members apart from their role as hosts of thousands of tourists each year.

20 SunWolf, 2007.

21 We point this out not to blame men for failing to act, but to reinforce our claim that aunting is a gendered practice. Nurturing is still framed as feminine in the dominant U.S. culture, and our data clearly demonstrated that in the vast majority of cases, women choose and maintain chosen kin ties. Of course, evidence exists that gay men do choose families of their own, but in predominantly heterosexual communities and among lesbians, women's kin choices largely prevail.

22 Weston, 1991.
23 Muraco, 2006, p. 1320.
24 Friedman, 1989, p. 290.
25 For a discussion on the perfomative nature of gender, race/ethnicity, and other identities that we tend to treat as natural or fixed, see Butler, 1990.
26 Bourdieu (1986) expanded the Marxist concept of "capital" to include cultural, social, and symbolic resources. Building on Bourdieu's work, "capital" was defined by Ebaugh & Curry (2000, p. 190).
27 Friedman, 1989, pp. 286–87.

Chapter 3

1   For a discussion of this criticism, see Miller & Parks, 1982; Parks, 1995.
2   Our analysis draws on and contributes to emerging studies on how family ties are maintained despite limited interaction and long-distance relationships; see particularly Stafford's (2004) excellent overview of research on families with an adult member on military assignment or in prison. Other studies have focused on limited communication among college-aged children and their parents (e.g., Graber & Dubas, 1996) and grandparents (Harwood & Lin, 2000).
3   Sigman, 1991.
4   Sahlstein, 2004.
5   Sahlstein, 2004, p. 709.
6   This sanction relates to what has been called the "tender years" doctrine: that a child needs a mother's intense involvement during early development to realize human potential and there simply is no substitute. This doctrine guided family court decisions over custody since the mid-nineteenth century, and although it has been replaced by a "best interests of the children" doctrine, it remains firmly embedded in American common culture.
7   In research on contact between nonresidential and/or noncustodial parents and their children, frequency of contact has been a major (and sometimes the only) indicator of relationship. However, frequency alone is not a strong predictor of the strength of these relationships (Stafford, 2004; Arendell, 1997). While relationships with aunts are radically different from relationships with parents, this research suggests that there are other, more important, ways of understanding the value and impact of distanced relationships.
8   A child's perception of a relational bond and symbolic contact with a noncustodial parent (e.g., through remembrances on holidays or birthdays) can be just as important to the child's well-being as frequent and

continuing personal contact (Stafford, 2004; Buchanan, 2000). We caution again that we do not intend any correspondence between noncustodial parents and absent aunts. Yet these findings suggest that such perceptions may be important in understanding the quality of an aunt/niece/nephew relationship.

9   Koerner & Fitzpatrick, 2002.

10 Wellman, 1998.

11 Sandmaier, 1994; Troll, 1985.

12 The influence of parental experiences with siblings on parent-child relations has been studied as "intergenerational linkages" (see Kramer & Baron, 1995).

13 E.g., Sachs, 1999.

14 This may be part of the passage from childhood dependence to adult independence; that is, nieces and nephews may make their own relationships with extended family apart from their parents' relationships. In this way, they move beyond the nuclear family circle while remaining within the family network.

15 For research on communication in adolescent-parent relationships, see Socha & Stamp, 1995.

16 Afifi, 2003; Braithwaite, Olson, Golish, Soukup, & Turman, 2001.

17 For a social construction perspective on relationships, see Gergen, 1994; Gergen, Schrader, & Gergen, 2008; Rawlins, 2008; Shotter, 2008.

18 Scholars of politeness and face threats have noted that superficially polite interactions may save face in encounters between people who dislike each other. Civility is maintained by saying "hi" without stopping for an exchange, and this act both acknowledges the tension and avoids confrontation (and saves face). See Domenici & Littlejohn, 2006; Tracy, 2002.

19 Current commentary on the narcissistic generation, consumption-driven parenting, and cultural expectations over "perfect" parenting support the cultural expectation that children should be the center of family attention. See Twenge & Campbell, 2009; Warner, 2005. For an historical perspective on the emergence of the "priceless" child in U.S. culture, see Zelizer, 1994.

20 Expectancy violation theory suggests that the wrong gift violates both personal expectations of affection and indulgence, and cultural scripts about fawning relatives. See Burgoon, Stern, & Dillman, 1995.

21 Shopping as a sign of sincere affection suggests that the contemporary obsession with consumption and material possession has become a hallmark of relational quality. See Hine's argument that women express a primal responsibility for nurturing through shopping (2002, p. 37).

22 For an interesting historical perspective on how we have come to expect the family to deal with their children in terms of justice and fairness in

the context of larger state policies regarding the welfare and protection of children, see Rose, 1990.

23 In Folbre's (2001) analysis of the economic justice of family care, she argues that we learn about relations of affection, care, altruism, and justice in the context of family responsibilities and obligations.

24 Sigman (1991) distinguishes among the interactional, social, and semiotic levels of relationship enactment.

25 Younger adults' satisfaction with intergenerational conversation is decreased when topics are not enjoyable (Williams & Nussbaum, 2001).

26 See Giles, Coupland, & Coupland (1991) on Communication Accommodation Theory.

Chapter 4

1 E.g., Duck, 1998; Gergen, Schrader, & Gergen, 2008.

2 Wilmott, 2006.

3 Burgoon, Stern, & Dillman, 1995; SunWolf, 2007.

4 Decorating our territory constitutes a significant form of nonverbal communication, e.g., Wood, 2008; see also studies of gendered stereotypes in children's bedrooms and home environments: Sutfin, Fulcher, Bowles, & Patterson, 2008; Pomerleau, Bolduc, Malcuit, & Cossette, 1990; Rheingold & Cook, 1975.

5 di Leonardo, 1998.

6 Friday, 1997.

7 Duck, 1991.

8 Hayes, 1996.

9 Stone (1989) argues that family stories often highlight and sustain such identifications.

10 Duck, 1991. See also Rawlins, 1983.

11 Hays, 1989; cited in Duck, 1991. See related research on self-disclosure, reporting that both men and women self-disclose more to women (Dindia & Allen, 1992). At the same time, Wilmott (1995) argues that overemphasizing self-disclosure and relational talk neglects the rich relational meaning constituted in nonverbal interactions and events.

12 Our findings on aunts' ability and willingness to act as relational buffers between nieces/nephews and parents or other family members is supported by Milardo's (2010) similar findings about aunts and uncles as buffers.

13 Hochschild, 1979.

14 Interpersonal scholars have argued that politeness is integral to interpersonal power relations and face-saving (Domenici & Littlejohn, 2006). See also sociolinguistic theories of politeness, including the classic

formulation by Brown & Levinson (1987); also critiques of this classic model and reformulations emphasizing context and gender, i.e., Watts (2003) and Mills (2003).

15 Politeness in personal relationships shapes conduct because personal inclinations are disciplined by multiple forces including social ideologies, cultural norms, linguistic patterns, and structural factors; as a result, "we may exaggerate or misrepresent expression of our interest in someone or our relational feelings about them, as when we smile at boring strangers at parties or kiss embarrassing relatives at Christmas time" (Duck, 1998, p. 4).

16 See Postman (2002) for a discussion of the need for politeness as a mainstay for civil society.

17 Sturgis, 2004; Traeder & Bennett, 1998; Cunningham, 1997.

18 Leach & Braithwaite, 1996, p. 212.

19 Sotirin & Ellingson, 2006.

20 On pronatalism: Lisle, 1999; Lovett, 2007; Monach, 1993.

21 In traditional Catholic godparenting relationships, childless couples who nurture a godchild may hold expectations for assistance from the child during their old age (Ebaugh & Curry, 2000).

22 Muraco, 2006.

23 Stewart, 2002.

Chapter 5

1 This expression of the self in the context of family relationships is what Langellier and Peterson (2004, p. 115), following McLain & Weigert (1979), call the "enfamilied self," an identity situated within the lived experience of family life and deriving a larger sense of meaning from family relations and histories.

2 Stone (1989) makes a strong case for the development of individual identity in the context of family stories. See also Rosenwald & Ochberg (1992) and Langellier & Peterson (2004).

3 This theme is the basis for the feminist project of recovery in which women's stories are reclaimed as valuable and reframed for the alternative perspectives they offer on the meanings, values, and practices of everyday life and relations (e.g., see DuBois & Dumenil, 2005; Romberger, 1986). Cairns and Silverman (2004) report that such stories are often evoked by the family heirlooms and artifacts that women treasure.

4 Jorgenson & Bochner (2004) argue that while canonical stories often circulate through popular culture, personal family stories often resist the cultural conventions of such tales and "authorize and/or legitimate" alternative stories "that seek to reform or transform canonical ones" (p. 528).

5 The story was one of the 2006 StoryCorps broadcasts. StoryCorps is a

traveling audio oral history project sponsored by National Public Radio. See Kochhar & Simon, 2006.

6　The spinster is a well-ingrained cultural image with connotations of undesirability, ageism, and mental instability. For an interesting analysis of associations, see Baker, 2008.

7　Sotirin & Ellingson, 2007.

8　See Allen's (2004) overview of ageism and adultism and issues of inter-generational communication.

9　Sotirin & Ellingson, 2003.

10　These subtle moves in Robin's story call to mind Oliver's (2001) ethics of witnessing in that her story "bears witness" to the pathos of racial/ethnic oppression.

11　There is a debate among feminist scholars about such victim stories: while some scholars argue that we need such stories to make women's oppression visible, others argue that the approach itself victimizes women by portraying them as hapless victims (see Cole, 1999).

12　Mentoring has a much longer history, originating in the *Iliad* story of Mentor, whose role was to prepare Telemachus, the king's son, to meet his life's challenges (Homer, 1991).

13　Kram, 1988.

14　Bennetts, 1994, p. 4, cited in Buell, 2004, p. 57.

15　On "wo-mentoring" see hooks (2000); on feminist ethics of care, see Noddings (2003); Tronto (1993).

16　Aunting as mentoring could productively reframe feminist mentoring relationships, shifting from an oft-adopted model of mother/daughter or sister relation toward an aunt/niece/nephew relation. Notably, aunting relationships avoid the tensions of the mother/daughter and sisterhood models that are so problematic for many feminists. For instance, second- and third-wave antagonisms are often couched in terms of feminist mothers and daughters and the difficult psychodynamics of those rela-tionships. (For more on the psychodynamics of these relationships, see Orr, 1997; Detloff, 1997.) Further, the ideal of "sisterhood" has proven quite problematic for feminists, obscuring critical differences and mak-ing undue demands for camaraderie and consensus. Instead, aunting embraces differences, avoids the dense dependencies and identifications that make mother/daughter relations so difficult, and allows for consider-able separation and distance without denying sisterly connections (after all, an aunt is also a sister) (see Ellingson & Sotirin, 2008).

17　As Jorgenson and Bochner point out, family storytelling "is subject to the evaluation of others—its audience—and thus must draw on situated narrative conventions and cultural typifications to achieve intelligibility" (2004, p. 525). Telling us about their aunts as mentors may have encour-aged our participants to construct their stories as culturally normative.

18 Bourdieu (1984) argues that we acquire the habits that distinguish social
    class in these mundane enactments of cultural rules, dispositions, and
    comportments.
19 Wiltshire, 1998, p. 2.
20 Freedman, 1993; see also Parke & O'Neil, 1997.
21 We discuss this desire in chapter 6 as the impulse to "generativity" or the
    desire to ensure the continuity of families and communities. Freedman
    (1993) argues strongly for the importance of generativity as a motivation
    for older adults to engage in volunteer community activities like mentor-
    ing at-risk youth.
22 Stone, 1989.
23 Jorgenson & Bochner, 2004, p. 513.
24 As narrative theorists Rosenwald and Ochberg (1992) observed, "The
    culture 'speaks itself' through each individual's story," yet our personal
    dreams and desires strain against cultural dictates (p. 8).
25 Stone, 1989.

Chapter 6

1 Cherlin, 1999.
2 Popenoe, 1995.
3 Similarly, Milardo (2010) argues that uncles express generativity when
   they involve themselves in the lives of their nieces and nephews.
4 McAdams, 2004, p. 236.
5 Similarly, Milardo (2005, 2010) emphasizes reciprocal relations of generativity when aunts, uncles, nieces, and nephews involve themselves in
   each others' lives. Milardo's study emphasizes reciprocal generativity—
   caring about and for future generations and the ongoing well-being of
   family—in aunting and uncling relationships. It is mutual interdepen-
   dence and intergenerational generativity contibuting to the persistence
   of the family ensemble that he finds most significant about aunting and
   uncling. "Relationships framed by generative inclinations substantially
   and uniquely benefit parents, their children, and the aunts and uncles
   themselves. In this social landscape, a new understanding of generativity emerges, one deeply rooted in a convoy of personal relationships"
   (pp. 200–201). Our study supports an enriched conception of reciprocal
   generativity but unlike Milardo, we do not find generativity to subsume
   the meaning and potential of aunting. While we document reciprocity
   in aunting as friendship, mentoring, caregiving, and "paying forward,"
   we argue for the ways that the flexibility, multiplicity, and responsiveness of aunting reframes how we might understand and enact family and
   community life.
6 Langellier & Peterson, 2006a, 2006b.

7   Langellier & Peterson, 2006b, p. 109.

8   Langellier & Peterson (2006a) emphasize the often disjointed and incomplete aspects of mundane family storytelling that are nonetheless critical to a family's unique identity, culture, and history: "the interrupted and intertwined conversations and habits of daily life—fragmentary, fleeting, and fluid, embedded among tasks and talk" as well as "multiple and dispersed" storytellers and listeners and stories that "may be contradictory and incoherent or simply bits of memory, speech, image" (p. 110).

9   Stone, 1989; di Leonardo, 1987.

10   Sotirin, 2007; Bergmann, 1993.

11   Langellier & Peterson, 2006a, p. 110.

12   According to a 2000 poll by Maritz Marketing Research Inc., approximately 60% of the U.S. population is interested in family history, up from 45% just five years ago. The poll also showed that about 35 million people have used the Internet for family history research (http://www.genealogy.com, 2000). *Time* magazine named genealogy as one of the four most popular topics on the Internet in its April 19, 1999, cover article on genealogy, "Roots Mania" (Hornblower, 1999).

13   Rosenzweig & Thelen, 1998.

14   Rosenzweig & Thelen, 1998, p. 12. Their book, *The Presence of the Past*, documents a major project to understand the omnipresence of the past in American everyday life; as "historymakers," people start with their family relations and histories, moving into social groups and then broader historical narratives, particularly concerning race and religion.

15   Family stories are often inspired by family homes, heirlooms, and old neighborhoods. Cairns and Silverman (2004) describe the stories women tell about the character of their families and themselves based on treasured artifacts from previous generations. Communication theorist Sigman (1991) defines such artifacts as "spoors," referring to "an object that is left behind and that indexes the prior physical presence of an individual in some location" (p. 114).

16   Leeds-Hurwitz, 2006b; Pratt & Fiese, 2004.

17   Leeds-Hurwitz, 2006b, pp. 12–17.

18   Leeds-Hurwitz, 2006b; Langellier & Peterson, 2004; Milardo, 2010; Stone, 1989.

19   Stone, 1989.

20   Stone (1989) attributes her temper to a family trait exhibited by her great-grandfather and warns that families often typecast members by telling and retelling stories of events that seemingly confirm these identifications.

21   Pratt & Fiese, 2004, p. 3.

22   See McGoldrick, Gerson, & Shellenberger, 1999.

23 Narrative theorists emphasize that family stories often participate in larger cultural narratives, in this case, a narrative about the enduring significance of affective kinship bonds. According to Pratt and Fiese (2004), "Stories and narratives are not simple reproductions of personal life experiences, but rather are *reconstructions* of the past, through the use of interpretive 'plots' that are adapted from the repertoire of stories available and learned from the culture" (p. 9; emphasis in original).

24 The idea of repaying kindnesses by doing a good deed for a third party who must then pass on the favor to another and so on exponentially has gained considerable attention in popular culture. The expression "pay it forward" is the title of a popular book (Hyde, 2000) and movie (Leder & Dixon, 2000) as well as a charitable foundation, the Pay It Forward Foundation (see http://www.payitforwardfoundation.com).

25 See Erickson (1959) for a classic statement on adolescent identity and autonomy.

26 This impulse to generativity in younger family members may be of particular importance given research that indicates a tendency for elderly adults and those facing life-threatening illness to contract their social support networks (see Schmeeckle & Sprecher, 2004, p. 354).

27 See Rossi, 2001; also Freedman, 1993.

28 Folbre, 2001.

29 Langellier & Peterson (2004) argue that personal narratives about family meaningfully organize family experience "sequentially and consequentially" (p. 112), that is, in a chronological and evaluative order, in this case, relating current aunting experiences as a guide to future aunting relationships. Jago (1996) argues that telling family stories is a way of gathering and ordering details from past experience in order to cope with present issues and illuminate possibilities and directions for the future (p. 505).

30 Jago (1996) argues that performing such alternative stories is an important reflexive exercise in self-authoring, that is, exercising the power to recreate a more productive and rewarding life story out of the details of a negative or damaging narrative.

31 For a thorough overview of research on families and religion, see Chatters & Taylor (2005).

32 Chatters & Taylor, 2005, p. 520.

33 See Airhart & Bendroth, 1996; also Catholic ItalianAmerican (di Leonardo, 1987); Catholic Mexican American (Falicov, 1999; Falicov & Karrer, 1980; Sault, 2001); Jewish American (Leeds-Hurwitz, 2006a).

34 See López, 1999. Anthropologists have documented similar systems in countries such as Italy, Belgium, Greece, and Sri Lanka.

35 See Ebaugh & Curry, 2000, p. 192.

36 This suggests that aunts are particularly available for such "kinscription," meaning that they are positioned in terms of gender roles, family relations, religious traditions, and cultural expectations to be scripted (or conscripted) into this form of kinwork. See Stack & Burton, 1998.

37 Even without the formal godmother designation, some aunts play critical roles in continuing religious traditions among their nieces and nephews, as we consider in our discussion of aunts as mentors (see chapter 5).

Conclusion

1 See social commentaries such as Niedzviecki (2006) and Twenge (2006).

2 See Ellingson (2009, pp. 70–72) for a discussion of the distorting and constraining effects of dichotomous thinking in qualitative research.

3 As Kellas, LeClair-Underberg & Normand (2009) document, the terms of address used in stepfamilies can indicate the closeness of relationships but at the same time, are often inadequate to the lived realities of their emotional complexities.

4 Floyd, Mikkelson, & Judd, 2006.

5 There is a burgeoning literature on grandparenting; see Cherlin & Furstenberg (1992) for an initiating call for research on the changing "companionate" practices of contemporary grandparenting. For an examination of "uncling," see Milardo (2005, 2010).

Appendix

1 We collected television shows, movies, children's books, poems, photos, advertisements, classic and contemporary novels, nonfiction trade books, and Web sites. Reading and reflecting on these shaped our understanding of the cultural images of aunts currently in circulation. Although not included in this book, we have published elsewhere some of our analyses (Sotirin & Ellingson, 2007).

2 This is theoretical sampling, as commonly described in qualitative texts, e.g., Warren & Karner, 2009.

3 Interviewing one relational partner may obscure audience, situation, and event to highlight the personal narrator and the story structure (Langellier & Peterson, 2006a, p. 115).

4 Arnett, 2000, quoted in Pratt & Fiese, 2004, p. 6.

5 Habermas & Bluck, 2000, quoted in Pratt & Fiese, 2004, p. 13.

6 Grotevant & Cooper, 1998. "Adolescents' stories of important issues in their lives commonly involve family relationships, as well as peers, and as noted, adolescents typically tell these life stories to families or friends, who collaborate in the co-construction of these stories as they are told and retold" (Pratt & Fiese, 2004, pp. 14–15).

7   E.g., Gergen, 2009; Stewart, 2002.

8   Feminist texts that informed our project include the following: Butler, 1990; Collins, 2000; Coontz, 2000; Fox & Murry, 2000; Osmond & Thorne, 1993; L. Stone, 2000; Thorne, 1992; Wood, 2008.

9   Charmaz (2000, 2005) revised Glaser & Strauss' (1967) classic positivist method of grounded theory and situated it within social constructionist theory (Gergen, 1999). She posited that the constructed nature of all knowledge claims arises out of relationships; meaning resides not in people or in data, but *between* them. Hence, the method can be acknowledged as both rigorous and as involving intersubjective processes from which researchers' selves cannot be separated. Researchers can "form a revised, more open-ended practice of grounded theory that stresses its emergent, constructivist elements. We can use grounded theory methods as flexible, heuristic strategies rather than as formulaic procedures" (Charmaz, 2000, p. 510). Charmaz' formulation is particularly amenable to feminist commitments and to scrutinizing researchers' standpoints (e.g., gender, race, class, sexual orientation, [dis]ability, etc.) in relation to the themes or patterns they generate in their analyses.

10 As outlined by Strauss & Corbin (1990) and Charmaz (2000, 2005).

11 Strauss & Corbin, 1990, p. 41.

12 See the discussions of the role of theory in qualitative research (Ellingson, 2009, pp. 82–89) and of the necessity of researcher reflexivity in understanding the relationships among self, research participants, and findings (Ellingson, 1998).

REFERENCES

Afifi, T. D. (2003). "Feeling caught" in stepfamilies: Managing boundary turbulence through appropriate privacy coordination rules. *Journal of Social and Personal Relationships, 20,* 729–56.

Airhart, P. D., and Bendroth, M. L. (Eds.). (1996). *Faith traditions and the family.* Louisville, Ky.: Westminster John Knox.

Albrecht, T. L., and Goldsmith, D. J. (2003). Social support, social networks, and health. In T. L. Thompson, A. M. Dorsey, K. I. Miller, and R. Parrott (Eds.), *Handbook of health communication* (pp. 263–84). Mahwah, N.J.: Lawrence Erlbaum Associates.

Allen, B. J. (2004). *Difference matters: Communicating social identity.* Long Grove, Ill.: Waveland Press.

Arendell, T. (1997). The new father. In T. Arendell (Ed.), *Contemporary parenting: Challenge issues* (pp. 154–95). Thousand Oaks, Calif.: Sage.

Arnett, J. J. (2000). Emerging adulthood: A theory of development from the late teens through the twenties. *American Psychologist, 55,* 469–80.

Austin, J. L. (1962). *How to do things with words.* Cambridge, Mass.: Harvard University Press.

Baker, P. (2008). "Eligible" bachelors and "frustrated" spinsters: Corpus linguistics, gender and language. In K. Harrington, L.

Litosseliti, H. Sauntson, and J. Sunderland (Eds.), *Gender and language research methodologies* (pp. 73–84). Hampshire, England: Palgrave Macmillan.

Bastida, E. (2001). Kinship ties of Mexican migrant women on the United States/Mexico border. *Journal of Comparative Family Studies, 32*, 549–69.

Bennetts, C. (1994). *Mentors, mirrors and reflective practitioners: An inquiry into informal mentor/learner relationships.* Unpublished master's dissertation, University of Sheffield, England.

Berger, P., and Luckmann, T. (1966). *The social construction of reality.* Garden City, N.Y.: Doubleday.

Berger, S. B. (2004). Laundry. In I. Sturgis (Ed.), *Aunties: Thirty-five writers celebrate their other mother* (pp. 3–7). New York: Ballantine Books.

Bergmann, J. R. (1993). *Discreet indiscretions: The social organization of gossip.* (J. Bednarz Jr., Trans.). New York: Aldine de Gruyter. (Original work published 1987.)

Bould, S. (2003). Caring neighborhoods: Bringing up the kids together. *Journal of Family Issues, 24*, 427–47.

Bourdieu, P. (1984). *Distinction: A social critique of the judgment of taste.* (R. Nice, Trans.). Cambridge, Mass.: Harvard University Press.

———. (1986). The forms of capital. In J. G. Richardson (Ed.), *Handbook of theory and research in the sociology of education* (pp. 241–58). New York: Greenwood Press.

Braithwaite, D. O., Olson, L. N., Golish, T. D., Soukup, C., and Turman, P. (2001). "Becoming a family": Developmental processes represented in blended family discourse. *Journal of Applied Communication Research, 29*, 221–47.

Brody, E. M. (2004). *Women in the middle: Their parent care years* (2nd ed.). New York: Springer.

Brown, P., and Levinson, S. (1987). *Politeness: Some universals in language usage.* Cambridge: Cambridge University Press.

Buchanan, C. M. (2000). Adolescents' adjustment to divorce. In R. D. Taylor and M. C. Wang (Eds.), *Resilience across contexts: Fam-*

ily, work, culture, and community (pp. 179–216). Mahwah, N.J.: Lawrence Erlbaum Associates.

Buell, C. (2004). Models of mentoring in communication. *Communication Education, 53*, 56–73.

Burgoon, J. K., Stern, L. A., and Dillman, L. (1995). *Interpersonal adaptation: Dyadic interaction patterns.* New York: Cambridge University Press.

Butler, J. (1990). *Gender trouble: Feminism and the subversion of identity.* New York: Routledge.

Cairns, K. V., and Silverman, E. L. (2004). *Treasures: The stories women tell about the things they keep.* Calgary, Alberta: University of Calgary Press.

Charmaz, K. (2000). Grounded theory: Objectivist and constructivist methods. In N. K. Denzin and Y. S. Lincoln (Eds.), *Handbook of qualitative research* (2nd ed., pp. 509–35). Thousand Oaks, Calif.: Sage.

————. (2005). Grounded theory in the 21st century: A qualitative method for advancing social justice research. In N. K. Denzin and Y. S. Lincoln (Eds.), *Handbook of qualitative research* (3rd ed., pp. 507–35). Thousand Oaks, Calif.: Sage.

Chatters, L. M., and Taylor, R. J. (2005). Religion and families. In V. L. Bengtson, A. C. Acock, K. R. Allen, P. Dilworth-Anderson, and D. M. Klein (Eds.), *Sourcebook of family theory & research* (pp. 517–22). Thousand Oaks, Calif.: Sage.

Cheal, D. (1988). The ritualization of family ties. *American Behavioral Scientist, 31*, 632–43.

Cherlin, A. J. (1999). *Public and private families: An introduction* (2nd ed.). Boston: McGraw-Hill.

Cherlin, A. J., and Furstenberg, F. F. (1992). *The new American grandparent: A place in the family, a life apart.* Cambridge, Mass.: Harvard University Press.

Christiansen, R., and Brophy, B. (2007). *The complete book of aunts.* New York: Twelve.

Clinton, H. (1996). *It takes a village: And other lessons children teach us.* New York: Simon & Schuster.

Cole, A. (1999). "There are no victims in this class": On female suffering and anti-"victim feminism." *NWSA Journal, 11,* 72–96.

Collins, P. H. (2000). *Black feminist thought: Knowledge, consciousness, and the politics of empowerment* (2nd ed.). New York: Routledge.

Coontz, S. (2000). *The way we never were: American families and the nostalgia trap* (Rev. ed.). New York: Basic Books.

———. (Ed.) (with Parson, M., and Raley, G.). (1999). *American families: A multicultural reader.* New York: Routledge.

Cunningham, A. S. (1997). *Aunts: A celebration of those special women in our lives.* Chicago: Contemporary Books.

Davidson, B. (1997). Service needs of relative caregivers: A qualitative analysis. *Families in Society, 78,* 502–10.

Davis-Sowers, R. L. (2006). *Salvaging children's lives: Understanding the experiences of Black aunts who serve as kinship care providers within Black families.* Unpublished doctoral dissertation, Georgia State University.

Detloff, M. (1997). Mean spirits: The politics of contempt between feminist generations. *Hypatia, 12,* 76–99.

di Leonardo, M. (1987). The female world of cards and holidays: Women, families and the work of kinship. *Signs: Journal of Women in Culture and Society, 12,* 440–53.

———. (1998). The female world of cards and holidays: Women, families, and the work of kinship. In K. V. Hansen and A. I. Garey, 1998 (Eds.), *Families in the U.S.: Kinship and domestic politics* (pp. 419–30). Philadelphia: Temple University Press.

Dill, B. T. (1998). Fictive kin, paper sons, compadrazgo: Women of color and the struggle for family survival. In K. V. Hansen and A. I. Garey (Eds.), *Families in the U.S.: Kinship and domestic politics* (pp. 431–45). Philadelphia: Temple University Press.

Dindia, K., and Allen, M. (1992). Sex differences in self-disclosure: A meta-analysis. *Psychological Bulletin, 112,* 106–24.

Domenici, K., and Littlejohn, S. W. (2006). *Facework: Bridging theory and practice.* Thousand Oaks, Calif.: Sage.

DuBois, E. C., and Dumenil, L. (2005). *Through women's eyes: An American history with documents.* New York: Bedford/St. Martin's.

Duck, S. W. (1991). *Understanding relationships.* New York: Guilford Press.

———. (1998). *Human relationships* (3rd ed.). Thousand Oaks, Calif.: Sage.

Ebaugh, H. R., and Curry, M. (2000). Fictive kin as social capital in new immigrant communities. *Sociological Perspectives, 43,* 189–209.

Edwards, R. (2004). Present and absent in troubling ways: Families and social capital debates. *The Sociological Review, 52,* 1–21.

Ellingson, L. L. (1998). "Then you know how I feel": Empathy, identification, and reflexivity in fieldwork. *Qualitative Inquiry, 4,* 492–514.

———. (2009). *Engaging crystallization in qualitative research: An introduction.* Thousand Oaks, Calif.: Sage.

Ellingson, L., and Sotirin, P. (2006). Exploring aunt-niece/nephew communication. *Journal of Social and Personal Relationships, 23,* 499–517.

———. (2008). Academic aunting: Reimagining feminist (wo)mentoring, teaching, and relationships. *Women & Language, 31,* 35–43.

Erickson, E. H. (1959). Identity and the life cycle: Selected papers. *Psychological Issues, 1,* 5–165.

Falicov, C. J. (1999). The Latino family lifecycle. In B. Carter and M. McGoldrick (Eds.), *The expanded family life cycle: Individual, family, and social perspectives* (3rd ed., pp. 141–52). Boston: Allyn & Bacon.

Falicov, C. J., and Karrer, B. M. (1980). Cultural variations in the family life cycle: The Mexican-American family. In E. A. Carter and M. McGoldrick (Eds.), *The family life cycle: A framework for family therapy* (pp. 383–425). New York: Gardner Press.

Fass, S., and Cauthen, N. K. (2008). *Who are America's poor children? The official story.* Retrieved March 25, 2009, from http://www.nccp.org/publications/pub_843.html

Feld, S., Dunkle, R. E., and Schroepfer, T. (2004). Race/ethnicity and marital status in IADL caregiver networks. *Research on Aging, 25,* 531–58.

Ferguson, S. J. (2001). *Shifting the center: Understanding contemporary families* (2nd ed.). Mountain View, Calif.: Mayfield.

Fiese, B. H., Tomcho, T. J., Douglas, M., Josephs, K., Poltrock, S., and Baker, T. (2002). A review of 50 years of research on naturally occurring family routines and rituals: Cause for celebration? *Journal of Family Psychology, 16,* 381–90.

Floyd, K., Mikkelson, A. C., and Judd, J. (2006). Defining the family through relationships. In L. H. Turner and R. West, 2006 (Eds.), *The family communication sourcebook* (pp. 21–39). Thousand Oaks, Calif.: Sage.

Floyd, K., and Morman, M. T. (Eds.). (2006). *Widening the family circle: New research on family communication.* Thousand Oaks, Calif.: Sage.

Folbre, N. (2001). *The invisible heart: Economics and family values.* New York: New Press.

Fox, G. L., and Murry, V. M. (2000). Gender and families: Feminist perspectives and family research. *Journal of Marriage and the Family, 62,* 1160–72.

Freedman, M. (1993). *The kindness of strangers: Adult mentors, urban youth and the new voluntarism* (Repr. ed.). Cambridge: Cambridge University Press.

Friday, N. (1977). *My mother/my self: The daughter's search for identity.* New York: Dell.

Friedman, M. (1989). Feminism and modern friendship: Dislocating the community. *Ethics, 99,* 275–90.

Furstenberg, F. F., and Cherlin, A. J. (1991). *Divided families: What happens to children when parents part.* Cambridge, Mass.: Harvard University Press.

Gergen, K. J. (1994). *Realities and relationships: Soundings in social construction.* Cambridge, Mass.: Harvard University Press.

———. (1999). *An invitation to social construction.* Thousand Oaks, Calif.: Sage.

————. (2009). *An invitation to social construction* (2nd ed.). Thousand Oaks, Calif.: Sage.

Gergen, K. J., Schrader, S. M., and Gergen, M. (Eds.) (2008). *Constructing worlds together: Interpersonal communication as relational process*. Boston: Penguin Academics.

Gerstel, N., and Gallagher, S. K. (1993). Kinkeeping and distress: Gender, recipients of care, and work-family conflict. *Journal of Marriage and the Family*, *55*, 598–607.

Giles, H., Coupland, N., and Coupland, J. (1991). Accommodation theory: Communication, context, and consequence. In H. Giles, N. Coupland, and J. Coupland (Eds.), *Contexts of accommodation: Developments in applied linguistics* (pp. 1–68). Cambridge: Cambridge University Press.

Glaser, B., and Strauss, B. (1967). *The discovery of grounded theory: Strategies for qualitative research*. Chicago: Aldine.

Graber, J. A., and Dubas, J. S. (1996). *Leaving home: Understanding the transition to adulthood*. San Francisco: Jossey-Bass.

Grotevant, H. D., and Cooper, C. R. (1998). Individuality and connectedness in adolescent development: Review and prospects for research on identity, relationships, and context. In E. Skoe and A. von der Lippe (Eds). *Personality development in adolescence: A cross national and life span perspective* (pp. 3–37). New York: Taylor & Francis.

Habermas, T., and Bluck, S. (2000). Getting a life: The emergence of the life story in adolescence. *Psychological Bulletin*, *126*, 748–69.

Hacking, I. (1999). *The social construction of what?* Cambridge, Mass.: Harvard University Press.

Hansen, K. V., and Garey, A. I. (1998). *Families in the U.S: Kinship and domestic politics*. Philadephia: Temple University Press.

Harwood, J., and Lin, M-C. (2000). Affiliation, pride, exchange, and distance in grandparents' accounts of relationships with their college-aged grandchildren. *Journal of Communication*, *50*, 31–47.

Hayes, S. (1996). *The cultural contradictions of motherhood*. New Haven: Yale University Press.

Hays, R. B. (1989). The day-to-day functioning of close versus casual friendship. *Journal of Social and Personal Relationships, 7,* 21–37.

Hine, T. (2002). *I want that! How we all became shoppers: A cultural history.* New York: HarperCollins.

Hobbs, F. (2005). *U.S. Census Bureau, Census 2000, Special Reports, CENSR-24, Examining American household composition: 1990 and 2000.* Washington, D.C.: U.S. Government Printing Office. Retrieved March 25, 2009, from http://www.census.gov/prod/2005pubs/censr-24.pdf.

Hochschild, A. R. (1979). Emotion work, feeling rules, and social structure. *American Journal of Sociology, 85,* 551–75.

————. (2001). *The time bind: When work becomes home and home becomes work.* New York: Holt.

————. (2003). *The second shift.* New York: Penguin.

Homer (1991). *The Iliad.* B. Knox, Introduction (R. Fagles, trans.) (Repr. ed.). New York: Penguin Classics.

hooks, b. (2000). *Feminism is for everybody: Passionate politics.* Cambridge, Mass.: South End Press.

Hornblower, M., August, M., Aunapu, G., Black, C., Daly, M., Rutherford, M., and Woodbury, R. (April 19, 1999). Roots mania. *Time 153(15):* 7pp. Retrieved April 18, 2008, from http://www.time.com/time/magazine/article/0,9171,990751,00.html.

Hyde, C. R. (2000). *Pay it forward* (Repr. ed.). New York: Pocket Books.

Jackson, S. (1992). Towards a historical sociology of housework: A materialist feminist analysis. *Women's Studies International Forum, 15,* 153–72.

Jago, B. J. (1996). Postcards, ghosts, and fathers: Revising family stories. *Qualitative Inquiry, 2,* 495–516.

Johnson, C. L. (1999). Fictive kin among oldest old African Americans in the San Francisco Bay area. *Journals of Gerontology Series B: Psychological Sciences and Social Sciences, 54*(6), S368–75.

————. (2000). Perspectives on American kinship in the later 1990s. *Journal of Marriage and the Family, 62,* 623–39.

Johnson, C. L., and Barer, B. M. (1995). Childlessness in late late life: Comparisons by race. *Journal of Cross-Cultural Gerontology, 9,* 289–306.

Jorgenson, J., and Bochner, A. P. (2004). Imagining families through stories and rituals. In A. L. Vangelisti (Ed.), *Handbook of family communication* (pp. 513–38). Mahwah, N.J.: Lawrence Erlbaum Associates.

Karner, T. X. (1998). Professional caring: Homecare workers as fictive kin. *Journal of Aging Studies, 12,* 69–82.

Kearney, R. (2002). *On stories (thinking in action).* London: Routledge.

Kellas, J. K., LeClair-Underberg, C., and Normand, E. L. (2009). Stepfamily address terms: 'Sometimes they mean something and sometimes they don't.'" *Journal of Family Communication, 8,* 238–63.

Kochhar, P., and Simon, K. (2006, August 18). An expert's lessons on being an aunt. StoryCorps: Recording America series, Morning Edition, National Public Radio. Retrieved May 20, 2007, from http://www.npr.org/templates/story/story.php?storyId=5665799.

Koerner, A. F., and Fitzpatrick, M. A. (2002). Toward a theory of family communication. *Communication Theory, 12,* 70–91.

Kram, K. E. (1988). *Mentoring at work: Developmental relationships in organizational life.* Lanham, Md.: University Press.

Kramer, L. and Baron, L. A. (1995). Intergenerational linkages: How experiences with siblings relate to parenting of siblings. *Journal of Social and Personal Relationships, 12,* 67–87.

Langellier, K. M., and Peterson, E. E. (2004). *Storytelling in daily life: Performing narrative.* Philadelphia: Temple University Press.

———. (2006a). Family storytelling as communication practice. In L. H. Turner & R. L. West, *Perspectives on family communcation* (pp. 109–28). New York: McGraw-Hill.

———. (2006b). "Somebody's got to pick eggs": Family storytelling about work. *Communication Monographs, 73,* 468–73.

Leach, M. S., and Braithwaite, D. O. (1996). A binding tie: Supportive communication of family kinkeepers. *Journal of Applied Communication Research, 24,* 200–216.

Leder, M. (Director), and Dixon, L. (Writer). (2000). *Pay it forward* [Motion picture]. United States: Warner Brothers.

Leeds-Hurwitz, W. (2002). *Wedding as text: Communicating cultural identities through ritual.* Mahwah, N.J.: Lawrence Erlbaum Associates.

———. (2006a). "Be a mensch": Judaism as ethnic and religious identity. In W. Leeds-Hurwitz, 2006(b) (pp. 139–70).

———. (Ed.). (2006b). *From generation to generation: Maintaining cultural identity over time.* Cresskill, N.J.: Hampton Press.

Lehr, V. (1999). *Queer family values: Debunking the myth of the nuclear family.* Philadelphia: Temple University Press.

Lisle, L. (1999). *Without child: Challenging the stigma of childlessness.* New York: Routledge.

López, R. A. (1999). Las comadres as a social support system. *Affilia, 14,* 24–41.

Lovett, L. (2007). *Conceiving the future: Pronatalism, reproduction, and the family in the United States, 1890–1938.* Chapel Hill: University of North Carolina Press.

Mac Rae, H. (1992). Fictive kin as a component of the social networks of older people. *Research on Aging, 14,* 226–47.

Maritz Marketing Research Inc. (2000, May 16). Recent Maritz poll shows explosion in popularity of genealogy. Retrieved April 18, 2008, from http://www.genealogy.com/press-051600.html.

McAdams, D. P. (2004). Generativity and the narrative ecology of family life. In M. W. Pratt and B. H. Fiese (Eds.), *Family stories and the life course: Across time and generations* (pp. 235–57). Mahwah, N.J.: Lawrence Erlbaum Associates.

McCarthy, B., Hagan, J., and Martin, M. J. (2002). In and out of harm's way: Violent victimization and the social capital of fictive street families. *Criminology, 40,* 831–65.

McGoldrick, M., Gerson, R., and Shellenberger, S. (1999). *Genograms: Assessment and intervention* (2nd ed.). New York: W. W. Norton.

McLain, R., and Weigert, A. (1979). Toward a phenomenological sociology of the family: A programmatic essay. In W. R. Burr, R. Hill, F. I. Nye, and I. L. Reiss (Eds.), *Contemporary theories about the family: General theories/Theoretical orientations*, vol. 2 (pp. 160–205). New York: Free Press.

Milardo, R. M. (2005). Generative uncle and nephew relationships. *Journal of Marriage and Family, 67*, 1226–36.

———. (2010). *The forgotten kin: Aunts and uncles.* New York: Cambridge University Press.

Miller, G. R., and Parks, M. R. (1982). Personal relationships: Dissolving personal relationships. In S. W. Duck (Ed.), *Communication in dissolving relationships*, vol. 4 (pp. 127–54). London: Academic Press.

Mills, S. (2003). *Gender and politeness.* Cambridge: Cambridge University Press.

Monach, J. H. (1993). *Childless: No choice: The experience of involuntary childlessness.* New York: Routledge.

Muraco, A. (2006). Intentional families: Fictive kin ties between cross-gender, different sexual orientation friends. *Journal of Marriage and Family, 68*, 1313–25.

Niedzviecki, H. (2006). *Hello I'm special: How individuality became the new conformity.* San Francisco: City Lights.

Noddings, N. (2003). *Caring: A feminine approach to ethics and moral education* (2nd ed.). Berkeley: University of California Press.

Oliver, K. (2001). *Witnessing: Beyond recognition.* Minneapolis: University of Minnesota Press.

O'Reilly, A., and Abbey, S. (Eds.). (2000). *Mothers and daughters: Connection, empowerment and transformation.* Lanham, Md.: Rowman & Littlefield.

Orr, C. M. (1997). Charting the currents of the third wave. *Hypatia, 12*, 29–46.

Osmond, M. W., and Thorne, B. (1993). Feminist theories: The social construction of gender in families and society. In P. G. Boss, W. J. Doherty, R. LaRossa, W. R. Schumm, and S. K. Steinmetz (Eds.), *Sourcebook of family theories and methods: A contextual approach* (pp. 591–622). New York: Plenum.

Owen, B. (1998). *"In the mix": Struggles and survival in a women's prison.* Albany: State University of New York Press.

Parke, R. D., and O'Neil, R. (1997). Social relationships across contexts: Family-peer linkages. In W. A. Collins and B. Laursen (Eds.), *Relationships as developmental contexts: The Minnesota symposia on child psychology*, vol. 30 (pp. 211–40). Mahwah, N.J.: Lawrence Erlbaum Associates.

Parks, M. R. (1995). Ideology in interpersonal communication: Beyond the couches, talk show and bunkers. In B. Burleson (Ed.), *Communication yearbook 18* (pp. 480–97). Thousand Oaks, Calif.: Sage.

Pay It Forward Foundation. Retrieved October 11, 2001, from http://www.payitforwardfoundation.com/.

Pei-Chia, L. (2002). Subcontracting familial piety: Elder care in ethnic Chinese immigrant families in California. *Journal of Family Issues, 23*, 812–35.

Peington, B. A. (2004). The communicative management of connection and autonomy in African American and European American mother-daughter relationships. *Journal of Family Communication, 4*, 3–34.

Pomerleau, A., Bolduc, D., Malcuit, G., and Cossette, L. (1990). Pink or blue: Environmental gender stereotypes in the first two years of life. *Sex Roles, 22*, 359–67.

Popenoe, D. (1995, Summer). The American family crisis. *Phi Kappa Phi Journal*, 15–18.

Postman, N. (2002). The communication panacea. In J. Stewart (Ed.), *Bridges not walls: A book about interpersonal communication* (8th ed., pp. 52–55). New York: McGraw Hill.

Postman, N., and Pozzetta, G. E. (1991). *Immigrant family patterns: Demography, fertility, housing, kinship, and urban life*. New York: Garland.

Pratt, M. W., and Fiese, B. H. (2004). Families, stories, and the life course: An ecological context. In M. W. Pratt and B. H. Fiese (Eds.), *Family stories and the life course: Across time and generations*. Mahwah, N.J.: Lawrence Erlbaum Associates.

Putnam, R. D. (2001). *Bowling alone: The collapse and revival of American community*. New York: Simon & Schuster.

Rawlins, W. K. (1983). Negotiating close friendship: The dialectic of conjunctive freedoms. *Human Communication Research, 9,* 255–66.

——. (2008). *The compass of friendship: Narratives, identities, and dialogues.* Thousand Oaks, Calif.: Sage.

Rheingold, H. L., and Cook, K. V. (1975). The contents of boys' and girls' rooms as an index of parents' behavior. *Child Development, 46,* 459–63.

Rich, A. (1976). *Of woman born: Motherhood as experience and institution.* New York: Norton.

Riley, P. J., and Kiger, G. (1999). Moral discourse on domestic labor: Gender, power, and identity in families. *Social Science Journal, 36,* 541–48.

Romberger, B. V. (1986). "Aunt Sophie always said . . . ": Oral histories of the commonplaces women learned about relating to men. *American Behavioral Scientist, 29,* 342–67.

Roots, C. R. (1997). *Sandwich generation: Adult children caring for aging parents.* New York: Garland.

Rose, N. (1990). *Governing the soul: The shaping of the private self.* New York: Routledge.

Roseneil, S. (2000). Queer frameworks and queer tendencies: Towards an understanding of postmodern transformations of sexuality. *Sociological Research Online,* 5. Retrieved March 25, 2009, from http://www.socresonline.org.uk/5/3/roseneil.html.

Rosenthal, C. S. (1985). Kinkeeping in the familial division of labor. *Journal of Marriage and the Family, 47,* 965–74.

Rosenwald, G. C. and Ochberg, R. L. (Eds.). (1992). *Storied lives: The cultural politics of self-understanding.* New Haven, Conn.: Yale University Press.

Rosenzweig, R., and Thelen, D. (1998). *The presence of the past: Popular uses of history in American life.* New York: Columbia University Press.

Rossi, A. (Ed.). (2001). *Caring and doing for others: Social responsibility in the domains of family, work, and community.* Chicago: University of Chicago Press.

Rubenstein, R. L., Alexander, B. B., and Goodman, M. (1991). Key relationships of never married, childless older women: A cultural analysis. *Journal of Gerontology: Social Sciences, 46*, S270–77.

Sachs, L. (1999). Knowledge of no return: Getting and giving information about genetic risk. *Acta Oncologica, 38*, 735–40.

Sahlstein, E. M. (2004). Relating at a distance: Negotiating being together and being apart in long distance relationships. *Journal of Social and Personal Relationships, 21*, 689–710.

Sandmaier, M. (1994). *Original kin: The search for connection among adult sisters and brothers.* New York: Dutton.

Sault, N. L. (2001). Godparenthood ties among Zapotec women and the effects of Protestant conversion. In J. W. Dow and A. R. Sandstrom (Eds.), *Holy saints and fiery preachers: The anthropology of Protestantism in Mexico and Central America* (pp. 117–46). Westport, Conn.: Praeger.

Schmeeckle, M., and Sprecher, S. (2004). Extended family and social networks. In A. L. Vangelisti (Ed.), *Handbook of family communication* (pp. 349–75). Mahwah, N.J.: Lawrence Erlbaum Associates.

Shotter, J. (2008). *Conversational realities revisited: Life, language, body and world* (2nd ed.). Taos, N.M.: Taos Institute Publications.

Sigman, S. J. (1991). Handling the discontinuous aspects of continuous social relationships: Toward research on the persistence of social forms. *Communication Theory, 1*, 106–27.

Smith, H. (2008). Searching for kinship: The creation of street families among homeless youth. *American Behavioral Scientist, 51*, 756–71.

Socha, T. J., and Stamp, G. H. (Eds.). (1995). *Parents, children, and communication: Frontiers of theory and research.* Mahwah, N.J.: Lawrence Erlbaum Associates.

Sotirin, P. (2007). Bitching about secretarial "dirty work": The social construction of taint. In S. Drew, M. Mills, and B. M. Gassaway (Eds.), *Dirty work* (pp. 95–112). Waco, Tex.: Baylor University Press.

Sotirin, P., Buzzanell, P. M., and Turner, L. H. (2007). Colonizing family: A feminist critique of family management texts. *Journal of Family Communication*, 7, 245–63.

Sotirin, P., and Ellingson, L. L. (2003, October). *Performing aunting: Audio excerpts of interviews on having and being aunts.* Presented at Organization for the Study of Communication, Language, and Gender Conference, Ft. Mitchell, Ky.

———. (2006). The "other" women in family life: Recognizing the significance of aunt/niece/nephew communication. In K. Floyd and M. T. Morman (Eds.), *Widening the family circle: New research on family communication* (pp. 81–100). Thousand Oaks, Calif.: Sage.

———. (2007). Rearticulating the aunt: Feminist alternatives of family, care, kinship and agency in popular aunt figures. *Cultural Studies<=>Critical Methodologies*, 7, 442–59.

Stack, C. (1974). *All our kin*. New York: Basic Books.

Stack, C. B., and Burton, L. M. (1998). Kinscripts. In Hansen and Garey, 1998 (pp. 405–15).

Stafford, L. (2004). Parent-child relationships at a distance. In P. J. Kalbfleisch (Ed.), *Communication yearbook 28* (pp. 35–82). Mahwah, N.J.: Lawrence Earlbaum Associates.

Stewart, J. (Ed.) (2002). *Bridges not walls: A book about interpersonal communication*. Columbus, Ohio: McGraw-Hill.

Stewart, J. R., Witteborn, S., and Zediker, K. E. (2004). *Together: Communicating interpersonally, a social construction approach* (6th ed.). Cary, N.C.: Roxbury Publishing.

Stone, E. (1989). *Black sheep and kissing cousins: How our family stories shape us*. New York: Penguin.

———. (2000). Family ground rules. In K. M. Galvin and P. J. Cooper (Eds.), *Making connections: Readings in relational communication* (2nd ed., pp. 49–57). Los Angeles: Roxbury Publishing.

Stone, L. (2000). *Kinship and gender: An introduction* (2nd ed.). Boulder, Colo.: Westview Press.

Strauss, A., and Corbin, J. (1990). *Basics of qualitative research: Techniques and procedures for developing grounded theory*. Thousand Oaks, Calif.: Sage.

Sturgis, H. (2004). *Aunties: Thirty-five writers celebrate their other mother.* New York: Ballantine Books.

SunWolf. (2007). *Gift giving unwrapped: Strategies and stresses during the giving or receiving of gifts.* Unpublished manuscript, Santa Clara University, Santa Clara, Calif..

Sutfin, E. L., Fulcher, M., Bowles, R. P., and Patterson, C. J. (2008). How lesbian and heterosexual parents convey attitudes about gender to their children: The role of gendered environments. *Sex Roles, 58,* 501–13.

Thompson, L., and Walker, A. J. (1995). The place of feminism in family studies. *Journal of Marriage and the Family, 57,* 847–65.

Thorne, B. (1992). Feminism and the family: Two decades of thought. In B. Thorne and M. Yalom (Eds.), *Rethinking the family: Some feminist questions* (pp. 3–30). Boston: Northeastern University Press.

Thorton, J. (1991). Permanency planning for children in kinship foster homes. *Child Welfare, 5,* 593–601.

Tillmann-Healy, L. M. (2001). *Between gay and straight: Understanding friendship across sexual orientation.* Walnut Creek, Calif.: AltaMira Press.

Tracy, K. (2002). *Everyday talk: Building and reflecting identities.* New York: Guilford.

Traeder, T., and Bennett, J. (1998). *Aunties: Our older, cooler, wiser friends.* Berkeley, Calif.: Wildcat Canyon Press.

Trestrail, J. (2001, September 2). Overscheduled, overwhelmed: A calendar that's too full can drain kids' energy. *Chicago Tribune.* Retrieved May 31, 2007, from http://www.hyper-parenting.com/chicagotrib2.htm.

Troll, L. E. (1985). *Early and middle adulthood.* Pacific Grove, Calif.: Brooks/Cole.

Tronto, J. (1993). *Moral boundaries: A political argument for an ethic of care.* New York: Routledge.

Turner, L. H., and West, R. L. (2005). *Perspectives on family communication.* New York: McGraw-Hill.

———. (2006). *The family communication sourcebook.* Thousand Oaks, Calif.: Sage.

Twenge, J. M. (2006). *Generation me: Why today's young Americans are more confident, assertive, entitled—and more miserable than ever before.* New York: Free Press.

Twenge, J. M. and Campbell, W. K. (2009). *The narcissism epidemic: Living in the age of entitlement.* New York: The Free Press.

U.S. Census Bureau (2008, July 28). 50 million children lived with married parents in 2007. U.S. Census Bureau News. Washington, D.C.: Department of Commerce. Retrieved May 17, 2009, from http://www.census.gov/Press-Release/www/releases/archives/marital_status_living_arrangements/012437.html.

Warner, J. (2005). *Perfect madness: Motherhood in the age of anxiety.* New York: Riverhead.

Warren, C. A. B., and Karner, T. X. (2009). *Discovering qualitative methods: Field research, interviews, and analysis* (2nd ed). New York: Oxford University Press.

Watts, R. J. (2003). *Politeness.* Cambridge: Cambridge University Press.

Watzlawick, P., Beavin, J., and Jackson, D. (1967). *Pragmatics of human communication: A study of interactional patterns, pathologies, and paradoxes.* New York: Norton.

Wellman, B. (1998). The place of kinfolk in personal community networks. In K. V. Hansen and A. I. Garey, *Families in the U.S.: Kinship and domestic politics.* (pp. 231–39). Philadelphia: Temple University Press.

Weston, K. (1991). *Families we choose: Lesbians, gays, kinship.* New York: Columbia University Press.

———. (1995). Forever is a long time: Romancing the real in gay kinship ideologies. In S. Yanagisako and C. Delaney (Eds.), *Naturalizing power: Essays in feminist cultural analysis* (pp. 87–109). New York: Routledge.

Williams, A., and Nussbaum, J. F. (2001). *Intergenerational communication across the lifespan.* Mahwah, N.J.: Lawrence Erlbaum Associates.

Williams, M. (1922). *The velveteen rabbit.* New York: Avon Books.

Wilmott, W. (1995). *Relational communication.* New York: McGraw-Hill.

————. (2006). The relational perspective. In K. M. Galvin and P. J. Cooper (Eds.), *Making connections: Readings in relational communication* (4th ed.). New York: Oxford University Press.

Wiltshire, S. F. (1998). *Athena's disguises: Mentors in everyday life.* Louisville, Ky.: Westminster John Knox.

Wood, J. T. (2002). "What's a family, anyway?" In J. Stewart (Ed.), *Bridges not walls: A book about interpersonal communication* (pp. 375–83). Columbus, Ohio: McGraw-Hill.

————. (2008). *Gendered lives: Communication, gender, and culture* (8th ed.). Belmont, Calif.: Wadsworth.

Zelizer, V. A. (1994). *Pricing the priceless child: The changing social value of children.* Princeton, N.J.: Princeton University Press.

INDEX